Willis Abbot

Battle fields and camp fires

A narrative of the principle military operations of the civil war

Willis Abbot

Battle fields and camp fires

A narrative of the principle military operations of the civil war

ISBN/EAN: 9783337224875

Printed in Europe, USA, Canada, Australia, Japan

Cover: Foto ©ninafisch / pixelio.de

More available books at **www.hansebooks.com**

AND CAMP FIRES.

A NARRATIVE OF THE PRINCIPAL MILITARY OPERATIONS OF THE CIVIL WAR

FROM THE REMOVAL OF MCCLELLAN TO THE ACCESSION OF GRANT.
(1862—1863)

BY

WILLIS J. ABBOT

AUTHOR OF "BLUE JACKETS OF '61," "BLUE JACKETS OF 1812," "BLUE JACKETS OF '76,"
"BATTLE FIELDS OF '61"

ILLUSTRATED BY W. C. JACKSON

NEW YORK
DODD, MEAD & COMPANY
PUBLISHERS

INTRODUCTION.

IN this volume I have taken up the story of the military operations of the civil war, at the moment when the Army of the Potomac, scattered and dispirited, was withdrawing from the Virginia peninsula after the disastrous failure of McClellan's campaign against Richmond. At this point begins what I conceive to be the second period of the war for the Union. An almost unbroken series of victories in Virginia had greatly encouraged the Confederates. Though heavy reverses had been suffered in the West they were not irreparable. The policy of fighting a purely defensive war was now to be cast aside by the Confederates, and in the course of this volume we shall see them planning and executing such plans of invasion as Lee's Gettysburg campaign, and Bragg's invasion of Kentucky. The second period of the war, the period covered by "Battle Fields and Camp Fires," saw the Confederacy at the zenith of its power. This epoch in the history of the war ends with the accession of General U. S. Grant to the chief command of the Union forces.

In telling the story of this period I have confined myself to describing the chief battles, with but a brief survey of the strategy, maneuvers, and minor engagements leading up to them. It has been my aim to describe the salient features of the war, leaving out altogether the details of petty skirmishes, raids, demonstrations, and indecisive engagements which serve only to impede the course of the narrative, and to confuse the youthful reader who wishes to learn how the people of the South fought to achieve independence, and how the men of the North strove successfully to maintain the Union.

WILLIS J. ABBOT.

CONTENTS.

CHAPTER I.

PAGE

AT THE GATES OF RICHMOND. — POPE BROUGHT FROM THE WEST. — GENERAL HALLECK PUT IN SUPREME COMMAND. — THE PENINSULA ABANDONED. — MOSBY CARRIES THE NEWS TO LEE. — THE BATTLE OF CEDAR MOUNTAIN. — STUART'S RAID TO CATLETT'S STATION. — JACKSON'S MARCH TO POPE'S REAR, . 1

CHAPTER II.

JACKSON'S PERILOUS PREDICAMENT. — LONGSTREET'S MARCH THROUGH THOROUGHFARE GAP. — POPE'S CHASE AFTER THE CONFEDERATES. — THE BATTLE OF GROVETON. — THE BATTLE OF MANASSAS, SOMETIMES CALLED THE SECOND BATTLE OF BULL RUN. — A BATTLE WITH STONES. — THE DEATH OF KEARNY. — BATTLE OF CHANTILLY, 22

CHAPTER III.

THE INVASION OF MARYLAND. — HIGH HOPES OF THE CONFEDERATES. — THEY MEET A COLD RECEPTION. — THE LOST ORDER. — JACKSON'S CAPTURE OF HARPER'S FERRY. — MCCLELLAN IN CHASE. — BATTLE OF SOUTH MOUNTAIN. — BATTLE OF SHARPSBURG OR ANTIETAM. — LEE ABANDONS MARYLAND, . 45

CHAPTER IV.

THE WAR IN THE WEST. — HALLECK'S SIEGE OF CORINTH. — FORREST'S RAID ON MURFREESBORO'. — THE CONFEDERATES CAPTURE CHATTANOOGA. — BRAGG'S INVASION OF KENTUCKY. — BATTLE OF RICHMOND. — PANIC IN CINCINNATI. — BATTLE OF MUNFORDSVILLE. — BATTLE OF PERRYVILLE. — BRAGG ABANDONS KENTUCKY. — BATTLE OF IUKA. — BATTLE OF CORINTH, ... 81

CHAPTER V.

BRAGG IN TENNESSEE. — REVELRY AT MURFREESBORO'. — ROSECRANS IN COMMAND OF THE ARMY OF THE CUMBERLAND. — MORGAN'S RAID. — ROSECRANS'S MARCH. — BATTLE OF STONE'S RIVER OR MURFREESBORO'. — BRAGG'S RETREAT. — THE RAID ON HOLLY SPRINGS, 119

CHAPTER VI.

THE WAR IN THE EAST. — PROCLAMATION OF EMANCIPATION. — GENERAL MCCLELLAN DISMISSED. — BURNSIDE IN COMMAND. — CROSSING THE RAPPAHANNOCK. — FREDERICKSBURG BOMBARDED. — THE BATTLE OF FREDERICKSBURG. — THE FIGHT FOR MARYE'S HILL. — RETREAT OF THE ARMY OF THE POTOMAC, . . . 136

CHAPTER VII.

BURNSIDE'S ILL-FATED "MUD MARCH." — GENERAL HOOKER SUCCEEDS TO THE COMMAND OF THE ARMY OF THE POTOMAC. — REORGANIZATION OF THE ARMY. — DEVELOPMENT OF THE CAVALRY. — RAIDS OF FITZ-HUGH LEE AND AVERILL. — HOOKER TAKES THE OFFENSIVE. — HIS STRATEGY. — THE MARCH TO LEE'S REAR. — CHANCELLORSVILLE. — THE FOUR DAYS' BATTLES. — JACKSON'S FLANK MOVEMENT. — CONFEDERATE SUCCESSES. — STONEWALL JACKSON WOUNDED. — HIS DEATH. — UNION VICTORY AT MARYE'S HILL. — RETREAT OF THE UNION ARMY BEYOND THE RAPPAHANNOCK, 160

CHAPTER VIII.

Confederate Activity. — General Lee Determines to Attempt the Invasion of Pennsylvania. — Cavalry Battle at Brandy Station. — Lee's Northward March. — Panic in Northern Cities. — Hooker in Pursuit. — Meade Supersedes Hooker. — Gettysburg. — The Battle of the First Day. — Old John Burns. — Bayard Wilkeson's Heroism. — Incidents of the Battle, . . 195

CHAPTER IX.

Battle of Gettysburg. — Lee Determines to Attack. — Longstreet's Protest. — The Battlefield. — The Struggle for Little Round Top. — The Attack on the Peach Orchard. — The Sacrifice of Bigelow's Battery. — The Charge of Wilcox and Wright. — The Night Assault on the Union Right. — Charge of the Louisiana Tigers. — Battle of the Third Day. — Pickett's Great Charge. — Its Repulse. — Close of the Battle. — Retreat of the Confederates, 221

CHAPTER X.

Opening the Mississippi. — Sherman's Expedition. — Battle of Chickasaw Bayou. — Expeditions up the Yazoo and through the Bayous. — Grant's Movements West of the River. — Crossing the River. — Battle of Port Gibson. — Battle at Jackson. — Battle of Champion Hill. — Battle at Big Black River Bridge. — Vicksburg Invested. — The Siege. — Pemberton's Surrender. — Fall of Port Hudson, . 263

CHAPTER XI.

Maneuvering Bragg out of Tennessee. — The Chattanooga Campaign. — Rosecrans's Army in Peril. — Battle of Chickamauga. — Thomas to the Rescue. — Bragg's Plans Foiled. — Starving in Chattanooga. — Opening the Cracker Line. — Grant in Command. — Battle of Wauhatchie. — Battle of Lookout Mountain. — Missionary Ridge. — Bragg's Final Defeat, 298

CHAPTER XII.

PAGE

IN CHARLESTON HARBOR. — CONFEDERATE EFFORTS TO BREAK THE BLOCKADE. — GENERAL GILLMORE IN COMMAND. — UNION TROOPS ON FOLLY ISLAND. — A LODGMENT ON MORRIS ISLAND. — ATTACK ON FORT WAGNER. — BOMBARDMENT OF FORT SUMTER. — THE SWAMP ANGEL. — BOMBARDMENT OF FORT WAGNER. — VICTORY OF THE FEDERALS. — THE END, ... 334

ILLUSTRATIONS.

	PAGE
Rations at Vicksburg	Frontispiece
Looting Manassas Junction	17
Starke's Brigade Fighting with Stones	35
Death of General Kearney	43
Holding Turner's Gap	57
The Charge at Burnside's Bridge	75
The Surprise at Richmond	87
Burial of General Little	105
Storming of Battery Robinett	113
Gathering the Wounded from the Battle-field	131
The Stone Wall at Fredericksburg	151
Fighting it Out	157
Fording the Rapidan	171
Death of Jackson	183
Charge of Union Cavalry, Brandy Station	199
Wilkeson at Gettysburg	213
Climbing Little Round Top	229

ILLUSTRATIONS.

	PAGE
Around the Camp Fire	241
Raid upon a Baggage Train	257
Running the Vicksburg Batteries	273
A Shell in the Streets of Vicksburg	287
In the Trenches	305
Dragging Battery through a Marsh	317
In the Wake of Battle	331
The Charge at Fort Wagner	339
In a Monitor's Turret	343
Mortar Battery in Action	347

LIST OF MAPS.

Pope's Campaign	13
The Battle of Manassas (*Positions at Noon, August 29th*)	29
The Battle of Manassas (*Positions August 30th, 6 P. M.*)	38
Scene of Lee's Operations in Maryland	49
Map of Gettysburg	224

BATTLE FIELDS AND CAMP FIRES.

CHAPTER I.

AT THE GATES OF RICHMOND. — POPE BROUGHT FROM THE WEST. — GENERAL HALLECK PUT IN SUPREME COMMAND. — THE PENINSULA ABANDONED. — MOSBY CARRIES THE NEWS TO LEE. — THE BATTLE OF CEDAR MOUNTAIN. — STUART'S RAID TO CATLETT'S STATION. — JACKSON'S MARCH TO POPE'S REAR.

THE few Union people in Richmond in July, 1863,—there were such, for the Richmond papers of that day tell how "vandals" sometimes under cover of darkness wrote patriotic mottoes on the walls and fences of the Confederate capital—might occasionally hear the strains of national anthems, or perchance the tuneful notes of "John Brown's Body," borne to them on the wings of some favoring southeast wind. Far out beyond the Confederate lines, a few miles from the city McClellan's army, some ninety thousand strong, still lay encamped about Malvern Hill and Harrison's Landing. The army recovered quickly from the fatigues of the seven days' retreat across the peninsula. In the lazy life of the camp the soldiers forgot the dreary days of toil in the miry depths of the White Oak swamp, and the bottoms of the Chickahominy river. A lavish commissary department fed the Army of the Potomac as no army had ever been fed before. The storehouses and wharves groaned with provisions, and the huge corrals of beef cattle looked like the stockyards of a modern cattle market. The camp was a city in itself. Streets of tents and cabins covered acres of ground. Long wharves stretched out into the river to catch the steamers laden with troops and munitions of war that were constantly coming and going. Out in the stream the gunboats lay tugging at their anchors. Around the outskirts of the camp the batteries of artillery were parked, but ready for the first hint of an attack. Everywhere the stars and stripes were to be seen, and morning and evening, at inspection, guard mount and dress parade, the regimental bands, with great pounding of drums and braying of brass, made the Virginia woods resound with the stirring notes of our national songs.

Richmond was but a few miles away from the picket line of the Federal camp, but Lee's army blocked the path. Ever since the end of that day when the Confederate general hurled his troops madly and uselessly against McClellan's terraced batteries at Malvern Hill, the railroads leading to Richmond from the south had resounded with the rumble of trains bringing more men to stand between McClellan and the capital city of the South. The Federal general was in no haste to renew the offensive, the Confederates were zealous to take advantage of his delay, and so it happened that when the war authorities at Washington began to urge McClellan on to an advance, he found the numbers of his foes so greatly augmented that he declared that it would be folly for him to attack unless reinforced by 20,000 men.

Meantime there had been changes in the ranks of the Federal commanders in Virginia. Jackson's exploits in the Shenandoah valley had demonstrated that one general is apt to be better than three, so President Lincoln ordered the corps of McDowell, Banks, and Fremont consolidated, giving to the organization thus formed the name of the

Army of Virginia. To command this army he summoned from the west General Pope, who had been active and successful in military operations along the Mississippi. The choice was an unfortunate one. Fremont, who was Pope's senior in rank, promptly declined to serve under the officer thus suddenly put over him, and transferred his command to General Sigel. Pope himself gave great offense to the officers and soldiers under his command by signalizing his assumption of command by an address in which he covertly criticised the tactics of his predecessors, and rather vaingloriously promised better things of himself. But the sentence which chiefly irritated his troops was this: "I have come from the West, where we have always seen the backs of our enemies; from an army whose business it has been to seek the enemy and to beat him where found; whose policy has been attack and not defense." This the soldiers thought amounted to a simple declaration that the armies of the east were deficient in courage, and their resentment was greatly aroused.

The creation of Pope's command made two great armies in Virginia,—the Army of the Potomac and the Army of Virginia. The President determined to have a general-in-chief at Washington to fill this post, which had been vacant since McClellan had been deposed in March, 1862. Again he looked westward for an officer, and this time he chose Major-General Henry A. Halleck. This officer was then in command of the department of the Mississippi. The great success of the Federal forces in the west, the victories at Donelson, Island No. 10, and Shiloh had drawn the attention of the people to Halleck, who was then in chief command of the department in which these successes had been achieved. We know, to-day, that for these victories little or no credit is due to the department commander. Grant himself has left on record a declaration that he was hampered and embarrassed in his expeditions along the Tennessee and Cumberland rivers by General Halleck's steady opposition. But in that day people only knew that Halleck was in chief command in the west, and that in the west the greatest victories had been gained. And so from an army which contained a Grant, a Sherman, and a Sheridan, General Halleck was chosen to take chief command of the Union armies.

Halleck's first act was to withdraw the Army of the Potomac from the peninsula altogether. Abandoning the conclusions reached by his predecessor, he determined that Richmond was to be attacked best from the north. Though he visited McClellan at Harrison's Landing, and saw the noble army and the vast stores of provisions and munitions of war that had been transported thither at great expense, he felt that it was better to abandon all this, to count all the work done to secure a lodgment near Richmond as work wasted, and to begin the campaign anew upon fresh lines.

McClellan protested, but protested in vain. He was ready to abandon the attempt to force his way into Richmond through Lee's lines north of the James river, but he wished to cross the river and invest the city on the south. By doing this he would place himself between Richmond and the great territory of the Confederacy. He could effectually check the stream of reënforcements coming to Lee, and in time starve the Confederate city into subjection. It will be seen later that this was exactly the course by which General Grant took Richmond two years later. Halleck at first acceded to the plan, and promised the necessary reënforcements, but soon after his return to Washington became alarmed at some of Stonewall Jackson's characteristic maneuvers in the Shenandoah Valley, and peremptorily ordered McClellan to leave the peninsula and bring his army to Washington. With the promulgation of this order the peninsula ceased to be the theater of war in Virginia.

Meanwhile General Lee was watching every movement of his enemies, and carefully weighing the rumors which came to him daily from Washington as to the plan of the Federals. His army lay between the two widely separated wings of the Federal forces. He could strike either before the other could come to its assistance. He waited only to find out the plans of the Federals in order that he might plant the blow where it would do the Confederate cause the most good.

At Fortress Monroe lay a great flotilla of transports loaded with Federal troops and evidently awaiting only the order to weigh anchor. It was of the utmost importance that the Confederate commander should learn whether these troops were to reënforce Pope or McClellan, in order that he might attack and if possible defeat the army for which the reënforcements were intended before they could arrive. If the flotilla should turn into the James river it would mean that the troops were for McClellan; if into the Rappahannock, then Pope was relied upon to make the attack upon Richmond. For a time Lee was left in suspense, but one evening early in August a small steamer flying a flag of truce was seen coming up the James. It was found to be loaded with Confederate prisoners sent to Richmond for exchange. Among them was a man whose name was known throughout both armies as one of the most daring, audacious cavalry rangers that the Confederate army contained. His name was John Mosby, and his evident haste to get through with the formalities of the exchange and to be off might well have aroused the suspicion of the Federal officers who were there to attend to the details. Twelve miles under the broiling sun he walked, after the formalities which set him free were ended, and had fallen exhausted by the wayside when a mounted Confederate officer happened along and carried him to headquarters, where he soon told General Lee that at Fortress Monroe he had heard the order given to the commanders of some of the vessels of Burnside's flotilla to take their ships up the Rappahannock to Acquia creek.

General Lee had already sent Jackson to block Pope's advance, and he now dispatched word to that officer to press upon the Union lines, while he himself made preparations for moving his entire army from Richmond to the vicinity of Gordonsville, where Jackson's men were confronting the blue-coated brigades of Pope's army.

A glance at the maps of Virginia will show that Gordonsville is the point at which the railroad leading south from Washington divides, one branch going to Richmond and the other leading off to Charlottesville and the south. Here was Jackson with some twenty thousand men. The great body of Pope's army was at Culpepper Court House, a few miles nearer Washington on the same railroad. The ground between the hostile armies was swept over by the cavalry commands of each daily, and slight cavalry skirmishes had been of frequent occurrence ever since the two armies had come to that region.

About midway between Gordonsville and Culpepper there rises by the side of the wood a hill of considerable eminence known locally as Cedar Mountain, or sometimes Slaughter Mountain. Just beyond the foot of its northern slope is the deep ravine of Cedar creek crossed by the road to Culpepper. It was on the densely wooded slopes of Cedar Mountain that the two armies were destined to fight for the first victory in the campaign of Northern Virginia.

Jackson had advanced from Gordonsville at once, upon receiving his orders from Lee. Pope in his turn had speedily advanced to meet him. Gen. Banks commanded the advance of the Union line, and had 7500 men in his division. At Cedar Run he halted, and an aide bearing an order from General Pope overtook him. It is probable that the order Pope intended to give was that Banks should select a position and hold it against the enemy, sending back to the main body of the army for reënforcements if needed. But the order was a verbal one only, and when Banks asked the aide to put it in writing it was done in so ambiguous a phraseology that it seemed rather an order for an attack than for a mere stubborn resistance. Perhaps, too, General Banks was a little too ready to construe the order as an order to give battle to the enemy in any event. He was one of those eastern soldiers who had felt themselves aggrieved by the bombastic address of General Pope when that officer took command of the army, and he felt anxious to demonstrate to his superior officer that there was plenty of good fighting spirit in the Army of Virginia.

There had been a spluttering warfare for two or three days between the cavalry scouts of the two armies, and on the 9th of August Jackson found himself on the crest of Cedar Mountain looking down upon the camp of his foe. A line of skirmishers confronted the van of the Confederate army, and a Union battery on the banks of Cedar Run was throwing shells into the woods in which the Confederates were hiding. Jackson thought the outlook for a battle good, and he sent Ewell forward through the woods, while Early took position on the side of the mountain, two hundred feet above the plateau upon which the Federal troops were deploying and which his guns could sweep with a searching fire. He disposed his troops as though he had an army of at least his own strength to encounter. But as a matter of fact Jackson had over 20,000 men, while the Union troops numbered about 7500. General Banks had made one attempt to reënforce his army by sending hastily to Sigel at Sperryville to come immediately to his aid. But Sigel instead of marching sent a courier to ask what road he should take, and before Banks could answer that there was but one road from Sperryville to Cedar Run, the battle had been fought and lost.

For several hours the battle took the form of an artillery duel. From the slope of Cedar Mountain the Confederate batteries roared out their deep notes of defiance, which the Federals hurled back in their teeth. The Confederates were all the time pushing forward, but this they did so slowly and cautiously that their advance was hardly suspected. But the sharp fire of the Federal batteries, though inadequate to check the enemy's advance, yet inflicted serious loss upon his crowded ranks. General Winder was struck down by a flying bit of shell, and a host of less prominent officers were made to feel the accuracy of the Federal aim.

After three hours of artillery fighting Banks began to get restive. He knew not how large a force might be massed in the woods before him; and his orders from General Pope seemed to authorize him to keep on the defensive only. But the Confederates had been so cautious in their maneuvering that Banks felt convinced that they could not be greatly superior to him in numbers; and as for his orders, they were just sufficiently ambiguous to give him an excuse for attacking if he thought success certain. And so between his ignorance of the enemy's strength, and his gallant wish for victory, he committed the fatal error of determining to attack Jackson's army of 20,000 with his handful of troops. And it is worthy of note that the admirable plan of the attack, and the glorious daring of the boys in blue, came very near winning the day for the Union.

So with his handful of men General Banks moved forward to attack his enemy. It was five o'clock on the afternoon of a sultry day. The artillerymen, who had been serving their guns since noon, were begrimed with smoke and powder and almost prostrated by the heat, but the infantry had as yet done but little hard work, and came from the cool, shady depths of the woods about Cedar Run fresh and ready for the conflict. Crawford's brigade was on the right of the Union line, and the plan was that he should turn the left flank of the Confederate line while the brigades of Geary and Prince should attack in the center and on the right flank. Right well did Crawford perform the part allotted to him. Through the sheltering woods he led his column unseen by the enemy. The edge of the woods once reached, he saw before him a broad corn-field. The ripened grain had been harvested and the sheaves were piled up in stacks about the field, affording shelter to the skirmishers between the hostile lines. The Confederates were not slow to see the danger that was threatening them, and a storm of musket-balls and cannon-shot sought out the Union lines that were forming in the edge of the woods. The place was too hot for endurance. Desperate though the charge across the stubble-field might be, it was better to take the chance than to stand idly, to be mowed down in their ranks by the enemy's fire. So doubtless thought the blue-coated soldiers as with a cheer they dashed across the stubble-field where bullets hummed like bees. The men fell fast, but the field was quickly crossed. The Confederates on the extreme left of Campbell's brigade gave way in confusion. The Federals outflanked them, drove them back, won a position behind them, rolled them back in hopeless rout upon their supporting divisions. Meantime the brigades of Prince and Geary had been doing their duty well. They pressed so hotly upon the lines of Taliaferro and Early that made up the Confederate center and right, that these officers had all they could do to hold their men in ranks. But when the broken masses of Campbell's brigade came pouring down on Taliaferro's left hotly pursued by the exultant Federals, that brigade too gave way and Early was left alone to stem the flood of blue-coats that seemed destined to sweep Jackson's army back again to the Rapidan. At this moment the field was actually held by the Federals, for parts of two Virginia and one Georgia regiment alone withstood them; the rest of the Confederate army was worsted.

But meantime reënforcements from the teeming Confederate brigades in the rear were hastening to Early's aid. Ronald's division, which was nearest, reached the scene first and was led into action by Stonewall Jackson himself. The sight of that hero of the Confederate armies gave new spirit to the men who were on the verge of defeat. "Stonewall Jackson! Here is Jackson," they cried, and formed again their shattered lines. Crawford's brigade after all its hard fighting had to receive the shock of this new attack. Once the gray-clad line was rolled back, but Jackson rode to the front. He forgot that he was commander of the whole field. For the time he was again only a colonel at the head of his regiment. His eyes flashed. In a voice that rose above the thunders of the battle he cheered on his men. The old "Stonewall brigade," which had never failed to respond to the call of its leader, answered nobly. The Federals were beaten back. Geary was wounded. Prince was captured. Though Banks sent for his small reserve under Gordon, it was useless. Before the Confederates, constantly increasing in numbers, the Federals were forced back until at last they occupied the position behind Cedar Run which they had left at noon. Here they rallied and made so bold a show that Jackson halted, and the descending shades of night put an end to the battle. A few shells thrown from the Confederate batteries brought so lively a response from the woods in which the Union lines were formed that Jackson thought he must have the whole of Pope's army in his front, and soon after dark he fell back toward the Rapidan.

The victory in this hard-fought battle has been claimed by partisans of both the hostile generals. Jackson himself considered the victory his, though he did not follow it up with an advance. "On the evening of the 9th instant, God blessed our arms with another victory," he wrote in his report. Pope on his part sent to Washington a despatch which at least implied that the victory rested with him. "The enemy has retreated under cover of the night," he wrote. "Our cavalry and artillery are in pursuit."

As a matter of fact the battle was won by the Confederates. That they retired during the night does not alter the fact that they drove the Federals first from the field. But the victory they won was won by overwhelming numbers only. Until the Confederate reënforcements came up the field was in the hands of the Federals. Fierce, obstinate and sanguinary was the fighting on both sides, but too much praise can hardly be given to the Union soldiers for the valor with which they dashed into the fight, almost carrying the day with the first charge. It was a bloody battle too, in proportion to the forces engaged. The Union loss was 2393, of whom 1661 were killed or wounded. The Confederates had 1283 killed or wounded, with a total loss of 1314.

The scene of war was now to shift to a point much nearer Washington. The old dread lest the Confederates should enter the capital was about to be revived. The people of Richmond for a time were to miss the familiar sight of tented plains about the city, and to hear no longer the ceaseless rattle of the musketry along the picket lines. The region about Manassas which had been the scene of the first battle of the war was again to be trodden by the huge armies of the North and South.

August 15th had come. McClellan's troops on their way back to Washington from the peninsula had reached Yorktown. There was not a single armed enemy to threaten Richmond, and Lee had brought his whole army—75,000 men in all—out to Gordonsville to confront Pope. That officer, alarmed by the tremendous odds against him, fell back beyond the Rappahannock. Here he determined to make a desperate stand. Indeed, it was there that the battle for Washington must be fought, for with Pope once swept out of the way, Lee could march into the capital before McClellan's troops which were hastening from the peninsula to its defense could get there. General Halleck saw how essential the maintenance of the line along the Rappahannock was to the safety of the capital. "Defend every inch of ground," he telegraphed to Pope, "fight like the devil until we can reënforce you." And so for several days Pope manfully beat back every attempt of the enemy to force a crossing.

Thus unexpectedly checked, Lee grew restive. He had expected to ride roughshod over Pope's lines, but the strong defensive positions afforded by the Rappahannock were not to be easily taken. The soldiers in the Confederate army shared the discontent of their leader. Cold, rainy weather and a poor commissariat made life far from pleasant to the men on the south bank of the river. "We live on what we can get," wrote one in his diary, "now and then an ear of corn, fried green apples, or a bit of ham broiled on a stick, but quite as frequently do without either from morning to night. We sleep on the ground without any other covering than a blanket, and consider ourselves fortunate if we are not frozen stiff by morning. The nights are both stiff and cold."

While the two armies thus rested on their arms, watching each other across the narrow river and now and then exchanging greetings in the shape of a few shells or rifle-shot, that dashing trooper "Jeb" Stuart made one of his characteristic raids into the Union lines and came out triumphantly with information that made Lee expedite his advance. With a cavalry squadron of some 1500 men this adventurous officer left the Confederate camp and started to make a long detour to the rear of the Federal lines. As he was riding past Jackson's headquarters he met that other noted partisan ranger, Col. Mosby.

"I am going after my hat," sung out Stuart gaily as he saw his colleague. A few days before a Union cavalry expedition had come within an ace of capturing both Stuart and Mosby as they were sleeping in a house beyond the Confederate lines. The Confederates made their escape but left sundry trophies behind, among them Stuart's hat, which the raiders carried away in triumph.

Stuart led his troopers—picked men every one—by circuitous paths beyond the flank of the Federal picket line, and then around inside the lines to Catlett's Station, back of the center of the Union line and then occupied as headquarters by Gen. Pope himself. It was night when the raiders reached their destination, and a heavy thunderstorm blackened the sky and sent sheets of driving rain into the faces of the hardy adventurers. A flash of lightning betrayed them to the sentries, who fired a hasty volley and fell back, followed fast by the troopers, who charged through the darkness over unknown ground at a break-neck pace, and uttering the famous yell of the Southern soldiery. The affrighted Federals fled from their tents. The surprise was complete and they had no time to make any defense. General Pope, the chief prize sought by Stuart and his raiders, was not there, but his coat and hat fell into the hands of Stuart, who felt himself thus somewhat recompensed for the loss of his own raiment at the hands of the Union raiders. But a prize of far greater importance rewarded the bold invaders. Though General Pope escaped, his field quartermaster, with a portfolio containing all the commanding general's official papers, was captured. A hasty examination of these papers convinced Stuart that they should be placed in General Lee's hands without delay. So stopping only to burn a few stores he retraced his steps, and was soon safe again within the Confederate lines.

From the captured documents Lee learned the size and extent of Pope's army. He discovered that McClellan's troops were being brought up the Potomac to reënforce that army, and a copy of a letter written by Pope gave him the pleasant news that the Federal general foresaw nothing but defeat should the Confederates break his line at the Rappahannock before McClellan should arrive.

Lee had begun to doubt his ability to force a crossing of the Rappahannock in Pope's front, but he saw the need of striking a crushing blow before McClellan's arrival should enable Pope to do the striking. So looking for a way out of this dilemma, he hit upon an expedient which was in violation of all the principles of scientific warfare, which was perilous in any event, and which would have been impracticable had it not been for the presence with the Confederate army of the redoubtable Stonewall Jackson and his tireless veterans of the "foot cavalry."

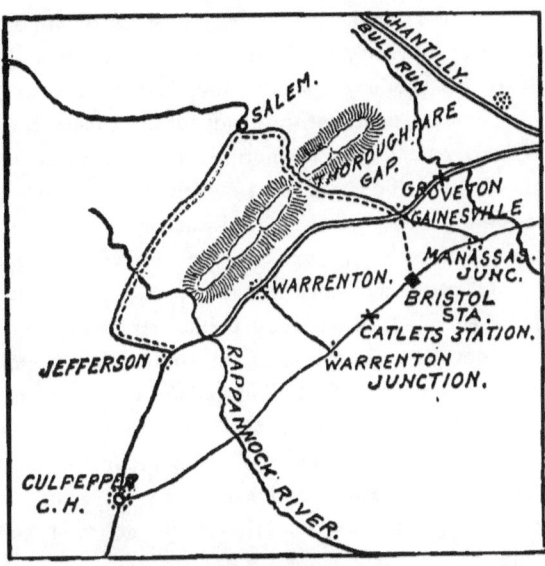

POPE'S CAMPAIGN.
(*The dotted line shows the course of Jackson's march to Pope's rear.*)

Lee's plan was to send Jackson by a long detour to the Federal rear, there to harass and attack Pope so as to create a diversion under cover of which Lee should slip across the Rappahannock.

It is morning of the 25th of August. In the camp of Jackson's division on the far left of the Confederate line all is life and bustle. The camp followers are packing wagons, teamsters harnessing refractory mules, artillery men greasing axles and getting ready for a long march. There is no stowing of tents, for "the tented field" was a sight little seen in the encampments of the Confederacy. Jackson's foot cavalry had no time for tent raising or striking. A blanket in a fence corner was good enough for the sturdy fellows whose commanding general did not scorn to bivouac himself snug under the lee of a log. There is but little packing of haversacks too. Provisions are scarce, and the tightly rolled blankets slung across one shoulder, in which the Confederate soldier carries all "traps" and provender, is chiefly filled with "traps" in the case of these ragged veterans who are about to make a march of near sixty miles to the enemy's rear.

The sun is not above the horizon when they take up the march. It is no holiday parade, the march of this gray-clad column. No harmonious band nor resonant drum cheers the men on. The quick-sighted enemy will be notified of the movement speedily enough by the great clouds of dust which a marching column always stirs up, without further attracting his attention by the sound of martial music. And so wi h guns at ease the veterans go trooping along, each at the gait that suits him best, but all keeping close in the column, for General Jackson doesn't like straggling and his officers and men all know it. So on in solid column, the infantry to the front, the artillery and wagons toiling painfully on in the rear, Jackson's thirty-five thousand men push their way along to the northwest until the range of hills called the Bull Run Mountains are between them and the Union army. Stuart and his cavalry have not yet left the borders of the Rappahannock, but they will do so speedily and overtake the column next day.

Meantime the signal officers and the scouts of the Union army are not asleep. They have seen the clouds of yellow dust rising above the tree-tops, they have heard the rumbling and creaking of the wagons and the artillery, and even faint sounds of human shouts and cries are wafted to their ears—the voices of the teamsters urging on their unwilling beasts. Where the column is going, and how great is its strength, are the chief questions which worry the Federals. The second is solved by a Union officer, Colonel Clark, who being out on picket far beyond the lines of his own command, hears the Confederate column approaching. Clambering up into a tree, he watches the long line pass before him. All day he clings to the branches, for he knows that to come down would mean discovery and certain death. At nightfall he makes his way back to his camp and reports that Jackson with thirty-five regiments and artillery has gone up the road toward the Shenandoah Valley.

Though puzzled to account for this apparently inexplicable maneuver, General Pope sees nothing alarming in it. He thinks only that Jackson has gone off on one of those raids down the Shenandoah Valley, which had made his name famous. But did the Federal commander but know the true destination of that flying column of gray-clad veterans, he would find that a brilliant if desperate move was being made against him by one of the first strategists of the war.

Behind the sheltering wall of the Bull Run mountains—a spur of the Blue Ridge—Jackson's column is speeding to the northwestward. Across open fields, pulling down fences that bar their path; by quiet country byways where hardly a wayfarer is met; past secluded homesteads where the women and the slaves come out to gaze wonderingly at the soldiers (for there were few other than women and slaves left in the homesteads of the South in that day); on under the burning sun, stopping neither to eat nor rest, nibbling ears of corn as they marched, weary, footsore, but brimful of enthusiasm, the soldiers plod on until at nightfall they bivouac near the little town of Salem. Just outside the village stands Jackson himself, looking with satisfaction on the well-filled ranks as they file past him, and answering the cheers of the men as they march past shoulder to shoulder with unwearying salutes.

That night the column rests in the fields about Salem. The Virginians in the ranks who know the country thereabouts draw maps in the dusty roads to show their comrades how great is the strategic value of the point to which "Old Jack" has led them. By the railroad which passes through Salem they might make a sudden descent upon Pope's great storehouse at Manassas Junction, cutting him off from his supplies and breaking his communications with Washington; or by following the same railroad in the opposite direction Jackson might lead his men again into the Shenandoah Valley through Manassas Gap; or should the general so desire he might desert the railway altogether, and by taking his forces down the turnpike fall on Pope's rear at Warrenton while Lee should re-attempt the passage of the Rappahannock in his front.

It is easy enough for the strategists in the ranks to conjecture what might be done, but not one of them knows what Jackson actually purposes doing until morning, when the head of the column is turned toward Thoroughfare Gap. Then every man in the ranks knows that they are to fall on the enemy's rear, to loot his provision depots, and to cut him off from Washington.

Thoroughfare Gap is reached and passed in safety. It is there in these mountainous defiles that Pope might have checked the raiders with a mere handful of men had he not lacked foresight. Once in the open country the column moves more swiftly. Stuart's cavalry hovers upon the right flank, capturing all Federal scouts and bringing in all persons who seem likely to carry news of the raid to Pope's headquarters.

It is eight o'clock in the evening when the van of the cavalry reaches the railroad between Manassas and Warrenton. The first thing to do is to cut the telegraph wires, which is speedily done; and the sudden cessation of the clicking of the instrument in General Pope's headquarters warns that officer that something is going wrong between his position and Washington. While the men are busy cutting the wires the thunder of a train coming from the south is heard, and before the track can be torn up it dashes by at full speed, heedless of a volley which is poured into it as it rolls by. Two other trains following close behind are thrown from the track by torn-up rails, and then the railroad is closed. The news of Jackson's approach has now doubtless reached Manassas, and thence been

LOOTING MANASSAS JUNCTION.

sent to Washington, but Pope is still in ignorance of the size and character of the force in his rear. How complete was his ignorance is shown by the fact that when his telegraph instrument stopped he ordered that one regiment be sent to Manassas "to repair the telegraph wires and to protect the railroad." One regiment to cope with Jackson's thirty-five!

However, it is not solely to wreck a railroad that Jackson has made his long and rapid march. Manassas Junction with untold stores of provisions and ammunition is his destination, and thither he turns his steps though it is nearly midnight and his men are fagged out. But the thought of the booty awaiting them lends those tired Confederates new vigor, and they step out as gaily as though on dress parade. Manassas is soon reached. The petty Federal force there stationed makes no resistance. A volley—a charge of Stuart's cavalry, and the vast storehouse of Pope's great army is in the hands of the Confederates.

What a prize it was, and with what zest did the half-starved Confederates set out to plunder the vast depot in which were housed the provisions for an army of 60,000 men! Jackson looked on indulgently as his men clothed and fed themselves from the spoil of the enemy. One precaution only he took. "The first order that General Jackson issued," writes Major Mason, "was to knock out the heads of hundreds of barrels of whisky, wine, brandy, etc., intended for the army. I shall never forget the scene when this was done. Streams of spirits ran like water through the sands of Manassas, and the soldiers on hands and knees drank it greedily from the ground as it ran."

" 'Twas a curious sight," writes another eye-witness, "to see our ragged and famished men helping themselves to every imaginable article of luxury or necessity, whether of clothing, food, or what not. For my part I got a toothbrush, a box of candles, a quantity of lobster salad, a barrel of coffee, and other things which I forget. The scene utterly beggared description. Our men had been living on roasted corn since crossing the Rappahannock, and we had brought no wagons, so we could carry away little of the riches before us. But the men could eat one meal at least. So they were marched up, and as much of everything eatable served out as they could carry. To see a starving man eating lobster salad and drinking Rhine wine, barefooted and in tatters, was curious; the whole thing was indescribable."

Though in the heart of his enemy's territory, with Federal troops on all sides save that by which he had entered—the narrow opening of Thoroughfare Gap—Jackson halted to let his troops enjoy this one brief hour of plenty. "In view of the abundance," writes one of the foot cavalry, "it was not an easy matter to determine what we should eat and drink and wherewithal we should be clothed; one was limited in his choice to only so much as he could personally transport, and the one thing needful in each individual case was not always readily found. However, as the day wore on, an equitable distribution of our wealth was effected by barter, upon a crude and irregular tariff in which the rule of supply and demand was somewhat complicated by fluctuating estimates of the imminence of marching orders. A mounted man would offer large odds in shirts or blankets for a pair of spurs or a bridle; and while in anxious quest of a pair of shoes I fell heir to a case of cavalry half-boots, which I would gladly have exchanged for the object of my search. For a change of underclothing and a pot of French mustard I owe grateful thanks to the major of the 12th Pennsylvania cavalry, with regrets that I could not use his library. Whisky was, of course, at a high premium, but a keg of lager—a drink less popular then than now, went begging in our company."

All too soon for the greedy soldiers the drums beat, and the order was given out to make a huge bonfire of all the stores that could not be carried away. Some idea of the extent of this task may be derived from an enumeration of the amount of arms and stores that were at Manassas when Jackson fell upon the place.

Forty-eight pieces of artillery were there, two hundred and fifty horses with equipments; two hundred new tents; ten locomotives; two railway trains of enormous size loaded with millions of dollars' worth of stores; fifty thousand pounds of bacon; one thousand barrels of beef; twenty thousand barrels of pork; several thousand barrels of flour, and an immense amount of forage.

Sorely did the Confederacy need this food for the supply of its armies. The pitiless blockade that shut out all communication with the outer world had begun to make itself felt, and that starving process which the South underwent for four years had already begun. But Jackson was within twenty miles of Washington, surrounded by hostile armies. He could not embarrass his movements with wagon trains, and so after setting the torch to the coveted treasure the Confederates took up their march again, rejoicing that they had enjoyed one "square meal," and wondering where and when they would get another.

CHAPTER II.

JACKSON'S PERILOUS PREDICAMENT. — LONGSTREET'S MARCH THROUGH THOROUGHFARE GAP. — POPE'S CHASE AFTER THE CONFEDERATES. — THE BATTLE OF GROVETON. — THE BATTLE OF MANASSAS, SOMETIMES CALLED THE SECOND BATTLE OF BULL RUN. — A BATTLE WITH STONES. — THE DEATH OF KEARNY. — BATTLE OF CHANTILLY.

THOUGH Jackson had thus accomplished his purpose of destroying Pope's supplies, thereby forcing that commander to fall back upon Washington for reënforcements, he had got himself and his own army into a most perilous position. Pope had by this time discovered the nature of the enemy in his rear, and was coming back horse, foot, and dragoons to fall upon the audacious pillagers and annihilate them before Lee and Longstreet could get to their aid. Hooker had come upon Early unexpectedly at Bristow, and had driven the Confederates from the field. Stuart's rangers had been out and brought in a captured dispatch which indicated that General Pope was using every effort to concentrate his army about Manassas, where Jackson then was. The roar of the Federal guns could be heard on every side, and the Confederate soldiers were beginning to wonder whether they had not, in their zest for plunder, got into a trap from which there was no escape.

Perhaps some thought of this kind flitted through the mind of the leader too, but if so he showed no sign of trepidation. It was while the storehouses were blazing, and the Federal guns in the distance roaring more and more loudly, that Major Roy Mason walked boldly up to Jackson and said:

"General, we are all of us desperately uneasy about Longstreet and the situation, and I have come over on my own account to ask you the question: Has Longstreet passed Thoroughfare Gap successfully?"

It was a decided violation of all rules of military etiquette for a subordinate officer to put such a question to the commanding general. Jackson smiled indulgently and replied:

"Go back to your command and say, 'Longstreet is through, and we are going to whip in the next battle.'"

But Longstreet was not through at that moment, and it was a bit of bad luck or bad management on the part of the Union commander that enabled him to get through at all. General Pope himself has written the story of the second battle of Bull Run, (to which all these maneuvers led up), but nowhere therein does he speak of having taken any steps to close Thoroughfare Gap against the advance of Lee. To have done so would have been an easy task. The Gap is a veritable Thermopylæ, capable of being held by a regiment and a battery against a whole army. At points it is scarce a hundred yards wide. Down the center rushes a turbid, tumultuous, mountain stream, and on either side the walls of the Gap rise steep and high. Huge bowlders and dense vines and undergrowth so cover the faces of the neighboring hillsides, that a battery or a regiment once posted could scarcely be dislodged.

It was at nightfall of the 28th of August that the head of Longstreet's column reached this pass, and learned that a Federal battery had just taken a position at the eastern end of the Gap. This was Ricketts's battery, which had been dispatched thither by Fitz John Porter. Had it remained there, the outcome of the second fight on the field of Bull Run might have been different, but Pope ordered it away; and so when dawn broke Longstreet, who had tried all night to find a trail over the mountains, found that the way through the pass was opened to his army, and marched through in ample season to reach Jackson's side when his aid was most needed.

While Longstreet was thus coming up to his aid behind the sheltering screen of the Bull Run mountains, Jackson had been seeking a spot whereon he might fight the battle which he knew Pope would force upon him. He sought a field which should afford him a strong defensive position, which was so situated as to enable him to escape with the remnant of his corps should the fight go against him, and which was so connected with Thoroughfare Gap as to make easy the junction of his force with that of Longstreet, should the latter arrive in time. All these characteristics he thought he saw in the country about Groveton, where the first battle of Bull Run had been fought. There he had won his title. He knew every fence and thicket and hillock on the field. Particularly he bethought him of a railroad embankment that crossed the field, and that would serve his troops in lieu of breastworks. So he sent his command by different roads to take a stand on the old field of Bull Run. General Pope followed fast behind the retreating Confederates. "If you will march promptly and rapidly at the earliest dawn upon Manassas Junction we shall bag the whole crowd," he wrote to McDowell on the 27th. The command was obeyed, but before the Federals had reached the Junction their bird had flown. "All that talk about bagging Jackson was bosh," wrote General Porter the next day. "That enormous gap, Manassas, was left open and the enemy jumped through." But though balked of his prey at the Junction, Pope still pressed eagerly on, feeling confident that he could yet catch and overwhelm the enemy. And indeed had he but blocked up Thoroughfare Gap with a proper force he might have done so.

On the afternoon of the 28th of August, King's division of the Union army and Jackson's right wing under Taliaferro and Ewell clashed near Groveton. It was but an accidental meeting. General Jackson had been sleeping in a shady corner of a Virginia snake fence when there dashed up to him a courier bearing Federal dispatches captured by a Confederate cavalry party. Rousing instantly from his slumber, Jackson seized the documents. They proved to be orders from General McDowell revealing Pope's intention of concentrating at Manassas. From them Jackson learned that one division of the Union army would soon pass along the Warrenton turnpike, which stretched out before his lines. Here then was a chance to snap at least one link in the iron chain with which Pope was threatening to bind him before his friends on the other side of Thoroughfare Gap could come to his aid.

"Move your division and attack the enemy," he said to General Taliaferro, who stood near him.

Then to Ewell, "Support the attack."

The two officers saluted, and gave the necessary commands. Their soldiers sprang from the ground at the sound of the drum. Soon they had taken up their position in a grove that fringed a field near the turnpike, and there waited for the column of the enemy to appear.

Soon King's column came plodding along toward Manassas Junction, expecting to find Jackson there. Had they but known it, Jackson was within a scant half-mile of them, but when an unseen battery in the woods near Groveton opened upon the Federals, they thought that it was but some isolated division they had encountered and not the right wing of the army they were seeking. For an hour or two the Union forces abandoned their advance toward Manassas to grapple with this unexpected foe; across a field, up a gentle slope straight to the edge of a clump of woods from which the Confederate batteries were spitefully playing, the blue-coated veterans charged. They had no plan of battle to carry out, no position to be held if they should be victorious in the fight. All they had to do was to drive the Confederates out of that neck of woods, and right pluckily they set about the task.

Two brigades, Gibbon's and Doubleday's, made up the Union line of battle; the Confederates had seven. Twenty-nine Confederate regiments with the advantage of position were about to be attacked by seven regiments of Yankees. If the Federals had but known it, they were about to stir up a hornet's nest.

Wheeling from the road along which they had been tramping toward Manassas, the brigades of Doubleday and Gibbon started for the woods, whence came a galling fire. A fence that barred their pathway was down in an instant. With cheers the waving blue line swept forward. Back of it the Union batteries wheeled into position and searched with their shells the thickets which hid the enemy.

For two hours and a half the fighting was stubborn and bloody. Neither side could make any headway. Standing up line against line, the hostile forces poured into each other bullet, shell and solid shot until darkness put an end to the fighting. It was a sanguinary encounter. Gibbon's brigade lost in the two hours of fighting 751 men, or over one-third of its total roster. The Confederate loss too was heavy, and among those hit were General Ewell, whose leg was amputated during the battle, and General Taliaferro. About midnight the Federals withdrew from the field and continued their march to Manassas, little thinking that the army they were leaving behind them was the very army for which they were seeking.

All that night there was marching and countermarching about the neighborhood of Groveton and Manassas. The lonely country roads were crowded with armed men, and resounded with the hoof-beats of galloping aides, or cantering troops of cavalry. Pope was making frantic efforts to find Jackson; the Confederate general in his turn was seeking an advantageous position, and far off to the westward the dusty columns of Lee and Longstreet were making all possible haste to reach Jackson in time to snatch him from the grasp of his intended destroyers. The thunder of the cannon in the battle of the afternoon had been heard in the Gap, and every report seemed like an appeal for aid.

Morning came—the 29th of August. Jackson had found the position he sought for—a steep railway embankment, running from Bull

Run to the Warrenton turnpike, along which Longstreet was to advance. The latter commander had passed the Gap, and was coming down the pike with rapid strides. General Pope had found the enemy he had sought unsuccessfully at Manassas and at Centreville, and by ten o'clock opened his attack.

A great battle does not often possess the spectacular features with which the fancy of the civilian is inclined to invest it. Occasionally some magnificent display of valor, some dashing charge in full view of both armies like the charge of the Guards at Waterloo or Pickett's charge at Gettysburg, decides by its success or failure the fortunes of the day. More often, though, a great battle is made up of a score of simultaneous movements, no two of which can be observed by the same spectator. Here a charging regiment; there a division stubbornly holding a critical position; at another spot a battery fighting an artillery duel with another battery a mile away; trees, hills or ravines hiding the supporting divisions one from the other; a hundred thousand men engaged and perhaps scarce a thousand visible at one time from one point of view. To direct such a contest demands the greatest genius on the part of the commanding general. The utmost he can hope for in the way of personal observation is a post on some eminence whence he can at least look down upon the woods and fields in which his men are fighting. Of the actual fighting he can see little or nothing. His ear must be tranied to catch the sound of cannon, that he may tell whether a battery at some decisive point is doing its duty. From the rattle of the musketry he must judge whether his lines are advancing or being driven back, and how fierce the fighting is at any point. A cloud of dust tells him of troops marching along a road, and he must have the topography of the battlefield and the positions of both armies well in mind, so that he may know whether the dust means reinforcements for the enemy or aid for himself.

The battle of the 29th of August, known generally as the battle of Groveton, was pre-eminently a contest such as here described. The field extended over a great expanse of wooded country, but little intersected by roads. Jackson's troops, as we have said, were posted along the line of an unfinished railroad that extended from the bank of Bull Run across the Warrenton turnpike. This roadbed was at some points an embankment, at others an excavation,—everywhere it was an admirable defensive work. Before it extended a dense strip of woods well filled with Jackson's skirmishers.

General Pope still hoped to fall upon Jackson and tear him limb from limb before Longstreet could come to his aid. The Union general knew that Ricketts had been driven from Thoroughfare Gap, and that a few hours at most would see the Confederate army united, but he hoped that in those few hours he might compass Jackson's destruction. All night he had been awake, sending dispatches to his division commanders and forming his lines, so that by daylight he had Jackson confronted by the greater part of the Union army. Sigel, who commanded on the Union right, had orders to open the attack at early dawn. His troops were wearied with hurrying to and fro in chase of Jackson. They had had scant rations for two days. Between hunger and fatigue they were in no fit condition to fight a great battle.

Morning dawns. Such of the soldiers as have slept turn out shivering from their damp beds. After a bit of hard tack and bacon the skirmishers start out rifle in hand to feel the enemy. The line of battle follows behind. The skirmishers reach the woods. The rifle shots begin to ring out. Men begin to fall here and there. Their comrades forget their hunger in the mad excitement of war and rush in to avenge them. The Union batteries in the rear drop their shells in the woods, preparing the way for the advance of the Union line. On the extreme left of the Union line the fighting lags. The artillery and the skirmishers have it all to themselves there. The combatants seem to prefer long range. Further to the eastward, though, the too-extended line of Carl Schurz's division tempts the gray-backs from their vantage-point. They dash out, and for a time spread confusion in Schurz's ranks. Here there is no long-range fighting. Muzzle to muzzle the muskets spit out their spiteful messages, and the bayonet searches out the vitals of its victims. Many of Schurz's men—most of them, indeed—are Germans, and they fight with desperate valor for their adopted country. Rallying, they beat back the Confederates. They follow them. Right up to the railway embankment the Germans swarm, and hold this point of vantage in the teeth of a furious Confederate fire until fresh troops come to relieve them.

The fighting begun on the Confederate left soon extended all along the line. Regiment after regiment of Union troops was brought up and plunged into the fight. The Confederates too were reënforced by the arrival of Longstreet, who reached the field shortly before noon. His arrival was unknown to General Pope, however, and there is nothing to show that his troops took any part in the battle of that day.

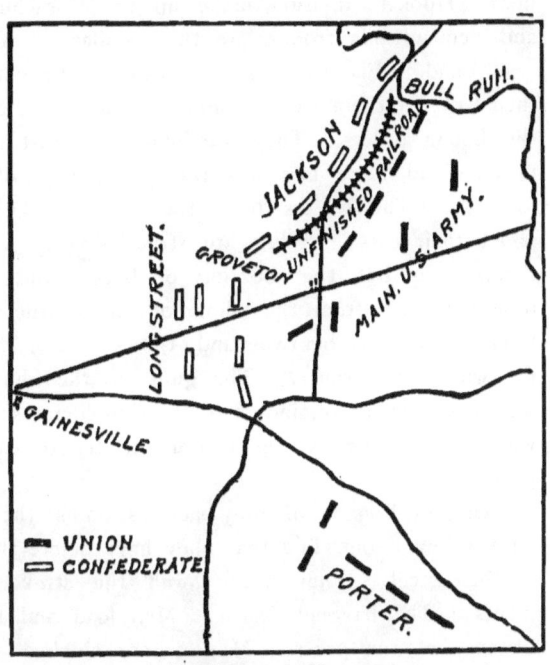

THE BATTLE OF MANASSAS.
Positions at Noon, Aug. 29th.

Mid-day brings a lull in the battle. Under the broiling September sun in Virginia there could be no furious fighting. And so for four hours only the skirmishers and the artillery are engaged. Meantime General Pope is getting ready for what he hopes will prove the finishing stroke of the day. He means to hurl a huge force of infantry against Jackson's left and center, pierce his line, and drive him in hopeless rout from the position he had held so firmly. This is the plan, good enough in conception, but which did not stand the test of execution.

It is against the center of Jackson's line that the storm breaks first. Hooker's division, made up of Massachusetts, New Hampshire and Pennsylvania troops, are the assailants. Grover's brigade leads.

"Load. Fix bayonets. Forward until you feel the enemy's fire, then halt, let them have it, and rush in with the bayonet!" Such are the Union orders. They are followed almost literally. With loaded muskets and fixed bayonets the gallant men of Grover's brigade step forward. The bullets from the enemy's skirmishers come singing about their ears. A few are struck down. No notice is taken of that; it is but the buzzing of bees. But now comes a sudden flash and roar from the whole of the hostile line. The bullets fly thicker, men fall by twos and threes. This is feeling the enemy's fire with a vengeance. The guns of the blue-coats are leveled and send back vicious rejoinders to the Confederates' harsh greeting. Then with a cheer they sweep forward to try to carry the day with the bayonet.

Gregg's brigade of gray-backs sustains the shock of the assault. Grover's men soon find that they have before them antagonists worthy of their steel. They firmly await the stroke of the charging regiments. The bayonets clash. Men load and fire at each other at a distance of ten paces. Muskets are clubbed and blows dealt right and left. The first line of battle of the Confederates is broken. The railway is reached and passed. A second line is met, and delivers a terrible fire. Then it too is swept away. Were there but more troops in reserve to dash in after Grover's gallant lads, the gap thus made in Jackson's lines might be enlarged until his whole army is split in twain. But no assistance comes, and a fresh body of Confederates, sweeping down upon the exhausted blue-coats, force them back little by little until all they had won at the expense of so much blood is lost again. It has been hot work on both sides. Grover took about 1500 men into the fight, and after 20 minutes came out minus 486 of them. At roll-call that night Gregg finds 613 of his men killed, wounded, or missing, including all the field officers except two.

Meantime on the extreme right of the Union line Kearny—gallant Phil Kearny, with a reputation as a fighter won on half a dozen hard-fought fields—is trying to turn the left flank of the enemy. For a time it seems as though the fierceness of his assault is going to turn the tide of battle. His first charge sweeps the Confederates from their point of vantage, the railway embankment, and rolls them back in confusion upon their line. But they rally, and with ranks strengthened by fresh troops from the brigades of Lawton and Early come doggedly back to regain the position from which Kearny had hurled them. For a time the center of the battle is shifted over there where Kearny and A. P. Hill are crossing swords. The woods resounded with the clash of musketry and were fairly choked with the smoke of gunpowder. The hills were flaming and smoking where the hostile batteries made deadly play. Up to the aid of Kearny comes Hatch, in command of King's division. He finds Hill rearranging his lines, and takes this for a sign that the Confederates are retreating. With three brigades Hatch hastens into the fray, hoping that a sudden blow may convert the retreat into a rout. Never was general more deceived. So far from retreating the gray-coats are getting ready to charge, and Hood's division of Longstreet's corps, being hurried forward, meets Hatch midway. The contest is sharp and bloody. "At one period," says a contemporaneous writer, "General Hatch sat complacently upon his horse, while every man who approached him pitched and fell headlong before he could deliver his message." For three-quarters of an hour this sharp work is kept up, then the Federals begin to withdraw. Their retreat is no less dogged than their advance. One cannon is so far to the front and so difficult to move that they see little chance of taking it with them. But they do not hastily abandon it. According to the testimony of one who led the Confederate advance, "this gun continued to fire, until my men were so near it as to have their faces burnt by its discharges." And when it became evident that the advance of the Confederates was irresistible, and that the gun could in no way be saved, the plucky Union gunners chopped its carriage to pieces and left it lying on the ground, useless for that battle at least.

With the withdrawal of Hatch and Kearny the fighting for that day ended. Night soon descended upon the field, and the hostile armies were glad enough to rest and reform their lines for the renewal of the conflict on the morrow. Here again Pope blundered through over-confidence. He thought he had won a victory, and sent off an enthusiastic telegram to Washington announcing it. As a matter of fact he had suffered defeat. He had gone into the fight with the purpose of annihilating Jackson before Longstreet could come to his assistance. In this he had signally failed. He had not even ousted Jackson from his snug position which he had held all day. And yet at midnight Pope telegraphed to Washington that he had driven the enemy from the field; and after sending the dispatch began to make his dispositions for renewing the attack on the morrow. It is sometimes said that keen appreciation of the moment when a retreat becomes advisable is the test of good generalship. This quality General Pope did not possess. With Jackson and Longstreet united in his front he still manfully held his ground. The next day's events showed the folly of this course.

Besides re-forming their lines for the struggle of the ensuing day, another and a sadder duty occupied both Federals and Confederates that night. Each side had come out of the battle with a loss of about 7000 men. Many of these were prisoners; many were dead. Still more perhaps lay on the battle-field, between the two armies, suffering from frightful wounds, racked with fever, groaning and crying for help. To bring the wounded in was the first duty of the men of both armies. "So soon as the fighting ceased," writes Private Goss in the *Century* magazine, "many sought without orders to rescue comrades lying wounded between the opposing lines. There seemed to be an understanding between the men of both armies that such parties were not to be disturbed in their mission of mercy. When the fire had died away along the darkling woods, little groups of men from the Union lines went stealthily about, bringing in the wounded from the exposed positions. Blankets attached to poles or muskets often served as stretchers to bear the wounded to the ambulances and surgeons. There was a great lack here of organized effort to care for our wounded. Vehicles of various kinds were pressed into service. The removal went on during the entire night, and tired soldiers were roused from their slumbers by the plaintive cries of sufferers passing in the comfortless vehicles. In one instance a Confederate and a Union soldier were found cheering each other on the field. They were put into the same Virginia farm-cart and sent to the rear, talking and groaning in fraternal sympathy."

Morning found the Confederate army posted along peculiar but formidable lines. Jackson retained his position of the day before behind the railway embankment, his left resting on Bull Run and his right reaching almost to the Warrenton turnpike. Longstreet's left flank joined Jackson's right, but instead of the line being prolonged in a line with Jackson's it stretched out at an angle, so that the lines of Jackson and Longstreet together formed a huge V; a sort of funnel into which the attacking army must charge.

Pope in his turn had his army massed on the hills which in the first battle of Bull Run had been held by the Confederates. Apparently he ignored the Longstreet arm of the Confederate V, and determined to attack Jackson only. He writes himself that he had little hope of victory, and only fought to delay the Confederate advance upon Washington. His troops "had had little to eat for two days, and artillery and cavalry horses had been in harness and under the saddle for ten days, and had been almost out of forage for the last two days." It might be thought that under such circumstances Pope would have taken up a defensive position behind Bull Run and waited for the enemy to attack him. Instead of this, however, he got it into his head that the Confederates were retreating, and made all possible haste to attack them, suffering a severe defeat for his pains.

Until near noon of that eventful Saturday, the 30th of August, silence reigned over the field on which the two great armies were to grapple once again. Not until twelve o'clock did General Pope order his divisions to advance. It is worthy of note that this order was for a "pursuit," not for an attack. So firmly did Pope believe that army to be in retreat, which in point of fact was massed behind embankments, snugly sheltered in railroad cuts, or ambushed on wooded hills waiting to slaughter the assailants.

Under the hot noonday sun the Federals advance to the assault. Heintzelman, Porter, Sigel, Reno and Reynolds are all in the attacking column. They advance north of the turnpike, little suspecting that they are marching straight into the jaws of the Confederate lion. The lower jaw—Longstreet's corps—is south of the turnpike. We shall soon see it close in upon the upper jaw, crushing the Union army between. Over on the Henry hill and Chinn hill, about three-quarters of a mile from Jackson's line, the Union guns are booming away, throwing their shells over the charging lines of blue and dropping them where the ranks of tattered gray-coats are lying close to the railway embankment for shelter.

Suddenly Reynolds, who of all the Union commanders is nearest Longstreet's lines, catches sight of a crowd of gray-backs in the woods on his left flank. He sends a courier to McDowell, who is commanding this operation which Pope was pleased to term a pursuit. McDowell orders him to abandon the charge, and change front to meet this flank attack. This he does while the rest sweep on to overwhelm Jackson.

STARKE'S BRIGADE FIGHTING WITH STONES.

Grandly and resistlessly the serried ranks of Porter's and Sigel's divisions sweep on toward the railway grade where the veterans of the Shenandoah valley wait to receive them. The Union cheer and the "rebel yell" voice the defiance of the foes. It is American against American,—a tug of war no less notable than that which comes "when Greek meets Greek." More than one of the men who weathered the leaden storm that day has left testimony to show the desperate bravery of the assailants and the dogged tenacity of the defenders of the railroad grade. General Bradley T. Johnson's brigade was posted in what was known as the "deep cut." Here the fighting was fiercest. "They stormed my position," he writes of the blue-coats under Porter, "deploying in the woods in brigade and then charging in a run, line after line, brigade after brigade, up the hill, on the thicket held by the 48th, and the railroad cut occupied by the 42d. . . . Before the railroad cut the fight was most obstinate. I saw a Federal flag hold its position for an hour within ten yards of a flag of one of the regiments in the cut, and go down six or eight times; and after the fight one hundred dead men were lying twenty yards from the cut, some of them within two feet of it. The men fought until their ammunition was exhausted, and then threw stones. Lieutenant ——— of the battalion killed one with a stone, and I saw him after the fight with his skull fractured. Dr. Richard P. Johnson, on my volunteer staff, having no arms of any kind, was obliged to have recourse to this means of offense from the beginning. As line after line surged up the hill, time after time, led up by their officers, they were dashed back on one another, until the whole field was covered with a confused mass of struggling, running, routed Yankees."

We shall see later that General Johnson is in error in giving Jackson's men the sole credit for hurling back those charging platoons of blue-coats, and we shall find Jackson himself calling for assistance lest he should be overwhelmed by those same "running, routed Yankees." But so far as the reported use of stones as missiles by the Confederates is concerned, there seems to be corroboration of the story. Lieutenant Healy of Brockenburgh's brigade writes: "Saturday we received urgent orders to reënforce a portion of our line in the center, which was about to give way. The troops occupying this position had expended their ammunition, and were defending themselves with rocks which seemed to have been picked or blasted out of the bed of the railroad, chips and slivers of stone which many were collecting and others were throwing."

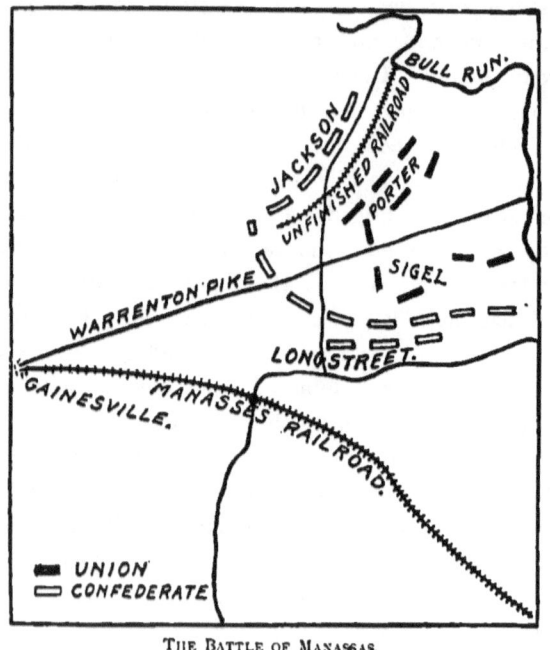

THE BATTLE OF MANASSAS.
(Positions Aug. 30th, 6 P.M.)

Of course a defense of this kind cannot long be maintained, and Jackson sends to Lee for reënforcements. Lee sends the courier on to Longstreet. That general is found sitting on his horse on the knob of the hill, whence he can watch the progress of the attack upon his colleague. The whole Union army, he says, "seemed to surge up against Jackson as if to crush him with an overwhelming mass."

"General Jackson is hard pressed, and General Lee directs that you send reënforcements to his aid," said the courier to Longstreet. The general nods, but sends no troops to Jackson's aid. He can do better than that. The spot on which he stands commands a magnificent view of the Union charge, and a battery posted there will sweep the ground over which Porter's men are charging. Three batteries are called up, twelve guns in all. The gunners bend to their deadly work with a will. Soon all twelve cannon are flaming and smoking and booming. The effect of this flanking fire upon the Federal forces is immediate. Thrice they are thrown into confusion, and thrice they reform their shattered ranks. Then while the guns are still hurling an iron storm against Porter's lines, Longstreet calls up his infantry, orders a charge, and this whole body of fresh Confederate troops goes sweeping down upon the wearied Union army.

Nothing is now left for Pope but to save what he can from the wreck; to get his army off the field and out of danger with the least possible loss. This he does with marked ability. The hill on which stands the Henry house—the very spot where the fighting was most vicious on the day of the first Bull Run—proves the key to the situation now. There Pope stations a regiment of regulars, against whose inflexible front the enemy beats in vain. Meantime the remainder of the Union army marches sullenly and sadly from the field, and wends its way through the smoky, rainy night, over rough and crowded roads, toward Centerville. It has been Bull Run repeated, save that in this second battle the retreat of the Union army was orderly, and not a rout.

There is some variety of usage among historians as to the names of these battles fought on the 28th, 29th and 30th of August, 1862. The last of the three is called uniformly by the Confederates the battle of Manassas, and more than one writer has suggested that the victors should at least have the right of naming the battle. Many Union historians, however, dub it the second battle of Bull Run. The battles fought on the 28th and 29th are most commonly classed as one contest and called the battle of Groveton. Sometimes, however, the second is spoken of as the battle of Gainesville.

The loss in these three battles was heavy, being about 14,800 for the Union army and 10,700 for the Confederates.

Few battles of the civil war have been so persistently fought over in time of peace as those of Groveton and Manassas. Smarting under the complete defeat inflicted upon him, General Pope sought for a scapegoat upon whom to lay the blame, and found one in the person of General Fitz-John Porter. It will be remembered that during the fighting of the 29th Porter with his division of 9000 men lay quiet, and took no part in the action. Pope declared that he had ordered General Porter to attack Jackson, and that by his disobedience in not responding to this order the opportunity to crush Jackson before Longstreet's arrival was lost.

Upon this charge General Porter was brought before a drumhead court-martial, tried, found guilty, and dismissed the service in disgrace.

But the matter did not rest here. General Porter devoted his life to clearing up the charges brought against him. He declared that Pope's order only directed him to attack in case Longstreet should not oppose him. That in point of fact Longstreet arrived almost as soon as the order did, and with 30,000 men blocked his way. That to attack Longstreet's overwhelming force with his own 9000 men would have been folly, and that he acted for the very best when he confined his operations to so maneuvering his men as to keep Longstreet constantly on the alert for an attack, and thereby kept him from giving any aid to Jackson.

Many years afterward General Grant thus summed up in two diagrams this historic controversy. The first diagram depicts the situation as General Pope conceived it.

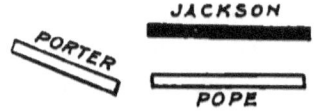

Clearly if this had been the way the armies stood it would have been Porter's duty to attack. But Grant's second diagram showed the situation as Porter saw it, and as it really was.

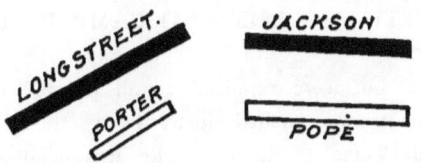

And this put a very different face on the matter.

After more than twenty-five years of constant effort General Porter convinced the United States Congress of the justice of his cause, and the rank and honors of which he had been deprived by drumhead court-martial in 1862 were restored to him by act of Congress in 1887.

Once again Pope and Jackson measured swords before the great army led by the former reached a haven of refuge at Washington. It was on the second day after the fighting at Manassas that the redoubtable foot cavalry came crowding down upon the Union right flank by the Little River turnpike from the northwest. Jackson had tried again his favorite tactics of making a long detour and falling upon his enemy's rear. But on this occasion his usual good fortune deserted him. His men, wearied with long marches and nearly a week of continuous and stubborn fighting, could no longer get over the ground with that celerity which had earned for them the title of the "foot cavalry." Ever since the day of fighting at Manassas, too, a cold, drenching rain had been falling, making the roads heavy with mud and breaking down the spirits even of Jackson's hardy veterans. So it happened that the march of the Confederate column was so deliberate that Pope was able to keep himself well posted as to its progress, and when Jackson seemed to threaten his rear he sent the fresh troops of Sumner to meet him at Chantilly, and ordered Reno, Hooker, and Kearny to support him.

It was near five o'clock of the afternoon of September 1st that Jackson's skirmishers encountered those of Reno, and a pitched battle soon began. The rain was still falling heavily, and the air soon became murky with the smoke of countless guns. The Confederates took the offensive, but were repulsed at all points with seeming ease Then the Union troops rushed forward in their turn, but were dashed back, while Isaac J. Stevens, who was leading the charge in person, was shot dead. It was while the fighting was at its fiercest that an officer commanding one of Jackson's brigades sent word to the commander that his men must retire, because the drenching rain was making their ammunition useless.

"Tell him to hold his ground," responded Jackson. "If his guns will not go off neither will the enemy's."

It was nearly nightfall when the battle began, and the armies had not been fighting long when it grew so dark that none could tell friend from foe. The darkness cost one brave Union soldier his life. General Philip Kearny, having in some way become separated from his command, set out to look for it, and rode straight into the skirmish line of the enemy. "What troops are these?" he shouted as he saw a group of soldiers rise up out of the fog and smoke before him. Then without awaiting an answer he wheeled his horse and started to escape. But the Confederates were as quick as he, and their bullets were speedier than his charger. A dozen musket-shots rang out, and brave Kearny fell dead from his horse. General Jackson sent his body into the Union lines next day with a military escort.

When the darkness at last put an end to the fighting the Federals had lost 1300 men, the Confederates 800. Neither side had gained any marked advantage, but as Jackson had tried to turn the Union flank and failed, the battle of Chantilly must be regarded as a defeat for him.

The next day the Union army withdrew within the cordon of forts surrounding Washington, and the career of the army under Pope was ended. The Army of Virginia which he had commanded was made part of the Army of the Potomac under McClellan, and General Pope returned to the west, where, as he said in his grandiloquent address, he had seen only the backs of his enemies.

DEATH OF GENERAL KEARNEY.

CHAPTER III.

THE INVASION OF MARYLAND. — HIGH HOPES OF THE CONFEDERATES. — THEY MEET A COLD RECEPTION. — THE LOST ORDER. — JACKSON'S CAPTURE OF HARPER'S FERRY. — McCLELLAN IN CHASE. — BATTLE OF SOUTH MOUNTAIN. — BATTLE OF SHARPSBURG OR ANTIETAM. — LEE ABANDONS MARYLAND.

F course while these stirring events were occurring in Virginia, there was fighting, and plenty of it, in the west. But for the sake of making our narrative continuous we will defer telling of the operations of the armies west of the Alleghanies until we have finished with the story of the moves made on the great checker-board about Washington, by the armies under McClellan and Lee in the fall and winter of 1862.

In Virginia the military prospects of the South were never so bright as in the pleasant autumn days of September, 1862. After long months of fighting the armies of the Union had been beaten away from the Confederate capital. For the first time in more than six months no hostile force threatened Richmond. McClellan first, and Pope after him, had been met and defeated. Now, instead of Richmond being surrounded by the muzzles of hostile cannon, it was Washington that was beleaguered, and the streets of the Federal capital were crowded with the stragglers and unattached soldiers who had lost their commands in the confusion attendant upon defeat.

But General Lee could not hope to take Washington by attacking it from Virginia. Not only the Potomac was between him and the capital city, but a cordon of forts on the Virginia side of the river made the approach of a hostile force impossible. Yet the Confederate general knew that it was his time to assume the offensive. His successes must be followed up. And so he determined to take his army over into Maryland, whence he might either proceed into Pennsylvania, or swing round and fall upon Washington in the rear.

This was a project full of importance for the Confederacy. For the first time the southern armies were to become armies of invasion. Hitherto the fighting had been confined almost exclusively to the soil of the seceded States. The policy of a defensive war outlined when the Confederacy was formed had been scrupulously adhered to.

But Lee now determined to let the heavy burden of war fall upon other people than Virginians. Ever since Sumter fell the hostile armies had been tramping back and forth through the Old Dominion, trampling down crops, burning fences, pillaging farm-houses. It was now harvest-time too, and if the theater of war could be shited to some northern State until Virginia had garnered her plenteous crops, all that store of corn and wheat would be saved for the granary of the Confederacy.

It is of course true that in entering Maryland General Lee did not consider that he was invading a hostile State. Maryland was southern in traditions and custom. Slaves were bought and sold within its borders. Though it had never seceded, it was generally reckoned as being one at heart with the Confederacy. The assault of the Baltimore mob on the Massachusetts troops early in the war, had been accepted as indicative of the temper of all the people of Maryland. It was a mistaken conclusion.

On the 5th of September the Confederate army waded through the cool waters of the Potomac at Noland's ford. General Jackson led the way, his head bare, his face grave and thoughtful, as though asking the blessing of Providence upon this expedition so fraught with importance to the southern cause. Some one started the southern army song, "Maryland, My Maryland," and the whole army caught it up and shouted out the melody until the woods on the banks resounded.

> Dear mother! burst the tyrant's chain,
> Maryland!
> Virginia should not call in vain,
> Maryland!
> She meets her sisters on the plain,
> "*Sic semper*," 'tis the proud refrain,
> That baffles minions back again,
> Maryland!
> Arise in majesty again,
> Maryland! My Maryland.

But the army had not proceeded far toward the interior of the State before General Lee found that the people of Maryland either had no liking for the Confederacy, or dared not show it. The recruits whom he expected would flock to his standard by hundreds came only by twos and threes. He reached the little village of Frederick, where he had hoped to find an ovation awaiting him and his army. Instead he found closed shops, locked doors, drawn shutters and empty streets. This quiet hostility where he expected warm greeting must have hurt the Confederate chieftain as much as the loss of a battle. And although he issued a dignified and eloquent address to the people of Maryland, only a few were stimulated by it to join the Confederate arms. It was in Frederick, by the way, that the incident upon which is founded Whittier's poem of "Barbara Frietchie" is said to have occurred. The genius of the poet has made the name of the patriotic old woman immortal, but there is reason to believe that she earned her immortality cheaply. The men who marched through Frederick that day have no recollection of how

> "All day long that free flag tossed,
> Over the heads of the rebel host."

Col. Douglass, who was in Maryland with Jackson, writes: "In Middletown two very pretty girls with ribbons of red, white and blue floating from their hair, and small Union flags in their hands, rushed out of a house as we passed, came to the curbstone, and with much laughter waved their flags defiantly in the face of the general. He bowed and raised his hat, and turning with his quiet smile to his staff, said: 'We evidently have no friends in this town.' And this is about the way he would have treated Barbara Frietchie."

Frederick sheltered the Confederate forces only a few days. The isolated garrison of Harper's Ferry, amounting to about 11,000 Union troops, tempted Lee sorely, and he determined to send Jackson off to capture that stronghold. Accordingly on September 9th the whole Confederate force except the rear-guard left Frederick and proceeded westward, Jackson making direct for Harper's Ferry and the rest of the division commanders proceeding at a more leisurely pace in the same direction.

McClellan meantime had pulled his army together and had left Washington, marching down to meet his enemy at Frederick. He reached the little town just in time to exchange a few shots with Lee's rear-guard, which was about to leave.

"From all I can gather," wrote McClellan when he had taken possession of Frederick, "Secesh is skedaddling, and I don't think I can catch him unless he is really moving into Pennsylvania." It seemed to be one of the failings of the Union generals of that day, that when they failed to comprehend the purpose of a movement on the part of the Confederate forces they immediately declared that the enemy was running away. However, General McClellan was not suffered to remain long in ignorance of the plans of the Confederates, for soon after his arrival in Frederick there came to him two soldiers bearing a bit of paper which they had found wrapped around three cigars in the house occupied by the Confederate General D. H. Hill. This paper proved to be a copy of General Lee's general order detailing the order of march and point of concentration of the Confedcrate army. McClellan was thus furnished with exact information as to the whereabouts and intentions of his foes. He learned that, instead of "skedaddling," Jackson had gone off to capture Harper's Ferry and the eleven or twelve thousand Union troops there stationed, and that when this was accomplished the Confederates were to rendezvous at Sharpsburg, and thence march into Pennsylvania.

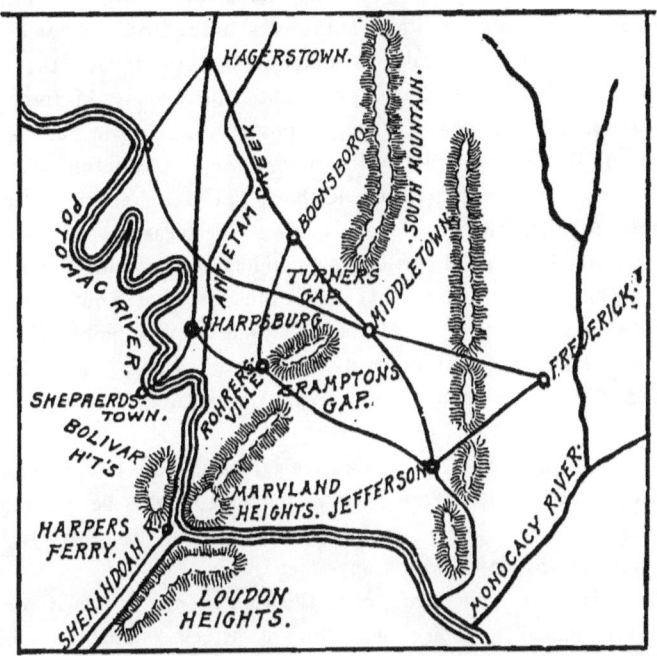

SCENE OF LEE'S OPERATIONS IN MARYLAND.

All this was made clear to General McClellan, who until the finding of this order had been completely in the dark as to his adversary's intentions. Now he had seen the hand of his antagonist, and could make his game accordingly. He saw at once that the Confederate army was split into two sections, separated by more than a day's march. Jackson, Walker and McLaws had gone to capture Harper's Ferry, while Longstreet had gone on to Hagerstown, and D. H. Hill was guarding the narrow and precipitous passes of Turner's Gap.

General McClellan determined to follow Longstreet with the main body of his army, forcing his way through Turner's Gap. Meanwhile Franklin was to go to the southwest, drive McLaws away from the slope of Maryland Heights, raise the siege of Harper's Ferry, and with the garrison hasten to join McClellan and complete the demolition of Longstreet. The best military authorities agree that the Union commander made a fatal mistake in determining, to follow the enemy through Turner's Gap. There he found the enemy in force, with a well-disciplined rear-guard strongly posted to dispute his advance. Had he on the contrary led his army through Crampton's Gap and taken the enemy in flank, he would have cut Lee's army in two and been able to demolish either part of it at his pleasure. It was this course indeed that the shrewder commanders among the Confederates feared. Col. Ruffin records that when the battle at South Mountain was at its fiercest, General Hill declared that he was highly pleased to know that McClellan's whole army was in his front. Knowing that Hill had but a few men to withstand the assault, Ruffin asked his reason.

"I had feared," said Hill, "that this attack was but a feint, and that the Union army at this very moment might be passing the mountains at some lower gap and thus cut in between Jackson's forces and the division under Longstreet."

That McClellan failed to crush the Confederate army is probably due to this mistaken choice of a line of attack. That he failed to save Harper's Ferry seems to have been due to the lack of pluck of the officer who commanded that post. Let us first consider the movements which led to the downfall of this historic Union stronghold.

Harper's Ferry lies on the low lands at the juncture of the Shenandoah and Potomac rivers. On every side the hills tower, offering scores and hundreds of places whence a hostile battery can pour its missiles down upon the town and its defenders. The spot is one incapable of protracted defense.

On the morning of the 13th of September, the Union pickets in the woods upon the hillsides about the town reported the appearance of the Confederates in force. All three divisions arrived at about the same time, and soon the signal flags were waving from Loudon Mountain and Maryland Heights. By the next morning the batteries were in position. The small Union force which held Maryland Heights on the north side of the Potomac was driven away by McLaws with but little trouble. And so, penned in by a cordon of Confederate cannon, the 12,000 boys in blue awaited the attack.

It was at two o'clock on the afternoon of the 14th of September that the guns of Walker's division opened fire from Loudon Heights. Soon their deepened thunder was echoed from Maryland Heights and the Bolivar hills, and the whole circle of batteries was in full play. At their elevated positions the southern soldiers could hear the booming of cannon over toward South Mountain and Crampton's Gap. They knew that in some way McClellan had divined their purpose, and was fighting his way through the mountain passes, and bringing help to Harper's Ferry. Every hour counted then, and the southern artillerymen worked their pieces with a will, creeping nearer and nearer to the enemy's stronghold as the Federals were driven from their outposts. Against a superior force which possesed an enormous advantage in the way of commanding positions, the Federals struggled manfully but hopelessly. They knew that help was coming, but how soon it would arrive no man could tell. When the sun went down that night only two or three Union cannon were answering the hoarse challenge of the Confederate batteries. The rest were silenced. By this time General Franklin, who led the Union relief force, had broken his way through Crampton's Gap and was firing signal guns to let the beleaguered blue-coats know that they might expect him early the next day. But the Confederate batteries on the hills kept up so constant a din that the signal guns were unheard. Jackson alone heard them, and he sent orders to his division commanders to carry Harper's Ferry by assault early in the morning.

That night the Confederates pushed their batteries still farther to the front, and massed their troops ready for the next day's assault. At dawn the cannonade was begun. The troops of A. P. Hill who were to make the assault began to deploy on Bolivar Heights. They thought they had hot work before them. A young lieutenant had been reconnoitering early in the morning, and brought back a disquieting report. "A few strides brought me to the edge of an abattis which extended solidly for two hundred yards," he wrote in telling the story afterward, "a narrow bare field being between the abattis and the foot of the fort, which was garnished with thirty guns. They were searching the abattis lazily with grape-shot, which flew uncomfortably near at times. I thought I had never seen a more dangerous trap in my life. I went back and Austin Brockenbrough asked, 'How is it?' 'Well,' said I, 'we'll say our prayers and go in like men.' 'Not as bad as that?' 'Every bit: see for yourself.' He went, and came back looking very grave. Meanwhile from the east, northwest and northeast our cannon opened, and were answered by the Federal guns from Bolivar Heights. We were down in a ravine, we could see nothing, we could only hear. Presently along came the words, 'Prepare to charge!' We moved steadily up the hill; the sun had just risen; some one said: 'Colonel, what is that on the fort?' 'Halt,' cried the colonel, 'they have surrendered.' A glad shout burst from ten thousand men."

The Confederates had good reason to shout. With the relieving force scarce four miles away, Harper's Ferry had surrendered, and 11,000 men, 73 cannon, and an immense number of small arms and munitions of war had fallen into their hands. Almost the last shot fired slew the Federal commander, Col. Miles, as he stood on the ramparts waving the white flag that the fog hid from the distant Confederate batteries. One Union officer alone won honor at Harper's Ferry. This was Col. Davis of the cavalry, who, learning that the place was to be surrendered, quietly led his command, numbering some two thousand men, out of the camp, across the Potomac river, and away to freedom under the very nose of the Confederate general, McLaws. More than this, on his way to join McClellan he captured a Confederate baggage train of 173 wagons, and with his troops and booty reached Sharpsburg in safety. The rest of the Harper's Ferry garrison was surrendered unconditionally to the enemy. Jackson's biographer, John Esten Cooke, thus tells the story of the surrender:

"Jackson had been up for the greater part of the night, and for many preceding nights had scarcely slept an hour, although he required more rest than any general in the army. He was now exhausted, and had no sooner satisfied himself that the place had fallen than he sat down on the ground, leaned his elbow on a log, and was asleep in a moment. Meantime General Hill had communicated with the Federal General White, who had succeeded to the command in consequence of a mortal wound received by Colonel Miles, and now came in company with that officer to arrange with Jackson the terms of the surrender. The contrast between General White's neat uniform and Jackson's dingy coat is represented as having been very striking; and the Confederate commander wore an old hat less imposing even than his yellow cap, of which some lady in Martinsburg had robbed him. General White probably regarded with some curiosity this singular specimen of a southern general, and allowed Hill to open the interview. The latter said to Jackson:

"'General, this is General White of the United States army.' Jackson made a courteous movement, but seemed ready to fall asleep again, when Hill added:

"'He has come to arrange the terms of surrender.'

"Jackson made no reply, and looking under his slouch hat, Hill found that he was asleep. He was again roused, and at last raising his head with difficulty said to the Federal commander:

"'The surrender must be unconditional, General. Every indulgence can be granted afterwards.'

"As he finished speaking Jackson's head fell, and unable to contend against his drowsiness he again fell asleep and the interview terminated."

So much for the success of Jackson's descent upon Harper's Ferry. Let us now return to the Union camp and see what McClellan has been doing while the Confederate guns have been thundering from the heights of Loudon, Maryland and Bolivar.

It is early dawn of Sunday, the 14th of September. In the Union camps about Middletown all is life and bustle. The men have had their early breakfast of bread and bacon and coffee, have struck their shelter tents, rolled up their few belongings, and are ready to take the road in pursuit of the Confederates. And now the long lines of blue-clad soldiers begin to move out slowly along the roads, looking like veritable torrents of men where the roads are in plain sight, and their course where the road passed through the woods marked by huge clouds of yellow dust rising high above the trees. Before the marching columns the hills rise by gentle slopes until at points they tower mountain high. It is the northern spur of the Blue Ridge, known thereabouts as South Mountain. Its highest crest is about 1000 feet in altitude, but at two points are depressions called gaps through which wind the rugged mountain roads that lead over the hills into Pennsylvania. The more northern of these gaps is called Turner's, the southern Crampton's Gap. A sharp-eyed spectator standing on the summit of the Catoctin mountain, east of Middletown, and provided with a good field-glass, might have seen this spectacle unfolded before him:

Directly beneath him, Middletown; nestling in the midst of a fertile valley, a clump of roofs and spires surrounded on all sides by fields of golden grain, green orchards, pastures covered with waving grass or dotted with grazing cattle. Clustered about Middletown, the white-topped wagons and ambulances of a great army. Everywhere beyond the village marching troops, on different roads, but all evidently going in one of two directions, either southwest or northwest. The former are Franklin's troops on their way to relieve Harper's Ferry; the latter form the major portion of the Union army, and are going to force their way through Turner's Gap. No foe at this hour seems to be opposing Franklin, who is plodding away in column of fours, but the van of the other division under Burnside is deployed in line of battle, and clouds of smoke and jets of spurting flame along the front would tell the observer that there was fighting there, even did not the rumble of the cannonade. And now if the field-glass is turned searchingly upon the rugged, wooded hills in front of the ever-advancing line of blue, there may be seen gray-clad regiments deployed among the trees, lurking behind stone walls, posted upon precipitous crags, and doing their best to beat back with leaden whips the onpouring flood of bluecoats.

So much for the scene in the forenoon as seen by an observer on a mountain top and out of range. Let us now go into the thick of the fighting with one of Burnside's soldiers.

A brigade of the Kanawha division of General Burnside's army is marching out of Middletown on its way to Turner's Gap. It is to support Pleasonton's cavalry, which is already on the way, and this small force is expected to sweep the Gap clear of all defenders. General McClellan knows that at Boonsboro' or beyond he will find the forces of Hill and Longstreet, but he has no idea that anything but a simple rear-guard will contest his advance through the Gap. As the brigade is crossing Catoctin creek it comes upon a Union officer, solitary and travel-stained, coming from the direction of the enemy's lines. He is at once recognized as Col. Moore, who had been captured by the enemy some days before.

"Where in the world did you come from, Colonel?" sings out an officer as he is recognized.

"Captured by the enemy three days ago. Paroled and sent back to-day," is the answer. "But where are you going?"

"Oh, up into Turner's Gap on a reconnoissance."

"My God! be careful," is Moore's exclamation as he sees the

slender force before him; then suddenly recollecting himself. "But I am paroled. I can say nothing."

He has just come from the Gap. He knows that instead of a puny rear-guard, it is defended by more than 12,000 men under Longstreet and D. H. Hill. Honor will not permit him to warn his comrades of the trap into which they are marching. He is on parole, and can neither fight nor give advice, but his hasty exclamation has aroused the suspicion of the Federals, and they take along another brigade of troops and advance warily.

The battle that follows is sharply fought. The Confederates are fighting for time. To hold the Union army in check twelve hours is victory for them. Though they are outnumbered—for when the battle has fairly begun the greater part of Burnside's division is engaged—the Confederates have the advantage of position.

A battle such as this at Turner's Gap does not admit of detailed description. The rugged ground, and the scarcity of roads, make any concerted plan of attack impossible. The affair is rather a series of disconnected skirmishes than a general engagement.

Cox's Kanawha division which we saw fording Catoctin creek goes into battle on the Federal right. It scales the rugged hillsides manfully in the face of the foe. About nine o'clock the bullets begin to fly, and the boys on both sides know that they are in for a hard day's fighting. As the blue-coats climb the mountain-sides their batteries, which cannot climb, throw shells into the woods ahead of the advancing line,—a sort of artillery service mightily affected in the early days of the war, and which was seldom of much aid to the friends or injury to the foes of the artillerymen.

The bullets begin to hum as soon as the blue-coats begin the ascent. Pickets and sharpshooters, dodging behind trees and crouched behind stone walls, make the climb very unhealthy for the men of the Kanawha division. But it is not until the summit is nearly reached that the fight becomes obstinate. There about a thousand Confederates—men from North Carolina—have taken up a position behind a

HOLDING TURNER'S GAP.

stone wall and are evidently ready to sell their lives dearly. Against this force Cox's Ohioans dash forward pluckily, but are beaten back more than once. Sheltered behind their stone breastwork the Confederates can take the situation coolly, aim well, and hold their fire until it can be delivered with telling effect. Cheering on the assailants is a young Ohio officer, the lieutenant-colonel of the 23d Ohio, one Rutherford B. Hayes, who in later years rose to be President of the United States. Just as he has led his regiment forward to the final charge which sweeps over the stone wall and breaks the enemy's center, a bullet strikes him down. But his men sweep on past him, cheering, breasting the storm of bullets, scaling the wall, clubbing their muskets and fighting hand to hand with the gray-coats they find there. General Garland, the Confederate commander, falls mortally wounded. His staff officers had repeatedly urged him not to expose himself, but he insisted upon sharing the perils of his men, and so met his fate. With his fall his line goes to pieces, and soon the victorious Federals are in possession of the crest at that part of Turner's Gap. It is now near noon.

For a few hours the fighting lags. The Confederates come back in force under Anderson to drive Cox away from the position he won in the morning, but Cox will not be driven. Meantime Federal reënforcements under Hooker are coming up the east slope of the mountain, while Confederate regiments under Longstreet have just reached the foot of the western slope. In the race Hooker is far ahead, but he little knows how slender a force is before him. Did he but press forward boldly, pushing his advance with the dash shown by Cox's brigade in the battle of the forenoon, he could sweep the Gap clear of its defenders before sundown. But instead he waits for reports from the engineers and for more troops. It is four o'clock before the Union attack is made in earnest, and by that time the head of Longstreet's column has arrived and the Confederate line is strengthened. And now the watchers in the valley, or on the distant range of Catoctin hills, can see the crest of Turner's gap wreathed in smoke, while lurid gashes show where the cannon are doing their deadly work. There are cleared spots, of course, where the hostile lines of battle stand boldly before each other, but much of the fighting is in the forests, where the cautious tactics of the Indian are brought into play. Batteries posted on commanding knolls sweep the roads, or search with shells the woods which are thought to be sheltering the enemy. A great battle, made up of countless petty skirmishes, is raging.

Through it all the Union lines are advancing steadily. The most casual observer can see that. There are long halts, men are falling thick and fast, but when any ground is lost it is the Confederates who have given way. A few more hours of daylight and the Pass will be fairly won. But the sun has gone down. Longstreet's troops are on the ground, and as if aware that darkness will bring them a respite, redouble their efforts. At no time is the defense so stubborn, the rattle of the musketry so constant, and the thunder of the cannon so heavy as at the moment when the twilight begins to deepen into night.

Now the Union advance is checked. Despite the best efforts of the officers, seconded by the ready courage of the men, not a foot of ground can be gained. General Reno, in command on the Union left, determines to go forward among the skirmishers, and view the Confederate position for himself. A sharpshooter picks him off, and his dead body is carried from the field. Then the battle dies away, though from time to time through the night a sudden crash of musketry tells that some incautious movement on the part of Federal or Confederate has brought on a skirmish along the picket line.

Late at night the wearied Confederate soldiers are roused from their slumbers. Silently they "fall in." Whispered commands are given. While the Union army sleeps its foes are retreating to Sharpsburg. Over two thousand southern soldiers were left behind, by far the greater part of them being prisoners. So wearied were the men of Lee's army that scores had crawled away into the woods to sleep, and when the time to fall back came they could not be found. The

Union loss in prisoners was but slight, only 22 men, according to McClellan's report. But in killed and wounded the Federal army has lost 1546 men.

Victory rests with the Federals, who hold the Gap, from which they have driven the enemy. But in checking the Union advance for a day and a night the defenders of the Gap have given Jackson time to swoop down on Harper's Ferry, and to get back to Lee in season to give battle to McClellan's army.

So much for the fighting at Turner's Gap. On the same day another Union column pushed its way through the Confederate lines at Crampton's Gap, six miles to the southward. The two battles, though separated by six miles of rugged and impassable mountain peaks, are generally classed together and called the battle of South Mountain.

The sharp-eyed man with a field-glass whom we left gazing from the towering crest of Catoctin Mountain saw one division of the Union army leave the main body and turn away toward the southwest. This was Franklin's force on its way to relieve Harper's Ferry. At the Gap Franklin encountered much such a reception as Burnside met at Turner's Gap. Stone walls, thick woods, steep declivities, all protected the enemy and made his 2200 men almost a match for General Franklin's 6500. Here again the Confederates were fighting for time, and though defeated and driven from their positions, they held Franklin in check long enough to enable Jackson to force the surrender of Harper's Ferry. Once the white flag was displayed from the defenses of that place, the Confederates spent no more time in fighting in that region, but marched away with all possible speed to join Lee at Sharpsburg before General McClellan could descend from the summit of South Mountain and crush him. It was about 8 o'clock of the morning of Sept. 15 when Harper's Ferry surrendered. By sunset not a gray uniform or a flag with the "stars and bars" was to be seen. All were off to Lee's assistance, with the exception of the officer left at the Ferry to parole the captured blue-coats.

Tuesday, the 16th of September, saw the two armies again confronting each other. McClellan had brought his legions over the mountains. Lee had seen Jackson and Walker return from the Harper's Ferry expedition, and needed only McLaws to reunite his army. Continued delays had defeated McClellan's plan of crushing Lee while the Confederate army was dismembered, and the Union commander was now about to give battle to the whole Confederate army on grounds of the enemy's own choosing. A retreat across the Potomac would have enabled Lee to escape without a fight, but he doubtless felt that such a course would cost him all the prestige won by his daring expedition into Maryland. So relying upon the advantageous position he had chosen to make up for the disproportion between his force and that of McClellan, Lee rested quietly and waited for the Federals to open that historic conflict known in the North as the battle of the Antietam, and in the South as the battle of Sharpsburg.

To the eastward of the little town of Sharpsburg, the Antietam creek flows through a devious channel, with many a bend but maintaining the general direction of north and south. The creek is sluggish and deep. The few fords by which it may be crossed were, at the time the hostile armies were arrayed along the banks, waist deep in water. Three bridges cross the stream near Sharpsburg.

The Confederate line was formed along a bold crest from which the fields and woods sloped away to the bank of the Antietam, a quarter of a mile to the eastward. The left flank of the line rested on the Potomac river, and that stream swept in a series of vast curves back of Lee's army and around until it almost touched his right flank. So with a deep creek covering his front, the Potomac protecting both flanks, a level turnpike and a good ford in his rear should a retreat be necessary, General Lee awaited the beginning of a battle which he had hoped to escape, but of which he was prepared to make the best.

For nearly a day the blue-clad regiments of the Union army came pouring down over the summit of South Mountain, and settling like a swarm of bees along the eastern shore of the Antietam creek.

All along the line of the creek they were massed, not far from 86,000 men in all. On every high hill the batteries were posted. By every bridge and ford were vigilant pickets to give prompt notice of any threatened crossing by the enemy, and determined detachments of infantry and artillery ready to beat him back.

It was about noon of the 16th that the cannon began to sing along both lines. A long ridge sheltered the Federals from the enemy's fire, and so long as they were content to rest quiet in their places no harm could come to them. But curiosity to see what was going on across the creek was strong, and reconnoitering parties even scaled the ridge and drew the enemy's fire. But though the cannoneers worked manfully away with their great guns, and the pickets kept up a constant exchange of bullets, most of the fighting on that day was in pursuance of no plan and amounted to but little. Late in the afternoon, however, McClellan played his first card. Hooker crossed the creek by the bridge and ford on the extreme right of the Union line, and turning southward, moved down upon the Confederate left flank. Then for a time the pulse of battle quickened. Hood's Confederate division was opposed to Hooker, and held its ground obstinately, fighting from behind stone walls and fences. But before either side could win the mastery darkness fell upon the scene and the fighting was ended.

There was little activity that night on the Confederate side. Lee had chosen his line of defense; his men were in position, and there was little for them to do save to rest while the pickets kept watch upon the enemy. But along the Union lines there was marching and countermarching. Through the black night columns of armed men were stealthily moving over to the right of the line, where the main attack was to be made on the morrow. General Mansfield with the Twelfth Corps crossed the river by the ford that Hooker had passed, and took up a position about a mile in Hooker's rear. Still remaining on the east bank of the Antietam within supporting distance was Sumner, the grizzled veteran whose march through the Chickahominy swamp saved the day at Seven Pines. There were no fires allowed along the Union lines that night, and one of the soldiers of Burnside's division tells how the soldiers mixed their ground coffee with sugar in their hands, and devoured the choking, powdery stuff. "I think we were the more easily inclined to this crude disposal of our rations," he writes, "from a feeling that for many of us the need of drawing them would cease forever on the following day."

Let us look more closely at that portion of the battle-field which lies in front of Hooker's men, as they bivouacked that chill September night. It was there that the most bitter fighting of one of the most desperate battles of the war took place.

Scarce a hundred yards in front of Hooker's pickets, who were facing south, was the picket line of the enemy. Back of this line and to the east was a clump of trees called the East woods, which sheltered a Confederate battery. A line of gray-clad soldiers, crouching behind roughly built breast works of fence-rails, extended from the East wood across the turnpike to the point where a spot of gleaming white, almost hidden in the trees, indicated the position of a little Dunker church, destined to gain a fame as permanent as that of another little county chapel that gave its name to the battle of Shiloh. Back of the Dunker church were the shady recesses of the West woods. Between the two woods was a rolling stretch of land cut up into cornfields. Right in front of Doubleday's division, which formed Hooker's right wing, was the roomy farmhouse of Mr. Miller. West of Miller's house was the cabin of farmer Nicodemus, and on a smooth hill near it a Confederate battery that could sweep the country in every direction with its shells.

The morning of the 17th was chill and damp. A dense fog hung over the hostile armies. The summits of the neighboring mountains were lost in the clouds. Cold and cramped with their bivouac, the soldiers of both armies unrolled themselves from their blankets and gulped down their coffee and bread. While they were eating the firing along the picket line began, then the Confederate battery near the

East wood began to boom out defiance to Hooker and his men. The challenge was promptly accepted, and Hooker pushed forward into the corn-fields between the East and West woods.

Meantime scores of Union cannon on the east side of the creek nearly a mile away had caught up the chorus of death, and were throwing solid shot into the woods that hid the Confederate lines. The enemy's guns replied stoutly, but were no match for McClellan's artillery. And on the hill about the Miller house the guns of the U. S. 4th artillery were banging away and throwing their shells over the heads of Hooker's advancing regiments and into the faces of the foe. It was hot fighting all along the line. With bull-dog tenacity the gray-coats held on to their position in the East woods, contesting bitterly the advance of Ricketts. It was there, on the Union left, that the only decided advantage won by any of Hooker's three divisions was gained, for Ricketts, aided by the Union artillery at the Miller house, and beyond the creek, succeeded in gaining the edge of the woods, and held that position even when he saw the right of Hooker's line driven back mangled and bleeding.

For it was on the right of Hooker's line that the carnage proved too great for veterans who had passed through the baptism of fire half a score of times to bear. Gibbon's brigade of Doubleday's division fell into a trap, and was suddenly taken in flank by a terrific fire from the Confederates in the West wood. Before the leaden storm men fell like grass before the scythe of the mower. A Wisconsin regiment upon which fell the full force of the withering storm made for the turnpike, where, lying down behind a fence of posts and rails, they strove their best to hold the enemy in check. The main body of Gibbon's brigade, however, leaped the fence and charged gallantly forward into the teeth of the storm. But brave though they were they could make no headway against the tempest. Men looked dazed as suddenly they found themselves standing alone, with their comrades shot down by scores right and left of them. Broken to pieces by the fire, the brigade broke and the survivors fled through the corn-field seeking shelter. Then the Confederates in their turn swarmed out of the woods and swooped down upon Gibbon's shattered ranks screaming the historic "rebel yell" that signalized so many gallant charges. But though sorely broken, Gibbon's lines still had fight in them. His cannon, double-shotted with canister, roared. His shattered lines closed up and met the enemy's assault with dogged determination. As the gray-backs recoiled, Patrick's brigade came up to Gibbon's assistance, and the Federals again swept forward to the very edge of the West wood, when another murderous volley beat them back. And so back and forth in that deadly triangle of plowed ground and standing corn the hostile armies swayed, cheering, yelling, cursing, screaming with pain, or shouting with exultation; every man daring death a dozen times a minute and death coming to one man out of every five, until by half-past seven through very exhaustion and loss of life each side is ready enough to cease its attacks, reform its shattered ranks and wait for reënforcements before trying once again to win that victory which neither was ready to relinquish. And so gradually something of a hush falls upon the bloody field, the rattle of the musketry dies away, and only the sullen booming of the artillery from every hill tells that the battle is not ended, but only lags for a time.

In his report General Hooker thus tells of one incident in the battle: "We had not proceeded far before I discovered that a heavy force of the enemy had taken possession of a corn-field (I have since learned, about a thirty-acre field) on my immediate front, and from the sun's rays falling on their bayonets projecting above the corn I could see that the field was filled with the enemy with arms in their hands, standing apparently at 'support arms.' Instructions were immediately given for the assemblage of all my spare batteries near at hand, of which I think there were five or six, to spring into battery on the right of this field and to open with canister at once. In the time I am writing every stalk of corn in the northern and greater part of the field was cut as closely as could have been done with a knife, and the slain lay in rows, precisely as they had stood in their ranks a few moments before. It was never my fortune to witness a more bloody, dismal battle-field. Those that escaped fled in the opposite direction from our advance, and sought refuge behind the trees, fences and stone ledges, nearly on a line with the Dunker church."

But though Hooker thus tells of the fearful carnage wrought by his guns in the ranks of the enemy, it was little greater than that which the Confederates in their turn meted out to the assailants. There was no monopoly of courage on either side that morning, nor could either one claim to have inflicted upon the other a much greater loss than it itself had suffered.

And so the first act in the monstrous tragedy of the Antietam ends. Two hours of desperate fighting had ushered in a day of blood. Hooker had won but little; he had beaten back the Confederate line a little space, and had won the East woods, but all the strong positions, all the commanding points were still held by the men in gray. On both sides, though, the loss had been heavy, the Federals suffering most in point of numbers, the Confederates having to mourn the fall of many of their general officers. More than a third of the men whom Ricketts led fell on the field of battle,—898 being wounded and 153 killed. Of the gallant soldiers under Gibbon, 380 were hit. Of Phelps's brigade nearly one half were shot down.

In the ranks of the South there was mourning. General Starke, who commanded the "old Stonewall" brigade, was killed. General Lawton, who commanded Ewell's division, was seriously wounded, and Col. Douglas, who commanded Lawton's brigade, was killed. In the brigades of Lawton and Hayes every second man was either killed or wounded, and in Trumble's brigade every third man. And when these sorely shattered commands were reformed, after falling to the rear, it was found that in all three brigades there were but two regimental officers uninjured.

Had there been no fresh troops to take the places of the sorely shattered regiments of Hooker and of Jackson, the battle would have ended then. But at this juncture Hood, whose line had been formed in Jackson's rear, came forward and took up his position in the edge of the West woods and about the Dunker church. On the Union side Mansfield, who had passed the night about a mile in Hooker's rear, pushed to the front, passing the bleeding remnants of Hooker's corps as it was slowly retiring from the field upon which it had fought so gallantly.

The conflicting reports of the commanding generals make it impossible to state at what time the Twelfth Corps under Mansfield went into action. But it was probably about 7:30 A.M., and Hooker had been fighting about two hours. Seven thousand men were in the corps, in two divisions commanded by Williams and Greene. Many of the regiments were new, untried and ill-drilled. There was delay therefore, in getting them deployed in order of battle, and their officers had some fears as to how the new recruits would stand their first experience under fire.

In the woods by the Dunker church, crouched behind ledges of rock, stone walls and fences, lying flat on their faces in gullies, or perched in the boughs of trees, were the men of Hood's Confederate division, far less in number than those who were coming to assail them, but possessing an inestimable advantage in position.

The Twelfth Corps goes into action on almost the same lines as those followed by the First Corps. The direction of the attack is a little more to the westward, because Ricketts has driven most of the Confederates out of the East woods, and the points of attack are now the corn-field, the West woods, and the Dunker church. In the corn-field the gray coats are swarming again, and their bullets come with angry hiss and an occasional spiteful spat among the Union soldiers who are forming their lines by Miller's house, ready to march into the valley of the shadow of death. There are plenty of brave men in Mansfield's corps,—they are going to show their bravery when they get down into that corn-field,—but this business of standing still and forming lines while an unseen enemy is peppering away only a few yards in your front is trying to recruits. Still they hold their ground gallantly, and are giving back to the Confederates as good as they send, when General Mansfield rides up. He sees his men firing into the corn-field where he had not expected to find any of the enemy. No colors are flying there. The uniforms of the men among the corn cannot be plainly seen. May they not be friends? He orders his men to cease firing, and himself rides forward to reconnoitre. Straight to the front he rides, a conspicuous object with his white hair streaming in the wind. An old Indian fighter, he knows no fear. As he comes to the front rank of a Maine regiment which leads the van, a captain and a sergeant beg him to go no further.

"See, general," they cry. "Those are the enemy. See their gray coats. They are aiming at you and at us now."

"Yes, yes, you are right," responds Mansfield, but before he can say more he is hit. He tries to turn his horse, but the animal too has been struck and will not obey the rein. Then the men lift the general from his steed and carry him tenderly to the rear, where it is discovered that his wound is mortal.

General Williams now succeeds to Mansfield's command. As he is about to order the advance General Hooker comes up to tell him what he learned during the fight of the morning, and to offer some suggestions. While they are talking Hooker suddenly faints. He had been wounded an hour before, but in the excitement of the battle had known nothing of it until weakened by loss of blood.

Williams led the Twelfth Corps over the same route that the soldiers of Hooker's corps had already marked out with their blood. Down the slope before Miller's house, through the corn-field, plodding along over the plowed ground, driving out of the East woods the few Confederates who still remained there, trying to drive out of the West wood the thousands of gray-coats who stubbornly refused to be driven,—act second in the tragedy of the Antietam was a mere repetition of act first, with a brand new set of characters to be slain. Had Hooker and Mansfield gone into the fight at dawn together their combined force would probably have swept Jackson out of their path. Had there been any reserves now to come to Williams's aid the victory might have been won for the Union. But as it was, a few minutes saw the Twelfth Corps mowed down by the pitiless fire of the enemy, particularly by that of a battery which the redoubtable Stuart had posted on a hill whence it took the Union column in the rear. And so, after a bare half-hour of plucky but profitless fighting the Twelfth Corps melted away, and its shattered fragments drifted back behind the Miller house, where Hooker's regiments were resting after the bloody doings of the early dawn, leaving a few tenacious regiments, together with some fragments of Ricketts's command, gallantly holding a position they had won in the corner of the woods not far from the Dunker church. It was then about nine o'clock.

Sumner came next to play the leading part in the third act of the tragedy of the Antietam. All the morning he has been resting quietly on the east bank of the creek, near enough to hear the sounds of battle; near enough to find the half-spent shot dropping among his men; near enough to see the wounded and stragglers from the Union forces going to the rear; plenty near enough to know that Hooker and Mansfield were being beaten. Why he was not ordered to cross the creek at daybreak and go into battle with Hooker has never been explained. But it was not until nearly nine o'clock that orders came to him to attack, and when he had crossed the stream he found that the enemy had beaten Hooker and Mansfield one after the other, and were ready to give him the same sort of a reception.

Sumner's line of attack was at right angles to that of the two corps that had preceded him. Instead of coming down from the north, he appeared on the field from the east, marching straight through the East wood, across the famous corn-field, where this time no Confederates were lurking, and on up to the West wood, where the enemy was supposed to be.

In this advance but one division—Sedgwick's—of Sumner's corps was concerned. Richardson's division was kept on the eastern bank of the creek waiting for McClellan to send other troops to take its place, and French's division had not yet come up. But Sedgwick's division was a division of veterans. Its commander had a well-earned reputation for gallantry, and he led his troops stoutly forward into battle. General Sumner, a gray-haired campaigner who had served against the Indians, rode into battle with the division.

As the Union troops move forward across the open space between the corn-field and the West woods a kind of lull falls upon the battle-field. Except for the artillery fire from Stuart's guns the Union advance is unimpeded until the edge of the woods is reached. But all this time they were marching blindly into an ambush. On the left flank was a country road, worn deep with ruts, and washed by the rain until it had become a gully. The ground rose sharply before it, and men could stand upright in the narrow lane and still be hidden from the sight of those in the Union lines. As Sedgwick's division, in three parallel lines, is moving steadily forward toward the West wood, the Confederates are stealthily sending regiment after regiment down into this sunken road to take Sedgwick in the flank and rear. He wonders that no hostile fire comes from the woods in his front. Just then an officer on the left of the Union lines catches a sight of the troops in the sunken road.

"General. Look. We are surrounded!" he shouts.

The alarm comes too late. Already the Confederate fire is delivered. Before the withering storm of lead, coming from so unsuspected a quarter, the blue-coats fall in heaps. Their lines are thrown into disorder.

"My God!" shouts Sumner, "we must get out of this," and he gallops up and down the lines seeking to form them anew. But it is too late. Little by little, the lines crumble away. The bravest soldiers in the army would be unnerved to find themselves suddenly in an ambush. The bravest in the world could not stand against that murderous fire. The Confederates advance. They press upon the Union flank. They swing around and take Sedgwick's men in the rear.

Sedgwick is struck by a bullet and falls from his horse. Sumner sees how the battle is going and gallops away to the nearest signal station. "Reënforcements are badly needed. Our troops are giving way," he signals to McClellan. Even while the flags that carry the message are waving the one-sided contest ends, and Sedgwick's division is practically wiped out. Over 2000 men have been killed or wounded without inflicting upon the enemy any material loss. From the time the Confederates sprang from their ambush and poured in their first volley, until the bruised and bleeding remnants of Sedgwick's division left the field, was scarce fifteen minutes. General Hood himself declared that the short and bloody combat was "the most terrible clash of arms that he had ever witnessed during the war."

Now up come the divisions of French and Richardson. Had they been on the field but a little sooner they might have averted the disaster which cost Sedgwick so many lives.

It is near the farm-house of Mr. Mumma that the lines of D. H. Hill and French clash. The Confederates are posted in a ravine near the house. Their sharpshooters are in the building, firing from every window, picking off French's skirmishers as they advance. But heedless of shrieking shells and whizzing bullets the dark-blue line comes pushing forward. It passes through an orchard, and the skirmishers who lead the advance dodge for shelter from tree to tree, firing as they go. Then a little graveyard is entered, and the headstones shelter the men from the enemy's bullets and serve for handy rests for their rifles. When the line has passed that little cemetery there are nearly as many dead above its green sod as below.

Before the persistent advance of the Union lines the Confederates fall back, first setting the torch to Mumma's house and leaving a blazing and melancholy monument of the miseries of war. A quarter of a mile to the south there is another rainwashed road,—Bloody Lane it is called to-day,—and there Hill's men take up their second position.

The repeated and gallant assaults of the men of French's division upon the Confederates in this position, and the tenacity with which the latter held their ground, form one of the most glorious incidents of American military annals. Even the historic corn-field, when the battle was over, did not show so many dead as the narrow road in which the troops of D. H. Hill had stood, and the ground before it across which French's regiments had charged. Though the Confederates stood gallantly to await the shock, the final charge of the blue-clad line was too much for them, and they were forced back through the fields and down to the southward with the Federals in full chase. Meantime Richardson has done as well in his assault upon Longstreet,—driven him from a strong position, and put his best soldiers to flight. Matters are looking serious for the southern army now, and if McClellan should send a heavy detachment to widen the breach that Richardson and French are making, it would soon be all up with Lee.

The Confederate leaders well knew how desperate was their strait. Lee was stripping his right wing of all available troops with which to strengthen his left. Jackson, Longstreet and Hill were everywhere. All sorts of expedients were resorted to, to cover up the weakness of the Confederate line. At one point which seemed to invite attack the teamsters, cooks, and other undisciplined and unarmed camp-followers were formed in line, in the hope that the sight of so large a body of men would keep the Federals from choosing that particular point for an attack. At another point two guns of the Washington artillery alone held the Federals in check at a most critical position. The guns were worked by officers of Longstreet's staff,—for all the regular artillerymen had long since been shot down,—and that officer stood quietly near by holding the bridles of his staff officers' horses. A North Carolina regiment was drawn up to support the little battery, and showed its colors boldly whenever the blue-coats showed signs of charging. And doubtless the battery would have been charged, and the Confederate center pierced, had the Union officers known that the regiment supporting the guns had in its cartridge-boxes not one single round of ammunition!

So on through the hot forenoon of a southern September day the battle raged. The ground won by French and Richardson, Longstreet strove to regain, but to no purpose. Trying to repeat the flanking maneuver which had resulted in the demolition of Sedgwick's corps, he sent a regiment around to gain the rear of Caldwell's brigade of Richardson's division. But as the regiment was stealthily proceeding on its way Col. Cross of the 5th New Hampshire caught sight of it, and instantly perceived its intention. Facing his regiment to the rear he started out on the double-quick to get first upon the ground that the Confederates were seeking. The gray-coats were ready enough for a race, and started off at a good pace. And so the two regiments went running along side by side, and keeping up a rattling fusilade, until the Federals gained the point of vantage first, and swinging into line beat their adversaries back.

It is unnecessary to say more in detail of the fighting around the region of the Dunker church. By noon it was ended. It had been marked by magnificent displays of daring on the part of the assailants, and admirable tenacity on the part of the Confederates. The bloodshed had been enormous,—as great, or greater, perhaps, in proportion to the numbers engaged, than that in any other battle of war. But when for the constant crash of the musketry and the shouts of charging men, the comparative quiet of an intermittent cannonade was substituted, the Confederates, though sorely shattered, were still unbeaten.

About three-quarters of a mile southwest of the town of Sharpsburg, a stone bridge spanned the sullen current of the Antietam. Near its eastern end were grouped the troops of Burnside's division. At its western end rows of Confederate guns posted on high hills, regiments of Confederate infantry behind stone walls, and scores of gray-clad skirmishers lurking behind every stump fence or bowlder that promised shelter, held it closed against all comers. With their artillery and their infantry, the Confederates were prepared to sweep the bridge clear of any northern troops who might venture to set foot thereon.

It was about ten o'clock in the morning that the order came from

THE CHARGE AT BURNSIDE'S BRIDGE.

McClellan to Burnside to carry the bridge. The staff officers who stood about the general shrugged their shoulders meaningly when they heard the order. A desperate commission it was indeed. First a long stretch of road on the river's bank, swept by the enemy's fire, had to be traversed, and then the bridge itself, on which Longstreet could concentrate the fire of all the guns in the division. The lay of the land on the side of the creek held by the Confederates was such that their artillery was perfectly protected. The batteries of Burnside's division could do nothing to clear the way for the advance of the storming party. The soldiers who were led to the conquest of the bridge had nothing to do but to push bravely forward through the pitiless hail of missiles, in the forlorn hope that when the bridge was crossed there would still be enough of them left alive to drive away the brigade of Toombs, that lay snugly sheltered under a hill awaiting the Federal attack.

Since early morning Burnside had been feeling the enemy's position, and he well knew its strength. He had seen his columns, marching on the road by the side of the creek, melt away before the flanking fire of the Confederates across the ravine. He had shifted his batteries from place to place on the heights which he held, seeking some point whence he might train his guns upon Longstreet's batteries and Toombs's riflemen. But all had been in vain, and now that the peremptory order for the passage of the brigade had come, he knew that dogged persistence and reckless dash alone could effect it.

To General Crook's brigade was first assigned the perilous task. Sturgis was to support Crook, and Rodman with his division was sent down the stream to look for a ford, and draw away the Confederate defenders from the head of the bridge by threatening to cross below and take them in the flank. But Crook's forces proved unequal to the task. No sooner had they appeared in the road than there burst upon him so fierce a fire from the enemy's cannon and muskets that he was fain to cease his advance, seek protection behind stone walls and fences, and respond to the attack as well as he could. Sturgis then, seeing that Crook's advance was checked, sent forward as a forlorn hope the Second Maryland and the Sixth New Hampshire regiments. With fixed bayonets the little band started off at the double-quick. On it fell the withering fire from the enemy's guns. For a time it seemed as though the unfaltering courage of these troops would carry them to the goal, but the high hopes of the Union officers watching the charge were destined to be shattered. Great gaps appeared in the column, there was a moment of wavering, of indecision, and the line began to go to pieces. Rallied by their officers and again started forward, the men again gave way. A third futile effort was made, and then the shattered columns were dispersed to form no more that day.

"The bridge must be carried at any cost. At whatever sacrifice of human life, we must get possession of the other side." Such was the order Burnside sent to Sturgis, and that officer prepared for a second assault.

New York and Pennsylvania troops, the 51st Regiment from each State, were chosen this time. They received powerful assistance from two guns which Crook had posted so as to bear on the enemy. Forward in double columns of fours, eight men to the front, the blue-coats charged. The enemy's guns made woful havoc in their ranks, but they kept on. The bridge was reached, and there the pelting storm of missiles was most tempestuous. Yet on through it all they pressed, leaving hundreds dead and wounded in their path, until the bridge was passed, and in a sheltering line of woods a moment of rest could be taken. It had cost 500 men to take the bridge; 200 of them then lay dead in the path over which the victorious band has passed, but with the way once cleared the rest of Burnside's forces quickly followed, until by two o'clock the greater part of the Ninth Corps had crossed the creek and was pressing hotly upon Longstreet's lines, and threatening to break through and take the town of Sharpsburg. In the very nick of time, however, for the Confederates, A. P. Hill with 2000 men arrrived from Harper's Ferry. Though wearied by his long march he plunged valiantly into the fight. This accession of fresh force invigorated the Confederates and struck consternation into the hearts of the Federals. Burnside's men were pressed back, relinquishing most of the ground they had gained. Frantic orders from McClellan kept them from recrossing the creek, but it was only on its banks that they halted. And so, when the sun went down, the men of Longstreet's division had won again most of the ground that had been wrested from them.

That night Lee and McClellan agreed upon an armistice, that the surgeons might go about the field and administer to the needs of the wounded. The rumble of the ambulance and the groans of the sufferers replaced the roar of battle. When morning came the strife was not renewed. The Confederates held their lines, alert, watchful, expecting every moment the shock of the Federal assault. But McClellan loitered in his tent. No advance was ordered. The shattered ranks of Lee's regiments, which could hardly have withstood another blow, were left unmolested. And when night came again Lee robbed McClellan of a possible overwhelming triumph by making one of those quick and orderly retreats for which the Confederates afterward became famous. Under cover of the darkness he withdrew his entire army across the Potomac, and when morning dawned McClellan's pickets saw in the fields before them no sign of life. Not a gray uniform, a cannon, a flag, or a wagon was to be seen. McClellan had allowed Lee to slip through his fingers, and the best opportunity the war had yet presented for crushing the Confederacy's greatest army was lost.

So ended the battle of the Antietam, or as the Confederates call it, the battle of Sharpsburg. It had been a hard-fought field. In deeds of gallantry each side vied with the other. The total force under Lee's command was scarcely one-half as great as the Union forces, but General McClellan's policy of sending in his divisions to attack one after the other, instead of descending upon the enemy with all his overwhelming force, had greatly reduced the odds against the wearers of the gray. On both sides the loss was heavy. McClellan's report fixed the Union loss at 12,469, of whom 2010 were killed, 9416 wounded, and 1043 missing. The exact loss of the Confederates is unknown, but it probably differed but little from that of the Union forces. In his report General McClellan states that 2700 of the enemy's dead were buried after the battle by the Federal soldiers.

Who were then the victors in this desperate and bloody battle?

So far as the immediate results of the fighting on the 17th were concerned, there could be no good claim to victory set up by either side. The Federals acted upon the offensive, but they certainly made no inroads of any serious extent upon the enemy's position. The Confederates, in their turn, had not repelled the attack all along the line, and were certainly too much weakened by the day's fighting to rightfully claim that they were victorious. When the sun set that night it put an end to a drawn battle.

But, as a historian of this campaign has well said, "for an invading army, a drawn battle is little less than a lost battle." So particularly was it in this case, for after confronting McClellan for one day, Lee abandoned the field and took his army out of Maryland again. The cherished plan for carrying the war into the Northern States had failed, and we shall soon see the tide of war sweeping back and forth again across the fields and through the forests of the Old Dominion.

CHAPTER IV.

THE WAR IN THE WEST. — HALLECK'S SIEGE OF CORINTH. — FORREST'S RAID ON MURFREESBORO'. — THE CONFEDERATES CAPTURE CHATTANOOGA. — BRAGG'S INVASION OF KENTUCKY. — BATTLE OF RICHMOND. — PANIC IN CINCINNATI. — BATTLE OF MUNFORDSVILLE. — BATTLE OF PERRYVILLE. — BRAGG ABANDONS KENTUCKY. — BATTLE OF IUKA. — BATTLE OF CORINTH.

LET us now turn again to the theater of war in the west, and see how the combatants were faring there while McClellan and Lee were battling upon the debatable ground between Washington and Richmond.

Readers of the first volume of this series* will recollect that after the battle of Shiloh the victorious Union forces moved southward in pursuit of the Confederates, who took refuge at Corinth. The extensive and formidable earthworks with which the Confederates had surrounded this town in anticipation of just such a contingency, effectually checked the Union advance. To drive the enemy from these works, General Halleck began a regular siege.

For nearly thirty days the men of Halleck's army worked in the trenches, throwing up parallels, building roads and regular approaches. The pick and the shovel took the place of the sword and the musket. Occasional skirmishes there were, — sharp encounters which in a war of less colossal proportions would have been reckoned notable battles.

Battle Fields of '61, by Willis J. Abbot. Dodd, Mead & Company, New York, 1889.

But the Union general had ordered his officers not to bring on a general engagement, while Beauregard for his part was not anxious for a battle, but was preparing to retreat.

It was toward the latter part of May that General Grant, who was second in command to Halleck and much underestimated and ignored by that commander, began to suspect that the enemy was getting out of Corinth with all the celerity possible. The rumble of trains entering and leaving the town was heard constantly, and experienced railroad men in the Union army declared that the noise indicated that incoming trains were empty, and the outgoing ones full. Somewhat puzzled they were by the loud cheers that greeted the arrival of each incoming train, as if the Confederates were being reënforced. But when on the 30th of May the victorious blue-coats marched unmolested into the enemy's works and found them untenanted, they learned that the cheering was but a ruse of the wily enemy, who had fled bag and baggage, leaving not a sick man, a gun or a flag as a trophy for the captors of Corinth.

The next two months were spent by the troops in surrounding the place with a system of earthworks so vast that an army of 100,000 men could scarce man them. The Confederates meantime had gone but fifty miles further south, and there were recruiting their army and preparing for a vigorous campaign. Some skirmishing there was, and some raiding by the daring cavalry leaders of the South, but the former had no bearing upon the fortunes of the campaign, while the latter, with other exploits of the cavalry rangers and partisans of the South, will receive attention in a later chapter.

After two months spent in recuperation the Confederates in the west determined to take the offensive. Kentucky was to them what Maryland was to their brethren in the east,—a State in the possession of their enemies, but in which they might fairly hope to find thousands of sympathizers with their cause. Many Kentuckians visited General Bragg, who had succeeded to Beauregard's command, at his headquarters at Tupelo, and urged upon him the wisdom of an invasion of

Kentucky. The State was with the South, they said, and it was only necessary for the Confederacy to make a show of its strength within its borders for Kentucky to cast its lot with the States that had declared for secession. Bragg lent a willing ear to these representations,—the more willing because he knew that Halleck had been called to Washington and was rapidly tearing to pieces the army which he had left under Grant.

One bit of Confederate cavalry service is worth attention here. At Murfreesboro, Tennessee, was a brigade of Union troops: two regiments of infantry, a company of cavalry and a small battery. The officers were at odds with each other, and had chosen to show their enmity for each other by encamping their forces so far apart that united action was impossible and an attack was fairly invited. Earnest friends living about Murfreesboro brought early news of this to the Confederate commander, and Col. Forrest with his cavalrymen swooped down upon the luckless blue-coats. The Federals were fairly caught napping. Watchful negroes had brought them the report that "Massa Forrest" was coming with a big army, but, occupied with their own petty quarrels, the Union officers had given no heed to the warning.

Early dawn of the 13th of July saw the woods about Murfreesboro swarming with cavalry troopers in gray. Stealthily they crept upon the Union pickets, and with a sudden rush overcame them before any alarm could be given. Only when the Confederates, with fierce yells and a prodigious clatter of hoofs upon the turnpike, came charging into the Union camp, did the soldiers there sleeping in their tents know of the blow that had fallen upon them. Then it was too late. Gen. Crittenden, in command of one Union regiment, was fairly captured in his bed. Col. Duffield, who at the first fire had sprung from his couch and rushed to rally his men, was shot down before his efforts were of any avail. Left thus to their individual judgment, the soldiers fought as skirmishers from behind fences and trees and houses. Some sixty or more took possession of the court house, and stubbornly resisted the attacks of the Confederates until the street before the building was dotted with many a dead body clothed in gray. But when this little band was dislodged from its stronghold, the assailants encountered no further serious resistance. The Minnesota regiment under Col. Lester, which was encamped at some distance from the Michigan regiment first attacked, made scarcely a pretense of showing fight. "The men were well armed, well disciplined, and were eager to fight," wrote an eye-witness to a Northern newspaper, "but their colonel faltered and dared not lead them on to victory."

And so, between the dissensions of the Union officers before the battle, and the cowardice of one of them after the shots began to fly, the Confederate cavalry had an easy task in depriving the North of the services of 1700 men, 600 horses, 4 cannon, and nearly a million dollars' worth of supplies.

"Few more disgraceful examples of neglect of duty and lack of good conduct can be found in the history of wars," said General Buell in an official address to his army on hearing the news.

Six weeks passed by. To Bragg's camp at Tupelo recruits were coming from all parts of the Confederacy. From Texas came rangers, long-haired, uncouth in dress and actions, but daring cavalrymen withal. From Missouri came long, lank, sallow, ungainly backwoodsmen, intractable and undisciplined, but keen-sighted and sure shots with the long muzzle-loading rifles that they carried. From Louisiana, Mississippi, Alabama and even the Atlantic States came reënforcements. The whole seaboard of the Confederacy was stripped that Bragg might have a great army to lead into Kentucky.

Grant's army, meanwhile, was being systematically weakened. From Washington, Halleck ordered that brigade after brigade should be detached upon some special service, until at last Grant found himself in danger of being left without men enough to defend his earthworks. A very large detachment was sent under command of General Buell to capture Chattanooga, and news of this movement coming promptly to the ears of General Bragg, he determined to forestall the Federals by seizing that city himself, for it was an important railway center, and of such military importance as to make quick and decisive action by either army most desirable.

It was only the old story repeated again. The Union troops march on deliberately. Buell's orders direct him to repair the railroad as he goes along, and he stops to do so. The Confederates find it an easy task to march around Buell, and get to Chattanooga first. Long before Buell gets to the goal the city is in the hands of the Confederates, who make it their base of operations for the invasion of Kentucky. Bragg splits his army into two parts. One under General Kirby Smith marches away to the northward through eastern Tennessee and Kentucky, while the other division under the personal command of Bragg himself keeps farther to the westward.

It was late in August when Kirby Smith's long columns of Confederate veterans emerged from behind the shelter of the Cumberland mountains, and after threading the tortuous defiles of Cumberland Gap struck out toward the northwest. They had before them almost a clear pathway to the Ohio river. Buell was far to the westward, and could not hope to intercept them, and to add to his perplexity the daring Confederate partisan John Morgan was raiding about Tennessee, cutting railroads, burning bridges, and completely concealing from Buell the location and the plans of the invaders.

At one point only did a Union force block the advance of Smith's columns. General Nelson, who commanded in eastern Kentucky, had a few thousand troops, mostly raw recruits just mustered in, stationed about Richmond, some twenty miles from Lexington. General Manson was in command, Nelson himself remaining at Lexington. On the 30th of August, the Confederates swooped down upon this force, outnumbering the blue-coats nearly two to one. The Union outposts were driven in, and the assailants followed swiftly after. Smith had other divisions some miles in the rear, but he went in, hammer and tongs, without awaiting their arrival. Outnumbered, undisciplined and badly commanded, the Federals were thrown into confusion. There were deeds of gallantry, and deeds of black cowardice. Many an officer was shot down while leading a desperate charge, and the newspaper reports of the battle tell of more than one shoulder-strapped poltroon who ingloriously ran away, leaving his men to lead themselves. Toward noon there was a lull in the conflict. The rattle of musketry ceased. The thunder of the cannonade gave place to an occasional sullen roar from some battery that was shelling a suspicious clump of woods. Men had time to look about them, to give aid to the wounded, to talk of the poor fellows who had been sent out of the world by the enemy's bullets, and to wonder whose turn it would be next.

At this moment General Nelson appeared among the Union troops. News of the battle had reached him at Lexington, and he had hastened to the field. He found his men routed, disheartened, half beaten already. "I know you are new at this business, boys," he said. "I'll show you how to whip the scamps." Up and down the lines he went, doing his best to instill new confidence and courage into the minds of his troops. Soon the storm of war burst again, and men fell thick and fast before the flying missiles. Nelson was in the thick of the fight. A man of colossal stature, he rode along the lines waving his hat and shouting:

"Boys, if they can't hit me, they can't hit a barn door."

But a stray shot soon brought him to the ground badly wounded, and his men fell back in hopeless rout before the advance of the victorious Confederates. After Nelson's fall the Union forces offered no more resistance. Every man for himself, was the cry. All semblance of military formation was lost. Scattering in all directions, the blue-coats fled before the foe, who followed in such hot pursuit that many a Northern soldier bit the dust during that disastrous retreat. Over three thousand prisoners rewarded the Confederates for their prowess that day, and in killed and wounded the Federals lost 900 more. The total Confederate loss was 790.

Had Jackson then been in Kirby Smith's place, there would have been dark days for the Union cause in the northwest. There was

THE SURPRISE AT RICHMOND.

now no hostile army in his path. The roads to Louisville and to Cincinnati lay open before him. It was a moment for audacity. A quick dash upon Cincinnati, the seizure of the city, the destruction of the railroads running east and west therefrom,—such a triumphant invasion of Northern soil would have been invaluable to the Confederate cause just at that time. But Kirby Smith lacked the quality of dash. His soldiers were not trained to make forced marches. He dared not forsake his base of supplies and his lines of communication as Jackson often did. And so, instead of pressing right on to the Ohio river, he halted at Lexington to recruit his army from young Kentuckians who thought the star of the Confederacy was in the ascendency. It was over two weeks before he led his army near enough Cincinnati to seriously threaten that city.

When General Kirby Smith annihilated General Nelson's force of new recruits at Richmond, Cincinnati was practically defenseless. But when, after his deliberate march northward, Smith was ready to attack the city, it was defended by works of no mean strength. A man whose name in later days is better known for his work with the pen than his exploits with the sword, had wrought the change. This was General Lewis Wallace.

The news of the Confederate victory at Richmond had scarcely reached Cincinnati when Wallace began putting the place in condition to resist a siege. He put the city under martial law, closed the business houses, and ordered all able-bodied male citizens to assemble on the Kentucky side of the Ohio river to work in the trenches. "Citizens for labor, soldiers for battle," was the rule of action by which he was guided, and for ten days citizens of every station worked with pick and shovel, throwing up fortifications on the high hills that skirt the southern bank of the river. Militia companies from all adjoining States, and thousands of unattached and undisciplined riflemen, flocked to the scene, and the citizens, seeing so many willing volunteers for the battle, did not seek to shirk the labor. Some doubters there were, as there are everywhere.

"If the enemy does not come after all this fuss," said one of them to the General, "you will be ruined."

"Very well," was his reply, "but they will come. And if they do not it will be because this same fuss has caused them to think better of it."

But the enemy did come. They came near enough at any rate to make it clear to the people of Cincinnati that their work of preparation had not been unnecessary; near enough for Kirby Smith to learn from his scout that the city was guarded by a line of frowning breastworks ten miles long, with plenty of cannon and seemingly plenty of men to defend them. On learning this, Kirby Smith halted, remained in position a few miles from Cincinnati for several days, and then fell back to join Bragg, who had entered Frankfort.

General Bragg on his part had marched across Tennessee, and nearly to the northern boundary of Kentucky, almost without firing a shot. Buell had raced with him the whole way, straining every nerve either to catch him and give him battle, or to reach Louisville before him. But the two armies did not clash, and as Bragg had the shorter route to travel, he only failed to capture Louisville because, like Kirby Smith, he neglected to seize a golden opportunity.

It was on the 20th of August that Bragg's column left Chattanooga, and after painfully scaling the heights of Walden's ridge, made a bee line straight away to Louisville, nearly four hundred miles off to the northwest. The cavalry squadrons of Forrest and Chalmers went raiding along on the left flank of the Confederate column, burning bridges, tearing up railroads, and effectually keeping the news of Bragg's movement from reaching the ears of Buell. Not until the 30th of the month did Buell learn the plans of his enemy, and then it was by a lucky chance that threw one of Bragg's dispatch-bearers into his hands. Then he set out in hot pursuit.

At Munfordsville, a little village on the railway leading to Louisville, Bragg found a small fort defended by a few hundred Union soldiers. The Confederate advance under Chalmers promptly attacked, but was beaten back with heavy loss. Early the next morning Chalmers made a demand for the surrender of the fort, but Col. Dunham stoutly refused. Thereupon the Confederates disappeared, and were seen no more for two days, when they suddenly returned to the field and made another unsuccessful attack. But, elated though the Union defenders were with their success, they saw all hope of final victory vanish when Bragg's powerful army appeared, coming to the aid of the slender force that had hitherto held the field alone. Matters then began to look desperate for the garrison, and Col. Dunham telegraphed to Louisville that he feared a surrender would be inevitable. Quick as the electric spark could flash came back an order for him to turn over the command to his junior officer, Col. Wilder. But Wilder himself saw no hope of a successful defense, and when Bragg sent a summons to surrender he was ready enough to parley. Bragg's summons told of his overwhelming force, and deplored any further shedding of blood. Wilder in his turn declared that if he could once be satisfied that resistance would be useless, he would resist no longer. Taking him at his word the Confederates sent a detail to escort him into their lines, where he saw 25,000 men drawn up ready for the assault, and with 45 cannon to support the attack. The fort was surrendered without more ado, all honors of war being paid to the capitulating garrison.

This was on the morning of the 17th of September. At that very hour, hundreds of miles away to the eastward, cannon were roaring and men falling on the bloody field of Antietam. It was a colossal struggle, and the extent of the theater of war was prodigious.

The stubborn resistance encountered at Munfordsville had detained Bragg for two days. It hardly seems probable that he ever intended to push on to Louisville, else he would not have stopped at so critical a moment to capture an unimportant post. At any rate, after the fort had been taken there was still time for the Confederates to march upon the great Kentucky city. Buell was coming up fast in the rear, but was not near enough to offer battle. The game was all in Bragg's hands.

But like Kirby Smith after the battle of Richmond, Bragg failed to seize upon his opportunity. Instead of pressing on to Louisville, he turned aside. At a little place called Prewitt's Knob he waited for Buell to come up. There the two armies maneuvered in full view of each other for two days; each inviting an attack and neither making one. Then Bragg took up the march again and led his army to Frankfort, the capital of the State, where he proposed to go through the empty form of inaugurating a secessionist governor for a State that had never seceded. Buell thereupon marched with alacrity to Louisville, there to re-equip his army, and take up the task of driving Bragg back to Alabama whence he came.

It is unnecessary for us to concern ourselves with the rather farcical proceedings at Frankfort, where on the 4th of October the Hon. Richard Hawes was inaugurated as governor with great pomp and ceremony, and six hours later fled in a panic from the city before the Union cavalry which was in advance of Buell's army coming out of Louisville to give battle to Bragg. But though the stay of the Confederate army at Frankfort was brief, it was long enough to convince the Confederate leaders that there was little sympathy for their cause in Kentucky. "We are sadly disappointed in the want of action by our friends in Kentucky," wrote Bragg to the Confederate government. "Unless a change occurs soon we must abandon the garden spot of Kentucky." And Kirby Smith added his testimony, writing: "The Kentuckians are slow and backward in rallying to our standard. Their hearts are evidently with us, but their blue grass and fat cattle are against us."

So it was. Kentucky was too prosperous to wish for war.

October 7 saw the hostile armies confronting each other near Perryville. For some days there had been skirmishing between the rear-guard of the retiring Confederate army and the advance guard of the Federals. So closely were the latter pressing upon the rear of Bragg's column that it became necessary for the latter to halt and strike a blow which should check the pursuit and give him time to gather together his troops and his wagons, heavy-laden with supplies from fertile Kentucky, preparatory to abandoning the State. For Bragg had already discovered that so far as getting recruits for the southern armies or bringing the State into the Confederacy was concerned, the invasion of Kentucky was a failure.

It was at Perryville that Bragg turned to strike back the foe that followed so persistently upon his heels. In that region the hot days of summer and the early autumn had caused a drought which dried up streams and rivulets, and made the question of securing water for the use of the Union army a serious one. At Perryville were some large springs, and it was about these that General Polk, who was in command of the Confederate army while Bragg was at Frankfort, massed his army.

About two o'clock in the afternoon of the 7th, reports from the Confederate picket lines indicated that the Federals were coming up. It was McCook's brigade of Sheridan's division that first appeared. The soldiers had been marching all day under a broiling sun, over dusty roads, and without a drop of water to cool their parched throats. They wanted water, and were ready to fight for it. In front of the Confederate lines was the channel of Doctor's creek, a little stream then nearly dried up, but with a few pools of muddy water standing in its bed. McCook sends out his skirmishers. They advance, exchange shots with the Confederate pickets, press on and fill their canteens at the stagnant pools. Others follow, and the Confederates, not wishing to bring on a general battle, withdraw. Bad though the water thus gained was, it was dearly prized. A Union staff officer relates that, being wearied of making his toilet with a dry rub, he proposed to use a dipper full of the water on his face, when General Buell, who had noticed his preparations, interposed, ordering him to pour it back into his canteen and keep it for an emergency.

Beyond a little rifle practice along the picket lines and some long range duels with the big guns, there was no fighting that day. Buell thought he had the whole of Bragg's army before him, and was cautious about bringing on an engagement, when by throwing in his whole force he might have swept the enemy from his path.

In the morning the Confederates take the offensive. Cheatham's division on their extreme right moves out and falls with terrific force on Terrill's brigade of Jackson's division. The Federal troops are raw, untrained soldiers. So far from expecting an assault from the enemy, they were preparing to make one themselves. The fury of Cheatham's assault, the ferocity of the "rebel yell," then heard by them for the first time, and the sight of their comrades falling on all sides, was too much for them. After one volley they broke and fled. At the very first fire General Jackson was killed. General Terrill soon afterward fell while bravely trying to rally his troops. The Confederates pushed on mercilessly, and the left of the Union line was thus thrown into hopeless rout at the very beginning of the battle. Nine guns from Parson's battery fell into the hands of the assailants, who turned them on the Union lines with fatal effect. Parsons himself had fallen ere his guns were taken. Revolver and sword in hand he stood by his guns, though his raw infantry supports went to pieces before the enemy's onslaught. Only when one of his men dragged him forcibly away would he leave his post, and as he retired a chance shot struck him. He lived, though, to fight through the war, and when the days of blood were over to enter the more peaceful service of the church.

By this time the battle was raging all along the lines. The cannon roared from every commanding hill, and the rattle of musketry was incessant. The combatants fought at close quarters, face to face with no sheltering breastworks or friendly stone wall to ward off the storm of bullets. In the fields the regiments of infantry were charging. From the neighboring clumps of woods the great guns were hurling their spiteful messages. Everywhere were wounded men, lying helpless on the ground or staggering to the rear to seek the aid of surgeons.

General Polk, who was actively engaged throughout the battle, had an adventure that nearly cost him his life, or at least his liberty. One of Bragg's staff officers thus tells the story in the *Century:*

"About dark, Polk, convinced that some Confederate troops were firing into each other, cantered up to the colonel of the regiment that was firing and asked him angrily what he meant by shooting his own friends. The colonel, in a tone of surprise, said:

"'I don't think there can be any mistake about it. I am sure they are the enemy.'

"'Enemy! Why, I have just left them myself. Cease firing, sir. What is your name?' rejoined the Confederate general.

"'I am Colonel —— of the —— Indiana. And pray, sir, who are you?'

"Thus made aware that he was with a Federal regiment and that his only escape was to brazen it out, his dark blouse and the increasing obscurity happily befriending him, the Confederate general shook his fist in the Federal colonel's face and promptly said:

"'I will show you who I am, sir. Cease firing at once.'

"Then cantering down the line again he shouted authoritatively to the men, 'Cease firing!' Then reaching the cover of a small copse, he spurred his horse and was soon back with his own corps, which he immediately ordered to open fire."

Successes were won and reverses sustained by both sides. The Confederate right had the battle all its own way; sweeping Rousseau away before it, capturing men and flags. To offset this the Union right was equally successful later in the day. There Sheridan commanded—the same gallant soldier who a year or two later won a fame only second to that of Grant. He saw a chance to deal the enemy a stinging blow, and, without waiting for orders from Buell, pushed his division forward, drove back the enemy, capturing many men and some wagons and artillery caissons. Gilbert too won laurels for the blue by a gallant advance made without orders. Buell was several miles away, and did not know that the battle was raging until it was over. The lay of the ground, or perhaps some peculiar atmospheric conditions, kept from his ears the sound of the musketry. The roaring of the cannon he heard, but thought it was but an artillery duel at long range,—a harmless kind of fighting to which both armies were much given in the earlier days of the war.

So when darkness descending put an end to the fray, the honors of battle were equally divided. Sheridan had beaten the enemy directly in his front, but so too had Cheatham on the part of the Confederates. And while the Confederates had failed in their purpose of annihilating McCook's division before the rest of the Union army could come to his assistance, the Federals in their turn had failed to seize their opportunity to crush Bragg's army then and there,—a task that would have been sufficiently easy had Buell but known of the battle that was going on within his very lines, and led into action the half of his army that stayed idle in its camp throughout the whole battle.

That night the pickets of the hostile armies could hear each other's steps as they cautiously moved through the woods. The most watchful vigilance was observed, for all thought that the morrow would witness a renewal of the fight. The dead and wounded lay thick upon the ground, for the battle had been fiercely fought and the casualties were heavy in proportion to the numbers engaged. General Buell reported a loss of 4340 men, of whom 916 were killed and 2943 wounded. General Bragg reported the total Confederate loss as being about 2500, but it is hard to believe this estimate not too low, for the Confederates were the assailants and should naturally have suffered most.

When morning dawned the Confederate pickets were still at their posts, but there seemed to be no signs of the battle beginning again. Soon they began to disappear, and the blue-coated skirmishers, pushing cautiously forward to investigate, discovered that there was no enemy confronting them. The woods, which the night before had swarmed with men in butternut gray, were now empty. Only the dead and wounded scattered about told of the enemy's former presence, and bore testimony, too, that his flight had been a hurried one, for he had left these victims of the battle behind.

The withdrawal from the field of Perryville marked the beginning of Bragg's retreat from Kentucky. He took his army first to Harrodsburg, where Kirby Smith joined him. The Confederates had learned by this time that their presence in the State created no great enthusiasm. They were received with indifference, and often with open hostility. No recruits flocked to their banners. The golden dreams in which they had seen Kentucky rising as one man to welcome the bearers of the Stars and Bars had faded. They were now in a parched and impoverished part of the State, which could not long sustain their army. Their way to the more fertile region was blocked by Buell, the temper of whose army they had tested at Perryville. All agreed that there remained no course open save to abandon the State.

Nevertheless the invasion of Kentucky had been in no sense a failure. The Federals had been pushed back again to the Ohio river, the line they held when Grant made his expedition against Fort Henry. Cincinnati and Louisville had been threatened, and the world shown that there was vitality and power in the Confederate armies in the west.

Nor in leaving Kentucky did Bragg go empty-handed. His foragers had been active, and the fertile fields, the pastures dotted with grazing cattle, the village stores with well-filled shelves, had all suffered from their visits. All the plunder was sent in advance of the army to the southward. Thousands of beef cattle, horses, sheep and swine were driven along by reckless Texans. An interminable train of wagons, heavy laden with all conceivable articles, followed. "The wagon train of supplies," said a writer in the Richmond *Examiner*, possibly with some exaggeration, "was forty miles long, and brought a million of yards of jeans, with a large amount of clothing, boots and shoes, and two hundred wagon loads of bacon, 6000 barrels of pork, 1500 mules and horses and a large lot of swine."

Said the Lexington *Observer*: "For four weeks while the Confederates were in the vicinity of Lexington, a train of cars was running daily southward, carrying some property taken from the inhabitants, and at the same time huge wagon trains were continually moving for the same purpose."

And so, heavy laden with supplies of inestimable value to the already sorely straitened Confederacy, Bragg made his exit from Kentucky via Cumberland Gap. Through those narrow and tortuous defiles Buell's army could not follow him with any hope of a successful pursuit, and the Federals therefore turned their steps toward Nashville. Thus a few weeks after the bloody encounter at Perryville the hostile armies turned their backs upon each other and took diverse paths, but only to clash again at a later date upon a field of battle far removed from the former one.

While Bragg had thus led his army into Kentucky and out again, the soldiers of the Confederate army of the southwest, whom he had left at Tupelo under command of Van Dorn and Price, had had their fill of fighting.

Van Dorn's army mustered some 16,000 men, and was scattered along the railroad from Holly Springs to Vicksburg. Price's troops, about equal in numbers, were concentrated at Tupelo. The commands were independent, but the two commanders were expected to co-operate cordially in discharging their prime duty,—preventing Grant from sending any reinforcements north to the aid of Buell in his struggle with Bragg for the possession of Kentucky.

Confronting the two Confederate generals was General Grant, with his headquarters at Corinth. He had under his command about 50,000 men, scattered between Memphis, Corinth, and Jackson. He for his part was on the watch to see that Price did not slip past him, and make for Kentucky, there to join Bragg's army of invasion.

For a time the two adversaries warily watched each other at a safe distance. Price moved first. Wishing to harass Grant as well as to get information from his rear, he sent out Armstrong with a cavalry troop 3700 strong to raid Bolivar, where some Federal troops were stationed. Armstrong laid his plans to surprise his antagonists, but found them on the alert. A battle followed in which the Union troops, though greatly outnumbered, more than held their own. Armstrong returned by a devious route without having accomplished anything of moment.

Not far from Corinth, on a line of railroad running east and west, is the little village of Iuka. Clear springs strongly impregnated with health-giving qualities bubble up from the ground beneath the shady canopy of a magnificent grove. Before the war it was a notable summer resort for the South, and a large tavern with spacious verandas and luxurious appointments was much frequented by the planters and neighboring gentry. Price thought Iuka a good place to hold. Its situation was such that he could make a descent upon Corinth or move off into Tennessee with equal ease. Accordingly he immediately transferred his army thither from Tupelo, ousting without a struggle the few Federal troops who were enjoying the salubrious air and pleasant waters of the little resort. The Federal officer in command on retreating neglected to destroy a large quantity of medical stores, provisions, and the like, so that the Confederates were able to revel in luxuries long unenjoyed, during the few hours they were left undisturbed.

Grant had not been napping during this time. Price's skirmishers had hardly entered Iuka before Grant, at Corinth, knew of it and was devising means to expel the Confederates from the point of vantage they had gained. He determined not only to recapture Iuka, but to get Price between two heavy detachments of Federals and grind him to atoms. Price had about 14,000 effective men in Iuka. Supposing him to be defeated, there were but two roads by which he could save the shattered remnant of his army—the Fulton road and the Jacinto road, both running south and almost parallel. Grant's plan of attack was to send Rosecrans with 9000 men to attack the enemy from the south, covering both these roads. Ord meantime, with 8000 men, was to fall upon him from the northwest. Thus beleaguered front and rear, Price would be brayed as in a mortar. "It looked to me that if Price would remain in Iuka until we could get there, his annihilation was inevitable," wrote Grant in his memoirs.

But unforeseen accidents sometimes defeat the most carefully formulated plans. Price had entered Iuka on Sept. 13. On the 18th the blue-coats who were to destroy him began operations. Ord went down the railroad to Burnsville, there left the cars, and took up the march. He proceeded to within two miles of Iuka, beat off the enemy's skirmishers, entrenched himself and waited for daylight, when he expected to begin the attack. Meantime Rosecrans was marching across country some miles to the south, seeking to get into a like advantageous position and be ready to join in the attack early in the morning.

Grant remained midway between the two. Couriers mounted on fleet steeds kept him informed of the progress of each wing of his army. Reports came fast from the northern wing telling of Ord's rapid progress, but not until midnight did an aide come galloping, his horse weary and covered with mud, bringing tidings from Rosecrans. The roads over which his route lay were deep with mud, said Rosecrans, the streams he had to ford were swollen, his men were weary, and he had only reached Jacinto. But, though fatigued with the wearisome march, his men would be able to reach Iuka by two o'clock next day.

Though greatly disappointed at the failure of Rosecrans to carry out the movement as planned, Grant strove to make the best of it. That Rosecrans could reach Iuka in time to attack at two o'clock he did not believe possible. So not knowing at what time the southern wing of the army would be ready to attack, he sent word to Ord to wait until he should hear the thunder of Rosecrans's guns, and then fall upon the enemy,—an arrangement which was faulty in that an adverse wind might—and did—carry the sound of the cannonade directly away from Ord.

Daylight saw Rosecrans's men rising from the damp ground, rolling up their blankets, getting coffee and making ready for the day's march. The sun was scarcely up before the column was tramping along the muddy road. Rosecrans rode at the head of the column. He was determined to keep his promise to Grant and take his men into battle by two o'clock.

One o'clock came. The cavalry troop in advance of the Union column suddenly came upon some mounted Confederates in the road, who gave a frightened glance at the sudden apparition, fired a few hasty shots, and galloped off. They were the Confederate outposts, and the news that the enemy was upon them was speedily carried to Price. The column of blue-coats swept steadily along the narrow road, which was flanked on either side by dense woods. A mile or so nearer town, the side road branched off by which half of Rosecrans's force was to cross over to the Fulton road. Until that road should be reached the Federals had to march in column of fours along a narrow road, in a region where the enemy might at any moment pounce down upon them. Though all knew that the foe could not be far distant, no attempt was made to deploy, and so the road for the space of nearly a mile was crowded with a long drawn-out column of infantry, artillery and cavalry.

Seeing some suspicious signs in the woods ahead, Hamilton, who commanded the leading division, pushed forward his skirmishers and rode close in their wake. Suddenly a shot from one of the skirmishers drew such a thunderous volley from an enemy concealed in the woods that Hamilton speedily saw that he had stirred up the foe in force. Wheeling his horse, he galloped back to the head of his column.

"Deploy your troops on both sides of the road and press forward," he cried to the regimental commanders. Three regiments were quickly put in line of battle. A battery was run into position on the right of the road, and responded with a will to the volleys of canister which the enemy was pouring into the Federal lines. Here, as in almost every battle of the war, the aim of the Union artillerists was the more effective. The enemy's shot "passed over our heads, doing no damage beyond bringing down a shower of twigs and leaves," wrote Gen. Hamilton some years later.

But now the Confederate cannon cease their roaring. The gray lines are sweeping forward to the assault, and are in the direct line of fire. Had the charge come a little sooner the Federals would have been swept away, rolled back on the column in the road below, routed, annihilated. But the Confederates had failed to grasp their opportunity, and now Hamilton with a battle line of three regiments is ready.

It is late in the afternoon, and the early autumn twilight is coming on. The Federals have the advantage of position, for their line of battle crowns the crest of a hill up which their assailants must charge. A battery of six guns—the 11th Ohio—is on the right of the Union line, and sends murderous volleys of grape into the faces of the advancing foe. Fiercely the gunners wield sponge and rammer. Scarce half a minute passes without the flame spurting from the muzzle of one of the guns. The Confederates see that the battery must be taken, and turn toward it. Volley after volley comes from their ranks. Men and horses began to fall around the guns with alarming rapidity. The fire of the battery begins to slacken. There are no longer men enough to man it. "In less than a half an hour after the battle began," wrote a war correspondent that night to the Cincinnati *Commercial*, "seventy-two of the battery men were placed *hors de combat*, being either killed or wounded, and every horse was shot from the caissons." Seeing this the Confederates charge forward, shoot down the few artillerymen left at the guns, and capture the battery. But there is no way to take the captured guns out of the battle, which is growing fierce thereabouts as Hamilton rushes other regiments into action, so they are spiked. The roar of the artillery then is heard no longer, but the shouts of the combatants and the crash of musketry make the woods reverberate. The hostile lines are not far apart, and pour destructive volleys into each other at short range. The commands of the enemy's officers can be heard in the Union lines. "My men were ordered by me to lie down, load, rise and fire," writes a captain of Missouri volunteers. "In this way I saved the lives of many men. After a few rounds were fired, a command was given by a rebel officer in a loud tone to fire low, when a leaden hail swept through our ranks, wounding several of our men and throwing my company into confusion."

By this time the steady, dogged advance of the Confederates had brought the hostile lines almost within bayonet reach. The blue-coats held their ground with admirable pluck, but fell fast before the fatal fire of the foe. At several places along the Union line the ammunition was exhausted, and the point of the bayonet alone was relied upon to hold the enemy in check. Twice, with bayonet charges, did the Union soldiers recapture the guns lost early in the battle, only to be driven away again by the enemy returning reënforced and with fresh determination. And so backward and forward, over the crest of the hill the surging mass of struggling, bleeding, fighting, cursing men went plunging until gathering darkness made it hard to tell friend from foe, and the strife lost something of its fierceness. Still in the deepening gloom the crack of the rifle and the occasional roar of a volley rung out, until the clear notes of a bugle gave the command "cease firing," and the battle was over.

Two hours had seen the battle begin and end. Scarce 4000 men on either side actually took part in the fray. Nevertheless it was a bloody field, for 141 dead bodies clad in blue, and 85 in the Confederate gray, lay on the ground. In wounded Rosecrans had lost 613, and Price 410. The Union loss was mostly in the brigade of Hamilton. Among the Confederate dead was General Little—shot through the head as he stood talking to General Price.

That night the Union soldiers bivouacked on the slope of the hill they had fought so fiercely to hold. Soon after dark a drenching rain began to fall, and the weary, half-famished soldiers rolled themselves in their blankets and huddled about the fires with gloomy anticipations of a night of discomfort in which to prepare for another day of battle. Few of the Union soldiers had the night undisturbed, for there was marching to and fro as Rosecrans rearranged his lines, sending to the rear the regiments that had borne the brunt of the first day's fighting, and bringing forward the fresh troops of Stanley's division.

The Confederates for their part slowly withdrew from the field, leaving pickets and skirmishers behind to mask their retreat. General Price knew that Ord was in his rear, that Grant was not far away, and that at any moment he might find himself caught between two fires. So only stopping to give the body of General Little a midnight burial by torchlight, and to set fire to the stores that the Federals had left in Iuka in their flight, he abandoned the village by the one road left uncovered. The sight of the blazing boxes, bales, and barrels of provisions was a sore blow to the Confederate host, who on entering the village had thought to revel in the good things provided for their enemies, and were now obliged to retreat leaving the provender almost untouched.

The next morning Rosecrans began his advance. He moved cautiously forward, expecting every moment to hear the crack of some Confederate picket's rifle. The enemy's dead and many of his wounded lay on the ground. Soon the skirmishers of the Union army passed the guns that the Confederates had captured the day before, spiked and abandoned. Then Rosecrans began to think the enemy had fled, and in a moment more a man with a white flag came into the lines, and reported that Iuka was deserted by Price and his soldiers. Ord, who had only received word of the battle at midnight, and to whose ears no sound of Rosecrans's cannon had come, reached the village about the same time as did the battle-scarred ranks of Rosecrans's division. It was then too late, however, to think of pursuing the enemy, and so Price's column, unmolested, went trailing off toward Tupelo, the soldiers consoling themselves for their defeat by plundering every house they passed, as though wholly oblivious to the fact that they were in a friendly country.

Three weeks passed. Iuka, deserted by all save a handful of Federals, relapsed into the sylvan quiet of a ruined summer resort. Ord

BURIAL OF GENERAL LITTLE.

had been sent to Bolivar, while Rosecrans with 19,000 men was tenanting the snug defenses which Grant had constructed inside the immense works built by Beauregard at Corinth. Upon Corinth the Confederates looked with a covetous eye. As a railroad center, it was of supreme strategetical importance.

Van Dorn, who ranked Price now in the command of the Confederate army in the southwest, says in his report:

"I determined to attack Corinth. I had a reasonable hope of success. Field returns at Ripley showed my strength to be about 22,000 men. Rosecrans at Corinth had about 15,000, with about 8000 additional men at outposts from 12 to 15 miles distant. I might surprise him and carry the place before these troops could be brought in. It was necessary for the blow to be sudden and decisive."

Though he had determined to attack Corinth, Van Dorn took every precaution to prevent his purpose from becoming known. Rosecrans was completely mystified by the apparently eccentric movements of the Confederates. For some time he was in doubt whether it was Bolivar or Corinth that was in danger. When he saw the blow was to be struck at the latter place, he was still in doubt as to the quarter from which it would come. But he kept busily on throwing up earthworks, digging rifle-pits, and putting up chevaux-de-frise in every direction, while all the time the cavalry—the eyes of an army—were scouring the country and bringing in reports of the enemy's movements.

A happy accident enabled Rosecrans to get wind of Van Dorn's designs, and then to lure him into a trap prepared for him. The Union general became convinced that some one in Corinth was communicating with the enemy.

Spies were set to watch the suspected persons, and before very long Rosecrans was in possession of a letter which a Miss Burton had tried to send to Van Dorn. Opening it, he discovered that it gave full information as to the strength of the Union forces, and the number of their cannon. The writer further suggested that the Confederates should attack on the northwest side of the town, where the defenses were weakest. With admirable shrewdness Rosecrans resealed the letter, sent it on to Van Dorn, and then went to work strengthening the earthworks on the northwest side of the town, keeping a vigilant watch upon Miss Burton meanwhile, to see that she found no means of warning Van Dorn against the trap that was being prepared for him. Before the cavalry scouts reported the enemy advancing in force, the ground which Miss Burton had called the weak spot in the Union line was well provided with revetted redoubts, rifle-pits, trenches, log breastworks and other defensive erections.

Friday, October 3d, sees the Confederates advancing in earnest, and by the northwest side of the town, sure enough. There has been skirmishing for two or three days, but this time the enemy pushes on so persistently that General Rosecrans feels sure that the day of battle has come. He sends forward Hamilton, the hero of the fight at Iuka, Davies, McArthur, and Crocker to meet them. Davies and McArthur get their men behind some old deserted earthworks—relics of the earlier Confederate occupation of Corinth—and make a stubborn resistance. They had been ordered only to make a sufficient resistance to force Van Dorn to show his hand, but McArthur's Scotch blood is up, and he makes so bitter a fight that Van Dorn believes he has encountered the main line of defense, and when he has carried the earthworks thinks that Corinth is already his. But before he passes that line, so hastily occupied, Van Dorn sees many of his bravest soldiers fall, while in the Union ranks Brigadier-General Hackleman is killed, and Brigadier-General Oglesby—Governor of Illinois many years later—is desperately wounded. Then the triumphant Confederates push on toward Corinth, until darkness checks their advance, and ends the running fight. "I saw with regret the sun sink behind the horizon," wrote Van Dorn in his report, "as the last shot of our sharpshooters followed the retreating foe into their innermost lines. One hour more of daylight and victory would have soothed our grief for the loss of the gallant dead who sleep on that lost but not dishonored field. The army slept on its arms within six hundred yards of Corinth, victorious so far."

But commenting upon this General Rosecrans says that he too saw with grief the sun setting, because one hour more would have given Hamilton time to complete a movement he was making to fall upon the Confederate rear and right flank, with the probable effect of throwing them into helpless confusion.

Whether the setting of the sun was disastrous the more to the Confederate or the Union case must remain undetermined. But certain it is that both armies utilized, to the fullest extent, the opportunity afforded by the night to reform their lines and strengthen their positions. By this Rosecrans unquestionably profited the more. He was fighting a defensive battle. His men could fight behind breastworks. All that night men worked by the light of torches, throwing up earthworks, digging trenches, and building redoubts of logs. One fort was built by fugitive slaves who had fled to Corinth to seek shelter under the flag of the Union. Long before daylight the pathway which the assailants had to tread to reach the town was a valley of death.

Dawn brings the opening of the conflict. A Confederate battery posted during the night on a commanding hill near town begins to shell the Union camp. The missiles drop among the soldiers' campfires and crash through buildings, sending the non-combatants flying for dear life out of town. After bearing it for an hour, the Federals return the fire from Fort Williams—one of the works put up during the night—and in a few minutes the Confederate battery is silenced and one gun deserted by the artillerymen.

Now for a time the skirmishers have it to themselves. The rattle of their musketry and the deliberate firing of batteries tell the educated ear of a soldier that as yet the battle has not begun. When the fighting begins in earnest the cannon will boom faster and the musket-shots will come in volleys.

Van Dorn has formulated a plan of attack. What would have been the result had it been followed cannot be told. It is not followed because General Hebert, who was to have opened the attack, is taken ill and fails either to carry out his orders or report his condition. About nine o'clock Van Dorn discovers why his assault is lagging and sends an officer to take Hebert's place. But the battle then takes the form of a direct attack upon a force of equal strength, sheltered by formidable earthworks. The result is inevitable.

Half-past nine o'clock. Suddenly the Union soldiers in the chain of redoubts that stretch from Fort Williams on the left to Fort Richardson on the right, see dense masses of troops coming down the Bolivar road. Upon the Confederates, thus massed in column of fours, the Union guns begin to play. Almost instantly the column opens, spreads out like a fan, and a long line of determined veterans comes sweeping forward, faltering not, marching sternly and steadily, determined to carry the Union works or fall before them. Now all the Union cannon are flaming and smoking. From Battery Robinett; from Forts Williams, and Richardson, and Powell spurt the jets of lurid flame that bid God-speed to the cannon's missive of death. Between the forts is the Union infantry, drawn up in line of battle and pouring volleys upon the advancing Confederates as fast as the smoking muskets can be loaded and discharged. Behind their log redoubts the Yates and Burgess sharpshooters pour in their deadly volleys, each bullet in which goes to its chosen mark.

Yet straight into the hurricane of death, with set faces and quick-beating hearts, the gray-clad veterans doggedly advance, closing up their lines where the enemy's cannon make the gaps too wide, and carrying their colors well to the front. "The enemy," wrote an eye-witness, "seemingly insensible to fear, or infuriated by passion, bent their necks downward and marched steadily to death, with their faces averted like men striving to protect themselves against a driving storm of hail."

The right of the Union line of defense is most advanced, and there the shock of battle is first felt. Fort Richardson belches forth its spiteful defiance in the faces of the advancing foemen. Davies's brigade is in line on either side of the fort, and from the muzzles of its thousand muskets the leaden bullets speed to scatter death in the ranks of the assailants. Yet the Confederates surge forward in one of those grand, breathless, desperate charges for which the men of the South were famous. They reach the crest of the hill. Another moment and they will plunge their bayonets into the bodies of Davies's men. But already the Union line is wavering. It crumbles away at the ends. Gaps appear in it not made by wounds or death. The men are straggling to the rear. Rosecrans sees that the line is going. Galloping to the spot he strives to hold the men at their post. Over the roar of battle his voice cannot be heard, but he waves his hat and points his sword at the enemy. But it is too late. All at once Davies's men give way and fall back, carrying Rosecrans with them, shouting, gesticulating, imploring, but all helpless in the midst of the panic-stricken rabble. The Confederate brigades of Gates and Cabell, sorely cut up, sweep on in pursuit. The redoubt of Fort Richardson, where the cannon are firing at point-blank range into the faces of the desperate men, checks them but a moment. Over the breastwork they swarm. The gunners are shot down or pierced through and through with bayonet thrusts. Brave Richardson, who gave the fort its name, falls dead among his guns. Fifty yards down the hill toward Corinth are the artillery horses. A score of Confederates run down to get them, but an Illinois regiment which has been in hiding suddenly rises and fires, and the horses fall dead, and most of the men who had gone to capture them meet the same fate. A number of the Confederates of Gates's command had penetrated as far as the outer streets of Corinth. They fight their way along from house to house, sheltering themselves behind trees and corners. At last they reach the house fronting on the public square which had been General Halleck's headquarters. They crowd into the house, on its piazza and into its yard. General Rosecrans is on the other side of the square. He brings up a battery and opens fire. In a moment the house is riddled with bullets and full of dead and wounded men.

But now the force of the Confederates' splendid charge is spent.

The Tenth Ohio and Fifth Minnesota regiments drive from the town such of the enemy as have come so far. The Fifty-first Illinois drives off the captors of Fort Richardson. Hamilton's veterans come up to aid in the work of wresting from the enemy the ground he had so magnificently won. A concentric fire from a ring of Union batteries is poured into the bleeding ranks of Gates and Cabell. Suddenly they retreat. It is a bitter disappointment to so soon lose the fruits of their daring charge. But the fortune of war is inexorable, and soon the ground before Fort Richardson is held only by the Confederate dead and wounded. There is no more fighting there that day.

After the battle was over General Rosecrans rode out on the field before the Union right. A wounded lieutenant of an Arkansas regiment attracted his attention. The general offered the sufferer some water.

"Thank you, general," was the response, "one of your men has just given me some."

"It was pretty hot fighting here," remarked Rosecrans as he looked about the field, over which the dead and wounded were plentifully strewn.

"Yes, general," said the Arkansan philosophically, "you licked us good, but we gave you the best we had in the ranch."

Meantime Van Dorn had made his assault on the Union center, and met no less warm a reception than that encountered by Price on the right.

Before Van Dorn lies even a more perilous path than that which the men of Price's command so bravely and so futilely trod. The ground is rugged, thickly studded with stumps, and covered with fallen trees. Van Dorn's men must go down into a ravine, up a hill, and through a tangled abattis bristling with sharpened spikes, and all the time they will be under the fire of Fort Williams and Battery Robinett and the supporting infantry. There are three 10-pound Parrott guns in Battery Robinett. The guns in Fort Williams are 30-pounders.

The Confederates waste no time in parade or formalities. Two

STORMING OF BATTERY ROBINETT.

brigades—Texans and Mississippians—come sweeping grandly forward in the teeth of the fire of the forts. In the front rank, towering high above the foot-soldiers, is a mounted officer. Though the cannon thunder constantly and the grape shot and the Minie bullets hum like a swarm of angry bees whose sting means death, the men of the South march gallantly onward. Every now and then the men in the Union lines see the Confederate colors go down, only to be caught out of the hand of the wounded color-bearer by some fresh volunteer. When they go down for the fourth time it is within a few yards of the ditch of Battery Robinett. This time the mounted officer leaps from his horse, grasps the standard of the colors, and with the flag in one hand and a revolver in the other, dashes forward, calling upon his men to follow him. The ditch is reached and crossed, and the plucky officer—Col. Rogers, of Texas,—has scaled the ramparts and stands there waving his colors, when a Union drummer-boy raises a pistol and fires. Backward into the ditch falls the gallant Texan, shot through the brain. Some of his men have followed close behind their leader, and though the guns of Robinett blaze fiercely it looks for a moment as though the redoubt would be carried. But back of the fort were 250 men of the Sixty-third Ohio, with muskets loaded, lying on their faces and awaiting their time. Their time has now come.

"Rise and fire!" shouts their colonel. As one man they rise and deliver a volley. Then another and another yet in quick succession. When six volleys had been fired the first line of the Confederate attacking force had been swept away. The ground before Battery Robinett is covered with dead men; the ditch is full; not a few lie within the rampart.

But now the second line of the Confederates draws near. Over the bodies of their luckless comrades who had fallen in the first assault the fresh troops march with steady tread. The Federals nerve themselves for this second shock. The guns of Robinett and Williams are thundering again. The Sixty-third Ohio swings around in front and to one side of Battery Robinett, so that its volleys will sweep the front of that work. All undaunted the assailants come on, breaking into a quick run as they get near the fort, and cheering each other on with that famous southern war cry, "the rebel yell." The cruel flanking fire from the Ohio troops throws the attacking column into confusion under the very guns of the battery. Many turn aside and plunge in among the Ohio men. A hand-to-hand fight follows. Muskets are clubbed and fierce blows dealt. The bayonets make bloody play on either side. There is no time to load a gun, but the pistols crack fast and often. Even fists are used in the mad rage of battle.

Some of the assailants meantime have got into Battery Robinett. They raise a shout of triumph as they see its defenders fly before them. But their joy is short-lived. The guns of Fort Williams command the interior of Battery Robinett. Before the battle it was ordered, that should the Confederates force their way into the latter work the defenders should retire, and the task of driving out the intruders be left to artillerymen in the other fort. So now the guns of Fort Williams begin to sweep every nook and corner of Robinett with grape and canister. The Confederates see that all their gallantry has only carried them to a point still under the enemy's guns. Their ranks have been too sore shattered for them to think of carrying the second battery by assault. So Robinett is abandoned, and the gallant assailants are soon in full retreat down the slope up which they had so bravely charged and to such small purpose. Pitilessly the storm of death from the muzzles of cannons and muskets beats upon their backs as they retreat, and as many men, almost, fall in fleeing from Battery Robinett as had fallen in charging upon it.

Van Dorn now sees his army beaten, cut to pieces, broken to fragments against the impenetrable wall of the Federal line of defense. On the right, on the left, in the center—everywhere that an assault had been ordered it had been made with unexceptionable gallantry and had been repulsed with great loss of life. The spirit of the

Confederate army was broken. A battle of scarce three hours had cost three thousand men. There was no course left to the Confederate commander but an immediate retreat.

Though prompt and pitiless pursuit would have spread still further disaster in the sorely shattered ranks of the retreating foe, the Union soldiers were too greatly exhausted to undertake it. Lovel's Confederate division, which had not been in the battle, was a rear-guard not to be despised, and Rosecrans had no fresh troops to cope with it. So a night of rest was given to the victors, and rations for five days were issued, so that on the following morning the pursuit could be begun.

Into the details of that pursuit it is useless to go. It is enough to say that Van Dorn led his army away successfully, with but one serious contest with his foe. At the fords of the Hatchie river General Ord fell upon the flying Confederates and captured three hundred of them with two batteries of artillery. The rest of the pursuit—which extended over sixty miles—was a mere matter of skirmishing between the Confederate rear-guard and the Union van.

The defeat at Corinth was a crushing blow to the Confederate cause in that region. It was to the Confederate campaign in northern Mississippi what Antietam was to Lee's invasion of Maryland, and what Perryville was to Bragg's invasion of Kentucky—it marked at once the culmination and crushing of the hopes of the Confederates. A bloody battle it was, too. The Union loss according to Rosecrans was 315 killed, 1812 wounded, and 232 missing; total 2359. As to the Confederate loss a contradiction in reports leads to doubt. Van Dorn reported 505 killed, 2150 wounded, and 2183 missing. But Rosecrans declared that he took 2268 prisoners, and his medical director states that 1423 Confederates were buried by Union soldiers on the field of battle. It is safe to assume that the figures of Van Dorn are too small.

A major-general's commission rewarded Rosecrans for his victory, and soon after he was sent north to command the Army of the Cumberland, from the command of which Buell had been relieved. As for Van Dorn, the weight of Jefferson Davis's anger over the lost battle fell heavily upon him, and he was deprived of his command. But he demanded a court of inquiry, and was fully exonerated from all charges of negligence or incompetency. Nevertheless, Van Dorn was not restored to his former station, but served until his death, in 1863, in command of a division under Generals Pemberton and Bragg. It is a curious fact that this dashing trooper, after exposing himself to the terribly destructive volleys of his foes at Pea Ridge and at Corinth, finally met his death in a duel.

CHAPTER V.

BRAGG IN TENNESSEE.—REVELRY AT MURFREESBORO'. — ROSECRANS IN COMMAND OF THE ARMY OF THE CUMBERLAND. — MORGAN'S RAID. — ROSECRANS'S MARCH. — BATTLE OF STONE'S RIVER OR MURFREESBORO'. — BRAGG'S RETREAT. — THE RAID ON HOLLY SPRINGS.

AFTER his retreat from Kentucky, General Bragg concentrated his army at Murfreesboro', a small village in Tennessee near the Kentucky line, and about thirty miles from Nashville. His presence there threatened the safety of the Tennessee capital, but when November came, and the Confederates showed no signs of activity, but went on preparing to meet the winter at Murfreesboro', the people of Nashville and the surrounding regions concluded that there was to be no more fighting until spring. The officers of Bragg's army gave themselves up to a round of social pleasures at Murfreesboro'. Jefferson Davis came from Richmond, and remained some time as Bragg's guest in a fine mansion which a wealthy sympathizer with the southern cause had placed at the latter's disposal. Balls, banquets, receptions and card parties followed each other in rapid succession.

The little Tennessee town was as gay as Brussels the night before the battle of Waterloo, when

> There was a sound of revelry by night.
> . . . .
> And all went merry as a marriage bell.

Nor was the marriage bell missing from the festivities at Murfreesboro'. That famous rough-rider and guerrilla John Morgan chose this time to be married. The officers brightened up their uniforms, and the belles of the town donned their gayest costumes. Leonidas Polk, who had discarded the surplice of an Episcopal bishop to become a Confederate general, now doffed his shoulder-straps and brass buttons, and arrayed in his episcopal robes pronounced the wedding service. Jefferson Davis was present, and congratulated the wedded pair. After the ceremony there was dancing, and the story goes that the rooms were carpeted with United States flags, that the dancers might show their contempt for the Union by trampling upon its banner.

The gayety at Murfreesboro', however, was chiefly on the surface. The higher officers might dance, and banquet, and flirt with the village girls, but the army as a whole was anything but contented. The men were disappointed in being forced to abandon Kentucky, and charged their failure to capture Louisville and Cincinnati to the incompetence of their commanders. There was an undercurrent of discontent running all through the camp. Bragg was never popular with his men. Quarrelsome with his equals, he was overbearing and severe with his inferiors. Some sentences of death which he pronounced upon some of his soldiers added to his unpopularity. The stories of his severity spread about the country. One of his staff officers says that one day the general, riding with his staff in the neighborhood of Tupelo, some time after the battle of Murfreesboro', met a man of whom he asked some information. The man replied intelligently, and after conversing for some time, the general inquired if he did not belong to Bragg's army.

"Bragg's army?" was the unexpected response. "He's got no army. He shot half of them himself up in Kentucky, and the other half got killed at Murfreesboro'."

The general laughed and rode on.

But not in dancing and gayety were the Confederates destined to spend the winter. Invitations were issued for at least one ball which was never danced. When the night for the entertainment came around, many of the bidden guests lay cold and stark on a hard-fought battle-field near Murfreesboro'.

The Union army which, while Bragg's men were tripping in the mazy waltz, was gathering at Nashville, was Buell's old army reorganized and under a new commander. Though Buell had driven Bragg from Kentucky, his conduct of the campaign was not satisfactory to Halleck, who then ruled supreme over the army of the United States, and so Buell was deposed and Rosecrans, who had just won the battle at Corinth, was appointed to his command. Thereafter the army was known as the Army of the Cumberland. Without moving his army from its comfortable quarters at Murfreesboro', Bragg thought to drive Rosecrans out of Nashville by sending out cavalry parties to cut the railroads which brought to the Union army its supplies from the North. For this service the veteran raider Morgan and the dashing cavalry leader Forrest were of course chosen. Both were familiar with the ground and with the nature of the task before them. In August, Morgan had been dispatched on a precisely similar errand. That time he captured a train of freight cars, ran them into a tunnel, tore down the timbers which supported the roof of the tunnel, set the cars on fire, and fairly let the mountain down upon the railroad. It took months for the Federals to repair the damage. But in the autumn, Rosecrans so well protected his railroad communications that neither Morgan nor Forrest could do any material damage. The audacity of Morgan was not to be wholly balked, however, and he managed to capture 1500 Federals who were encamped at Hartsville. For this exploit he was made a major-general.

About noon on the 26th of December, the Confederates at Murfreesboro' were unpleasantly surprised to get word by swift couriers that the Union army had left Nashville at six o'clock that morning, and was coming to offer battle. There were some festal invitations out then that were destined never to be accepted.

Scarce two miles from Nashville the Union columns encountered the Confederate outposts, and there was skirmishing all along the front as great torrents of blue-clad men went streaming along by three almost parallel roads toward Murfreesboro'. By the 29th of the month, however, the whole army was within attacking distance of Bragg. That general for his part had come out to meet the foe, and was encamped on the further side of a little creek called Stone's river. The day was spent by both armies in choosing their lines for the battle of the morrow and resting their men. A slight advantage was gained by each. Rosecrans, having been informed that the enemy was evacuating Murfreesboro', pushed forward Harker's brigade in hot pursuit. Harker came near rushing into the very jaws of the foe, for Bragg had indeed evacuated Murfreesboro', but only to advance and meet the Federals, not to retreat as Rosecrans had imagined. Luckily Harker only encountered a weak regiment, which he speedily routed and a large portion of which he captured. His prisoners warned him of the danger of proceeding further, and he retired with the trophies of his victory. The Confederates, for their part, devoted the night of the 29th to one of those dashing raids around the Union army. How successful the raiders were may be judged from the fact that a Union staff officer estimates the damage to the Federal army at "700 prisoners and nearly a million dollars' worth of property"; and declares that at the scene of devastation "the turnpike as far as the eye could reach was filled with burning wagons. The country was overspread with disarmed men, broken-down horses and mules," and that the raiders carried back to camp "a sufficient number of Minie rifles and accoutrements to arm a brigade."

Through the dreary, rainy night of the 30th of December the two armies lay on the cold, damp ground confronting each other. Each was expecting to begin the battle at daybreak, and by a singular coincidence the plans of battle chosen by Bragg and Rosecrans were identical. Speaking generally, the lines ran north and south, through a country in which fallow fields and dense clumps of cedar alternated. A railroad and a turnpike, straight as arrows, cut through both lines at an acute angle. Stone's river flowed sluggishly along, following the same general direction as the lines of battle, but separating the hostile armies nowhere. Rosecrans was at first surprised that Bragg had not seen fit to make this stream his line of defense. He discovered the next morning that it was not a line of defense to which the Confederate general had been devoting his mind.

From left to right the Union line was made up of the divisions of Crittenden, Thomas, and McCook. Confronting them—reaching from right to left, were the Confederate brigades of Breckenridge, Polk, and Hardee. In strength the two armies were about equal, the effective force of each being about 30,000 men.

That night there was a council of war in Rosecrans's tent. The three division commanders were there. The plan of battle was unfolded. Spies had kept the Union general well informed of the disposition of the enemy's troops. He knew that the weakest force confronted Crittenden; the most powerful was hidden in the cedars about five hundred yards before McCook's pickets. The plan was then to push forward Crittenden, fall upon Breckenridge's weak division; cross the river and outflank the enemy. Thomas was then to follow and the whole Union army, save McCook's division, which was the pivot, was to execute a mighty right wheel; swinging around to the southeast, sweeping through Murfreesboro' and rolling the foe away before it. Two conditions were necessary to the successful execution of this plan,—the charge must be dogged, dashing and irresistible, and the pivotal division—McCook's—must stand "like a stone wall."

"Be cool," said Rosecrans as the conference closed. "I need not ask you to be brave. With God's grace, and your help, I feel confident of striking this day a crushing blow for the country. Do not throw away your fire. Fire slowly, deliberately—above all fire low, and be always sure of your aim. Close steadily in upon the enemy, and, when you get within charging distance, rush upon him with the bayonet. Do this, and victory will certainly be yours."

And so with hearts beating high, and the blood coursing more quickly in their veins, the three generals went away to finish the night with their benumbed soldiers in the sodden, fireless trenches.

Now Bragg too had formulated a plan of attack. There is no evidence that he held a council of war, but had he done so his three division commanders, Breckenridge, Polk, and Hardee, would have listened to words almost identical with those in which Rosecrans had outlined his strategy. Bragg's left was to attack at daylight; it was to beat back, envelop, and outflank McCook; the center under Polk was to follow hard after; the whole Confederate army was to execute a great right wheel, with Breckenridge for a pivot, sweeping the Federals away to the northward.

The two commanders had chosen identical plans, and had the attacks been made simultaneously and the battle fought as planned, the singular spectacle would have been presented of two great armies revolving slowly upon a fixed pivot.

Early dawn saw the Confederates of Hardee's division falling in; their belts tightened, plenty of ball ammunition in their cartridge-boxes, and every man in that state of nervous exhilaration that comes upon the soldier going into battle. Quietly they took up their march, which lay through a dense forest of cedars. The long line composed of the brigades of McConn and Cleburne curved and wavered, as the men made their way with difficulty through the woods, but when they came out on the edge of the clearing it was straight in an instant. The Union pickets were on the watch, and the quick, warning reports of their rifles rang out sharply on the quiet morning air. But the onward rush of the assailants was too impetuous for the alarm to be of any avail. At the sound of those shots the men of Johnson's and Davis's brigades spring from their coffee-pots and their camp-fires to catch up their rifles and throw themselves in the path of the foe. But it is too late. The fury of the charge cannot be checked by a hastily rallied force. The Union right is outflanked and falls back. Men fall fast, for the range is short, and the Confederates are using their muskets as though there was no such thing as a scarcity of powder in the Confederacy. Goodspeed's battery loses three guns, for the Confederates charge right in among them and there are no horses to drag them away. When that gray line broke from the front of the cedar thicket the battery horses were being watered at a neighboring creek, and there was no time to bring them up. In Kirk's brigade full 500 men were shot down; Willick's lost nearly as many, beside its commander, who was captured. There was hand-to-hand fighting for a while. Clubbed muskets and bayonet thrusts made the battle less noisy, but no less terrible. In three-quarters of an hour the divisions of Johnson and Davis were routed, and the Confederates made themselves masters of that part of the field.

Rosecrans, who is three miles away on the extreme left of the Union line, superintending the advance of Crittenden's division, has no idea of the danger which threatens his right. He hears the din of the battle, but feels no doubt of McCook's ability to hold his ground. At that very moment, however, McCook's right has been cut to pieces; his cannon have been captured and turned against him; the Confederate troopers of Wharton's cavalry had got around to the Union rear, and were capturing stragglers and guns and wagons,—all this had been done in three-quarters of an hour, and the Confederates, flushed with victory, were preparing to assault a second Union line which had hurriedly been formed to check their onward course.

" The new line is formed at right angles to the one which had been swept away. Seven thousand men now confront the gray-coats.

There were no trenches, no redoubts. Save for a rail fence which covered a portion of the line, the men stand with breasts bared to the bullets of the foe. Ten thousand men are in the attacking column. Though Hardee's brigade sweeps forward thrice in desperate charges, the blue-coats still hold their ground. General Sill is shot dead while leading a counter-charge. Sheridan's brigade, being out of ammunition, obeys the order of that fearless soldier to stand and receive the assault of the enemy on the point of the bayonet. But at last the Confederates outflank the stubborn defenders of the Union, and there is nothing for it but to give way. The first part of Bragg's plan is now completed. The Union right has been crushed, and the wheel of battle is to swing around as the Confederate general had planned it.

Swift couriers gallop away through the fields and woods, thronged with panic-stricken stragglers, to carry the news to Rosecrans. He is at the ford of Stone's river, sending Van Cleve across to move on Murfreesboro'.

"Tell General McCook to contest every inch of ground," says Rosecrans. "If he holds them we will swing into Murfreesboro' and cut them off."

Then he sends Rousseau's division, composed largely of regulars, to McCook's assistance, and a few minutes later, becoming convinced that disaster is lurking on his right, recalls Van Cleve and sends him on the same errand.

Rousseau marches quickly off toward the sound of battle. He has not gone far when he sees signs that matters are going badly in the front. First, stragglers are passed going to the rear, then companies, then regiments. Now Sheridan's division comes by in full retreat, dragging a few pieces of artillery. Rousseau hears that more guns have been left behind, that 1800 dead or wounded soldiers lie on the ground about the abandoned guns, and the enemy is following close upon the retreating soldiers of the crushed right wing. Rousseau concludes to halt where he is and await the enemy's onslaught.

Against this new obstacle the hostile lines dash themselves for a time in vain.

But now Rosecrans comes galloping down to where the fighting is thickest. It is time indeed. So long has he been seeking to offset the Union reverses on the right by striking a fierce and final blow with his left, that the reverses have become well-nigh irreparable. The stoutest-hearted among his division commanders think that the battle is lost. But, heedless of danger, never once admitting the possibility of defeat, the old soldier plunges into the fray. The manner in which he snatched victory from the very jaws of defeat must ever challenge the admiration of military critics. He forms a new line. With a soldier's practiced eye he chooses every point of vantage. His regulars are where the fighting is sure to be the fiercest. His batteries are on the crest of every hill. Every clump of cedars that offers the slightest concealment, shelters a line of Federal infantry.

Fearing nothing for himself, Rosecrans shows little pity for his associates to whom the fortunes of war bring death or wounds Some one tells him that Sill is dead.

"Never mind," he responds, "brave men must fall in battle."

He rides up to a brigade that is holding an exposed position. The men are going fast. The spat of the round shot, the thud of the bullet, the sharp cry of the wounded, tell how great is the peril in which every man there stands.

"Stand firm, boys," says the general, as he shares their danger, "cross yourselves and fire low."

A Catholic by faith, as his words show, the religious code which Rosecrans observed on the battle-field was not unlike that of the Puritans, who "put their trust in Providence and kept their powder dry."

By this time a line has been formed that may fairly be expected to hold the Confederates in check for some time. Rosecrans suddenly thinks that there may be danger of an attack on his left flank, and gallops off to the ford, which he thinks the enemy may try to pass. He finds there a regiment of Union troops.

"Who is in command here?" he asks.

"I am," responds an officer, Col. Price, coming forward.

"Will you hold this ford?"

"I'll try, sir."

"Will you hold this ford?" repeated the general with meaning emphasis.

"I will die right here."

"Will you hold this ford?" thundered Rosecrans for the third time, in a manner that left no doubt that what he wanted was a direct answer.

"Yes, I will."

"Good. That will do," and the general gallops back to the scene of the battle.

The new line is formed by this time, and stretches at right angles to the first one. Sheridan is there, and shows on that bloody field the bull-dog qualities which put him in the front rank of American soldiers; Thomas, cool and inflexible, holds his men rigidly to their task; Hazen with his brigade of Ohio boys; Shepherd with his brigade of regulars, whose professional pride would never let them leave a field while a volunteer dared stay; Rousseau, with his brigade tried in the fiery furnace of Corinth,—all these are there shoulder to shoulder, and at intervals along the line the guns of Loomis, Guenther and Stokes are at work filling the air with smoke made lurid by the powder's flash.

The enemy's guns are not idle, though, and many a gap is made in the long blue line as some roaring round shot or hurtling charge of canister goes through. Rosecrans, who is riding everywhere, has more than one narrow escape. A shot strikes the haunches of a horse directly in line with him. The rider is thrown twenty feet, but the shot is deflected from its course and Rosecrans is unhurt. A little later a round shot takes off the head of his friend and aide Garesché, who rode close at his side. Some one, seeing the blood which plentifully bespatters the general's uniform, asks if he is wounded.

"No, it's Gareschè's blood, poor fellow. But no matter. Death may come to any in battle."

It were idle to tell of the gallant but fruitless efforts that the Confederates made to break down this line of iron hearts; how with their batteries blazing in the rear they pressed forward with all the fiery dash of men of southern blood; how they met the storm of iron that dashed against them and were mowed down by it,—undaunted, but unable to make headway against the deadly blast; how the battle standards went forward, wavering now and then when some volunteer standard-bearer snatched the staff from the faltering grasp of one falling before the enemy's stroke, and then drifted back again; and how, withal, the plucky assailants gained not one inch of ground, nor moved the Union line one jot. Elated and certain of victory at first, the Confederates became irritated at this unexpected check, then doubtful of success, then despairing. When the sun went down it left the Union army still holding its position, and a feeling was abroad in the ranks of the foe that from that position it was not to be driven. At noon Rosecrans was being beaten everywhere; the Confederates were driving his choicest divisions before them like sheep; he had lost half his field of battle and seemed fated to lose the remainder. But by sundown he had formed a line which had withstood the rudest shocks of battle, and though the general results of the day's fighting had been against him he held the field and made ready for an attack on the morrow.

All night the searching parties with torches and litters wandered about the battle-field seeking the wounded. They found plenty of work, for the day had been a bloody one, and the ambulances that lumbered away on the roads to Nashville and Murfreesboro' were heavy laden.

All night, too, the commanders of the hostile armies were busy re-forming their lines, and laying their plans for the morrow. Rosecrans rode over the ground. There had been some talk at headquarters of retreating, but the general determined to first see for himself how strong was the ground he held. This done he sent for more powder and shot and declared he would fight where he was. "It's all right, boys," said he to some soldiers who looked inquiringly at him as he passed; "Bragg is a good dog, but Holdfast is a better."

But when day dawned—New Year's Day, 1863—no sign of any desire for more fighting was shown on either side. The two lines of pickets, pushed within a stone's throw of each other, kept vigilant watch upon each other's movements, but neither showed any inclination to advance. "God has granted us a happy new year," telegraphed Bragg to Richmond, and all day he watched eagerly for signs of the retreat which he felt confident the Federals were going to make. And there is little doubt that when the sun rose on the morning of the 2d, and he saw the thin blue line of Federal pickets still in his front, he was bitterly disappointed.

Now against the advice of his officers Bragg determines to reopen the battle. He finds that during the day before the Federals have not been idle, and that Van Cleve has crossed the river and established himself on a hill-top whence his artillery can enfilade Polk's line. Either Polk must retreat or the position must be carried, and Bragg chooses the latter course. To Breckenridge is assigned the task; four brigades and ten Napoleon guns are given him to discharge it with. His orders are to carry the hill, post his artillery there to enfilade the Union line, then press on and fall upon the Federals beyond the river. Polk protests against the plan as being impracticable, but accepts the duty. Until four o'clock he is massing the troops for the assault.

Four o'clock. A gun somewhere along the Confederate lines booms out the expected signal. From a narrow skirt of woods the first line of Breckenridge's attacking force appears. Before them an open field some six hundred yards wide slopes gently upward to where Van Cleve's men stand waiting the assault. The assailants set out on their perilous journey, and despite a fierce fire from the blue-coats on

GATHERING THE WOUNDED FROM THE BATTLE-FIELD.

the top of the hill, and a vicious rain of iron coming from the Union batteries beyond the river, they reach the crest of the hill. The defenders strive valiantly to hold their ground, but the odds are too great, and the exultant shouts of the Confederates tell Bragg that the first trick has been taken. Thus far all has gone well. In his report of this part of the battle, Breckenridge declares that he "after a brief but bloody conflict routed the opposing lines, took 400 prisoners and several flags, and drove their artillery and the great body of their infantry across the river." But his triumph is destined to be short-lived. As he pushes along down the hill in pursuit of his fleeing enemy, he thinks that no foe remains to dispute his progress on this side of the river. He little knows that, down under the shelter of the river's bluff, Miller's brigade is lying down out of sight, and waiting for an effective moment to deliver its fire. The moment comes when the last of the Union fugitives is out of the way, and then the concealed brigade rises suddenly, and pours its volleys into the faces of the advancing foe. Before this unexpected attack the men of Breckenridge's command waver and halt. It needs only that this cruel blow should be followed by one equally ferocious, to put them to hopeless rout. The second blow comes quickly. From the other bank of the river General Crittenden had seen the discomfiture of the Union troops, and has summoned his batteries to their aid. At this moment the guns open, fifty-eight of them, all flashing and roaring away, firing not less than a hundred shots to the minute. The Confederates seem fairly to melt away before them. When the carnage in their ranks is at its worst, the Federals begin to cross the ford and march upon them. In but a few minutes the Union line is re-established on the crest of the hill, and the woods again shelter all of Breckenridge's command save 1500 brave men who lie on the field of battle. An hour has been enough to put an end to all Confederate hopes in that quarter.

For another night the armies bivouacked on the battle-field. But Bragg was all the time preparing to retreat. He knew that his foe had been largely reinforced, and he felt that for him the opportunity had passed. By eleven o'clock the next night his whole army was in retreat, and the next day the Union troops entered Murfreesboro', to find the whole town a huge hospital, for not less than 2500 of Bragg's wounded had been left behind.

The loss had been heavy on both sides. The fighting was fierce and the number killed or wounded unusually great. Bragg had lost 1025; of these 9000 were wounded or slain. Rosecrans had 1553 men killed, 7245 wounded, and 2800 made prisoners. Moreover, the Federals lost 28 pieces of artillery and a great amount of their baggage train. But they held the field, and though in the chief day of the battle Bragg carried almost everything before him, yet Holdfast proved to be the better dog, and the Confederates by retreating confessed that to them the battle of Murfreesboro', or Stone's River, was really a serious reverse.

Before closing this chapter, so full of Confederate reverses, let us chronicle one exploit in which the wearers of the gray were successful, even though their success was due more to the negligence of a Union commander than to their own skill or daring.

In December the little village of Holly Springs, Miss., was a thriving and a bustling place. It was full of northern speculators who had come south to buy cotton. It was the headquarters of the merchants who supplied the sutlers of Grant's army with their merchandise. All the rabble of non-combatants that always follows in the train of a great army had settled down at Holly Springs. The place was the base of supplies for Grant's army, and was garrisoned by 1800 men under Col. Murphy, the same officer who had abandoned Iuka without destroying the stores gathered there.

Van Dorn determined to attempt the capture of this place, and led a column of some 5000 men against it. Grant heard of the movement and despatched reinforcements to Murphy's assistance, but before they arrived that officer had been surprised and had surrendered the town. For several hours the men of Van Dorn's command reveled in plunder. The great depots of army supplies were sacked. The cotton speculators were relieved of their money, and all the cotton which had been gathered in the town was burned. The sutlers' shops were broken open, and their contents devoured by the tattered Confederates. Then setting fire to everything he could not carry away, Van Dorn paroled his prisoners and made his escape in safety. The raid cost the United States 1,809,000 fixed cartridges, 5000 rifles, and 2000 revolvers; 100,000 suits of clothing and other quartermaster's stores to the value of $500,000; 5000 barrels of flour and other commissary stores valued at $500,000; one million dollars' worth of medical stores; $600,000 worth of sutlers' stores, and 1000 bales of cotton.

CHAPTER VI.

THE WAR IN THE EAST. — PROCLAMATION OF EMANCIPATION. — GENERAL McCLELLAN DISMISSED. — BURNSIDE IN COMMAND. — CROSSING THE RAPPAHANNOCK. — FREDERICKSBURG BOMBARDED. — THE BATTLE OF FREDERICKSBURG. — THE FIGHT FOR MARVE'S HILL. — RETREAT OF THE ARMY OF THE POTOMAC.

HAVING thus described the chief battle-fields in the West in which the soldiers of the North and the South contested for the mastery during the latter half of the year 1862, let us return again to the roads and fields of Virginia, so steadily trod by the armed hosts of Lee, and the several generals whom the North in turn chose to beat him.

We left the Confederate army of Virginia after the complete failure of its invasion of Maryland, and its crushing defeat at Antietam, safe once more on the south bank of the Potomac. It had escaped once again the fatal blow which might have been dealt it by a swifter hand than McClellan's, but it had returned to Virginia and brought the war with it. The Virginians had fondly hoped to see the tide of war surge over on to Northern soil, but now that their burden came upon them again they took it up with a cheeriness impossible save for a people thoroughly convinced of the justice of their cause. It was the unhappy fate of the "Old Dominion" throughout to bear the brunt of this determined conflict.

BATTLE FIELDS AND CAMP FIRES.

Toward the latter part of November, 1862, the Army of the Potomac and the Army of Virginia were watching each other from opposite banks of the Rappahannock river at Fredericksburg, a little Virginia town in the district which had been so often countermarched by the hostile armies. There had been no serious encounter between the two since the Antietam battle, but there had occurred some great events which we may pass over hastily.

Five days after the Antietam battle, President Lincoln had issued his proclamation of emancipation, giving freedom to every slave within the States then in arms against the Union. In the North, except among a small and bitter political faction, it was hailed with loud acclaim. In the South, where black men were property, and to free them would ruin many a planter, it created the same anger and hatred that an order confiscating all the planters' estates would have caused. Among the negroes themselves it was received with wonder, incredulity, or indifference. Many did not know what freedom meant; many knew but did not wish it. Those who were not far from camps of United States soldiers generally showed that they comprehended the general purport of the proclamation, by promptly running away and seeking the protection of the troops.

Among those who did not like the proclamation was General McClellan. He feared that it would raise up a party in the North hostile to the war, and he believed that it would force the Southerners to fight still more bitterly and with no thought of suing for peace so long as their right to their slaves was menaced. Cherishing these beliefs, the general was free to utter them. His criticisms irritated many of the foremost advisers of the President. McClellan was at odds with the Secretary of War; his over-caution had aroused the hostility of that large class of the populace which was always shouting "On to Richmond," and seldom giving a thought to the obstacles in the path; finally he was a democrat. Of these three causes the result was, that on the night of the 7th of November, when McClellan was sitting in his tent near Salem, Virginia, studying some maps preparatory to a battle which he expected to have with Lee in a day or two, there came in to him two officers, General Burnside and General Buckingham. The latter was a stranger in the camps of the Army of the Potomac, and as McClellan rose to greet him and took from his hand a sealed official envelope, he must have felt that the visit portended some evil thing. And so it proved, for the envelope contained a curt order directing McClellan to turn over the command of the Army of the Potomac to Burnside, and himself proceed to a town in New Jersey to await the orders of the War Department. Handing the letter to Burnside, the deposed chief of the Army of the Potomac said simply, "You command the army," and then strove to turn the conversation that followed into other channels.

There was mourning in the tents of the Army of the Potomac next day when the news of McClellan's removal spread among the soldiers. Despite his disputes with the authorities at Washington—or because of them perhaps—he was a prime favorite with the men under his command. Long afterward they mourned his departure, and any shortcoming of any later commander was sure to raise the cry "Give us Little Mac again."

The Confederates had a word to say, too, for when the news of McClellan's downfall reached General Lee, he said with a sort of grim humor that he rather regretted parting with McClellan, because "we understood each other so well. I fear they may continue to make these changes until they find some one whom I don't understand."

So, followed by the regret of his soldiers and the hostility and unmanly suspicions of the War Department, McClellan went away into retirement. Never again was he the commander of even a corporal's guard. Whether he was properly punished for timidity and dilatoriness, or was a martyr to political prejudice, is hard to decide. It is enough to say that his immediate successors to the command of the Army of the Potomac did not do so well with it as he.

On the south bank of the Rappahannock river stands the little, closely built city of Fredericksburg. The river's banks are steep there, and the houses skirt the very crest of the bluffs. On the opposite side of the river is the village of Falmouth, and from it a short line of railway leads to the harbor of Acquia creek on the Potomac river. It was this harbor and this railway that decided Burnside to take the army of the Potomac thither, and use Fredericksburg as a base from which to begin his campaign against Richmond,—for the chief end and aim of all the Union armies that ever entered Virginia was to accomplish the downfall of the capital city of the Confederacy.

On the arrival of the Union army at Falmouth, only a contemptible force of the enemy was ensconced in Fredericksburg. Though the only bridge was down, it would have been easy to cross the river by a ford, disclosed by a wading herd of cows. But though Sumner, who led the advance, asked permission to cross the river, Burnside refused it. He feared lest a sudden rise in the river might make it unfordable, after a part of the troops had crossed, and he determined to wait until the materials for building pontoon bridges arrived. But by the time the pontoons arrived, the greater part of Lee's army was there too, and the passage of the river, which might have been won so easily, cost many precious lives.

On the afternoon of the 21st of November, the head of Lee's army, under command of General Longstreet, appeared in sight of Fredericksburg. The troops did not occupy the town. About a mile from the river a low range of hills bounded the level plateau in which the city stood. These hills Lee thought afforded the best line of defense, and on them he posted his batteries, dug his rifle pits, and aligned his regiments. Only a few regiments of sharpshooters were established in the town, and they were there rather to harass the Union troops than with any expectation that they could hold the river against an attempt to cross it.

Now for a time the two armies rested on their arms. Lee well improved his time throwing up breastworks, until his whole line, which measured over five miles, was underground. Burnside, being planning an offensive campaign, had no defensive works to construct, and he was fretting and fuming over the delay which was enabling his antagonist to strengthen his position daily. But the pontoons had not yet arrived, and without them the river could not be crossed. So Burnside suffered the mortification of being kept idle for two weeks.

Besides the men of Lee's army, one other class of people found advantage in this unexpected delay. The inhabitants of Fredericksburg, who had thus unexpectedly discovered themselves hemmed in by two armies about to grapple in bloody fight, were not slow to seize the opportunity to escape. Sumner had threatened their town with bombardment, when he first appeared on the other bank of the river, but was dissuaded by the fact that the Confederates were not going to occupy the place. But though freed from this peril from their enemies, the people of Fredericksburg were still exposed to danger from the side of their friends, for Lee's batteries would undoubtedly open fire on the place as soon as the Union columns should begin marching through it to attack him. Thus caught between two fires, threatened alike by friend and foe, the unhappy citizens saw that flight alone could save them. For days the roads leading out of town were choked by throngs of fugitives on foot and in wagons. The rumble of the wagon trains carrying away the household goods of the unfortunate people was as heavy as that of an army's artillery train. The woods and fields out of the line of fire were soon tenanted by the camps of the fugitives. The city began to look empty, and the Confederate sharpshooters who held it found themselves almost the sole inhabitants of a city of closed stores and locked-up houses.

December 10th comes. The pontoons are at hand. Burnside's army is all enthusiasm, and the whole North is crying "On to Richmond!" The general determines to cross the river at once. Five bridges must be built,—three opposite the town, two a mile and a half down the river. All the batteries of the Union army—one hundred and fifty guns all told—are posted on the high ground overlooking the river and the town on the other side. The engineers work all night, and by daylight the bridges are half done. The Confederate sentries have heard the noise and half suspect the cause, but a heavy fog adding to the darkness of the night made it impossible for them to discover what is going on.

But daylight discloses the pontoon bridges stretching out into the stream and reaching nearly across. Now is the time for Barksdale's Mississippi sharpshooters to show themselves worthy of their name. They fairly swarm along the river front of Fredericksburg. Sheltering themselves in every possible way, they begin coolly to pick off the men working on the bridges. Few shots are wasted. The smoke puffs from windows of houses, from behind trees and fences, and every time there is a puff of smoke a blue-coated soldier falls from the bridge. All the efforts of the Federal sharpshooters to retaliate are unsuccessful. Only a few men at a time can be employed upon each bridge, and those few are picked off by the Confederate riflemen before their work begins to show any signs of progress. The river begins to display some ominous red stains, and work on the bridges before the city is stopped for a time. When the Union engineers think that the sharpshooters are off their guard, a pontoon is hastily set afloat. A dozen men carrying planks run out to the end of the bridge and work is again under way. But before a nail can be driven, or a stake set, the deadly rifles ring out, and a sudden stop is put to the bridge-building. Eight trials are made, and eight times the Federals are foiled. One o'clock comes, and the bridges still lack eighty yards of spanning the river.

But now the spiteful swarm of hornets has stung the Union army into a fury. General Burnside sees with rage his bravest engineer battalions sacrificed in the attempt to build the bridges. "Concentrate your batteries and batter that town down," he sternly orders his chief of artillery. In a few minutes one hundred and fifty guns are roaring on the river's brink, and their iron messages are falling thick in the streets of Fredericksburg. It is but short range—scarce 500 yards at most—and the missiles do dreadful havoc in the closely built streets. For an hour or more the guns blaze, and smoke and thunder until seventy tons of iron have been thrown into the streets of the stricken city. Then the bridge-builders begin their work once more, only to encounter the same withering fusilade that had balked all their previous efforts. Sheltered in the cellars of the city, the sharpshooters had survived the cannonade, and were still obstinately bent upon disputing with the Federals the passage of the Rappahannock.

But the plans of General Burnside are not to be defeated by so paltry an obstacle as 3000 Mississippi riflemen. They must be swept out of the way. It is time for a forlorn hope.

The soldiers of the Seventh Michigan regiment volunteer to cross the river in boats and dislodge the riflemen. It is a perilous task, but they eagerly seek the honor. They rush down the bank and swarm into the boats, while the Confederates, not knowing what to make of this new move, hold their fire for a moment. But the instant the first boat pushes into the stream the bullets come whistling about, and many a man is hit before the shelter of the further shore is reached.

Into one of the boats with the rest of the Michigan men climbs drummer boy Robert Hendershot. He is not a very old soldier— twelve years old this very first day of the battle of Fredericksburg—but where his regiment goes, there he proposes to go too. And so he clambers into the boat in the most matter-of-fact way with his drum strapped to his back. His captain catches sight of him.

"Get out of this," he orders him gruffly. "You're too small for this sort of business."

"May I help push off the boat, Captain?" asks the boy, as if eager to do something."

"Yes."

So Robert clambers out again and with others gives the boat a push which sends it out into the channel. But he clings to the gunwale, and so, floating in the icy water, is dragged across the stream. As he comes out of the water on the other side a bit of shell tears his drum from his shoulder. Then he seizes a dead soldier's musket and takes his place with his regiment.

The steep bank of the river protects the storming party from the bullets of the riflemen, and in its shelter they huddle until the boats come over again with reënforcements. Then, with a cheer, they rush up the hill, regardless of flying lead, and drive the sharpshooters from their lurking-places. Some of the Mississippians are captured in the cellars where they have taken refuge, but most of them fight in the streets, dropping back from house to house and making a fierce resistance. At last the town is cleared of the last of them, and the work of building the bridges goes on without molestation.

So all that day and night and much of the next day the blue-coated regiments are marching across the floating bridges. Franklin's grand division crosses by the lower bridges, Hooker and Sumner by those opposite the town. All around the town on a commanding range of hills are Lee's batteries, yet not a shot is fired into the town crowded with 50,000 soldiers. All the Union officers expect a bombardment, and many guesses are hazarded to explain the silence of the enemy's guns. "I'll tell you why Lee didn't keep us out," said one grizzled color sergeant. "He wanted us here. We've got a river behind us and all the best batteries in the rebel army in front of us, and the Johnnies know they can gobble us up whenever they get ready."

The sergeant's idea is not wholly absurd. Lee's position is in fact one which the practiced eye of the soldier sees to be formidable indeed. A chain of hills starts from the Rappahannock river about two miles above the city and runs southeast, until it almost touches the river's bank three miles below the city. All along the crest of the hills the Confederates have thrown up earth-works. Many of the hill-sides being precipitous, and heavily wooded, form a complete defense in themselves. Others slope upward more easily, and about these the Confederates have massed their artillery, and exerted their engineering talent to the utmost.

The hill which of all others seems to invite the Federal attack stands directly back of the city and about half a mile from its outskirts. On its crest stands the pillared mansion of Mr. Marye, and from this the hill derived its name. Marye's hill will live in military annals for many a year yet to come. For half a mile from the city extends a rolling plateau, commanded at every point by the guns which frown from Marye's hill and the adjacent heights. Just where the hill begins to rise from the plateau, is a road skirting its base. The road is sunken somewhat beneath the level of the plateau and separated from it by a stone wall faced on the outer side with banked up dirt. No one walking across the fields would suspect that either wall or road is there.

Now Marye's hill being neither very steep, nor very densely wooded, Lee suspects that it is against it that the enemy will turn their attack. McLaws's division—tried veterans of a hundred battlefields—are to hold the hill for the Confederacy. To aid them some of the strongest batteries of the Army of Virginia are posted in commanding positions. Cannon are everywhere. From every hill their iron muzzles point down upon the plain across which Burnside's regiments must advance. No possible preparation is neglected by the Confederates. Riding about the heights, General Longstreet noticed an idle gun.

"Post that where it will bear on the plateau," he ordered.

"Why, general," responded his superintendent of artillery. "We cover that ground now so well that we will comb it as with a fine-tooth comb. A chicken could not live in that field when we open on it."

The gun is put in place, and when the time comes the truth of the artilleryman's confident assertion is amply proved.

December 13th dawns frosty and foggy. From their trenches on the crest of the hills the Confederates can see nothing but a sea of shifting, gray, impenetrable fog, covering Fredericksburg like a pall and cutting off all vision. But up out of the fog came martial sounds, that tell clearly enough to a soldier's ears that a battle is coming. The blare of the bugle, the roll of the drum, the occasional rumble of a battery,—not much of that, though, for most of the Union batteries are on the heights beyond the river—and the shouts of the soldiers as their officers exhort them to deeds of bravery, all float upward through the fog, carrying their story to the listeners on the heights. "We're in for it to-day, sure enough," think the ragged Confederates, and those of them who are on Marye's hill thank their stars they are not the fellows who have to charge across that fatal plain lying there below.

By ten o'clock the sun comes out brightly. Its rays are too much for the fog, and the gray curtain slowly fades away, leaving the martial pageant on the plains below spread out, clear to the vision of the Confederates. Lee and Longstreet are on horseback on a hill that commands a view of the whole scene. After the first glance they look meaningly at each other. Before Marye's hill not a Union soldier is to be seen, while two miles further south, arrayed against the hill which Stonewall Jackson holds, are the teeming regiments of Franklin's grand division, and two divisions from Hooker. Can it be, after all, that Burnside's assault is to be delivered against Jackson? Was all that massing of batteries about Marye's hill a useless precaution? But after a momentary consultation the two generals decide that Franklin's demonstration against their right is merely to cloak Burnside's true purpose. Then they give themselves up to watching the great military spectacle spread out before them.

Franklin's well-clad regiments are indeed a brilliant spectacle. The bright December sun dances gaily on twenty thousand gleaming bayonets and musket-barrels. The flags float in the breeze, the red stripes of "Old Glory," and the countless colors of state flags, regimental banners and guidons making bright patches of color against the blue background of the solidly massed troops. Mounted aides are galloping everywhere, and now and then some general officer with a gaily caparisoned staff gallops along the front of a brigade, and the cheers that greet him are born aloft on the breeze. Now the troops are moving. Soon, after much marching and countermarching, two long lines of blue appear and move forward toward the wooded slopes which shelter Stonewall Jackson and his tattered regiments of battle-scarred veterans. And then the Union batteries far away across the Rappahannock suddenly spring into full cry, and clouds of smoke arise over there, and from the woods where their shells are bursting. The battle is begun, but as yet Jackson makes no sign. But when the first line reaches the edge of the woods there is a crash of musketry, and Stuart's cannon begin to roar. Then Lee knows that his most trusty lieutenant is hard at work, and the ragged Confederates whom the battle has not yet reached wonder audibly "what old Stonewall is going to do with them fellers."

Let us go over to the right and see how the battle is going there. Sixteen thousand men are in the assaulting columns of the Federals. Of these a brigade of Pennsylvanians under Meade carry off the honors of the day. Disregarding alike the rapid and deadly fire of the Confederate infantry and the furious hail of grape-shot from the hostile batteries which beat against their faces, these brave men plunge into the woods, and push doggedly on. Their field artillery does good work in supporting their advance. An eye-witness says that the very first cannon-shot from the Confederate batteries was responded to so quickly that the return shot sounded like a missile. As the projectile came crashing in among the Confederate gunners, a boy who was helping serve one of the guns cried out in horror to General Stuart, who stood near, "General, their very first shot has killed two men."

Jackson rides along his lines encouraging his men to stand firm against the coming assault. Some of the soldiers who had marched with him through the Shenandoah valley and fought with him on the fields of Manassas and Antietam scarcely know him to-day. A few days before Fredericksburg, General Stuart bought him a new coat and cap of Confederate gray plentifully garnished with gold lace. To-day

General Jackson is resplendent in his new finery. The dingy surtout of gray and the battered cap are gone. The general has togged himself out for battle as daintily as though he were going to a ball. So unusual is the brilliancy of his dress that one of his tattered veterans is heard to say to a comrade, who pointed out this nicely dressed officer as General Jackson, "What! that finely dressed fellow Old Jack! No sir. You can't fool me that way."

Jackson soon finds plenty of work along his lines. A gap has been left between the brigades of Archer and Lane, and into this the Federals press with irresistible power. The line thus pierced begins to give way. General Gregg, trying to rally his troops, is mortally wounded. For a time things look desperate for the Confederates thereabouts, but Jackson coming up soon changes the situation. Without trying to rally his first line, he brings his second line into action. It is Early's brigade which now comes plunging through the underbrush on the double quick to the scene of impending disasters. The veterans are inclined to make sport of the men of Archer's brigade when they pass on their way to the front. "Here comes old Jubal!" they cry. "Let old Jubal straighten that fence! Jubal's boys are always getting Hill out o' trouble."

This time certainly Jubal Early's men do succeed in redeeming the day for the Confederates. They fall fiercely upon Meade's men, who, exhausted with long and gallant fighting, and exposed to a murderous fire from the Confederate batteries, begin to give way. Could Franklin but send reënforcements to their aid, the advantage so gallantly won might be held. But though Meade is the wedge that had made an opening in the Confederate lines, Franklin has no maul with which to drive the wedge in further and widen the breach. He has scattered his men over so extensive a line of attack that he has none near enough at hand to be sent speedily to Meade's support. And so, disheartened by the lack of aid which they had expected, Meade's men are beaten back, out of the woods and down upon the plain whence they came. Never again during the day do Franklin's forces succeed in making any impression on Stonewall Jackson's line. No second charge is made. The field artillery maintains the conflict aided by occasional volleys of musketry from the infantry. Most of Franklin's division are posted in secure positions. Some are lying down behind a slight elevation of ground, secure from the enemy's musketry, but slightly exposed to his batteries which are posted on the heights. One regiment was posted thus in fancied security, the men joking with each other on their good fortune in being able to lie down all the afternoon out of range, when suddenly a Whitworth gun that the Confederates had run into battery on a commanding hill opened fire. The second bolt narrowly missed the head of a soldier and ripped his knapsack all to pieces. Out of the knapsack flew a pack of cards, which were thrown on every side. "Oh, deal me a hand!" was the cry all along the line, and the owner of the property so suddenly scattered joined heartily in the laugh, thankful indeed that his head had been out of the path of the missile.

But it is not at this part of the field that the fighting is fiercest. It is not before Jackson's men that is to occur that horrid carnage that is to make Fredericksburg a name brimful of sorrowful memories to many a northern household. It is against Marye's hill that Burnside proposes to deliver his main attack,—Marye's hill, from which the Confederate batteries can rake the plain below as with a comb.

About the middle of the forenoon, when the noise of the conflict on the Confederate right seems to indicate that Jackson is being rather roughly handled, the Confederate gunners on Marye's hill open fire on Fredericksburg. The effect is like pitching stones at a wasps' nest. The shells have hardly begun to fall in the town when a column of troops appears, marching out of the streets, and deploying on the plain before the Confederate guns. The skirmishers scatter out to the right and left and march steadily forward, driving the Confederate pickets before them. The line of battle follows hard behind, French's division leading, Hancock's division in support, formed in two parallel lines. Grandly the great array, bristling with bayonets and gay with flags and banners, swings out under the fire of the enemy's guns and presses forward with quick strides. The Confederate gunners turn away from the town now. They have a more thrilling target than piles of brick and mortar. And so from all the semicircle of hills the cannon roar, and the hissing shot cut cruel lanes in the ranks of the advancing host. From Marye's hill the famous Washington artillery of New Orleans is pounding away. But though they are in the very hottest part of the field which Longstreet's chief of artillery declared he could rake as with a fine-tooth comb, yet it seems for a time that the gallant blue-coats are going to gain the slope of the hill after all. Faster and faster work the gunners on the heights, wider and more often do the gaps open in the Union line. But still the advance is unchecked until suddenly a line of men in gray seems to rise up out of the ground right in their faces. There is a crash of musketry, and the first line of the advance is gone. The bewildered blue-coats hesitate a moment. There comes another volley, so close upon the first that the echoes have had scarce time to die away, and the smoke still hides their unlooked-for assailants. Before this scorching blast of lead and flame, the Federals are swept away. When the smoke of the two volleys clears away their lines are seen to have gone to pieces, and the field is covered with men each seeking to save himself. Many take refuge in a railway cut which shelters them from the batteries on Marye's hill, but some Confederate artillerymen on Lee's hill see this, and turn their guns on the cowering, crowding mass of routed men. The shot and shell tear through the cut from end to end, spreading death in their path. Rushing from the cut the men seek shelter elsewhere and soon find it, behind a slight slope in the field which protected them from their enemies.

What was it that brought this sudden disaster upon the gallant men of French's and Hancock's division? The reader will remember the half-sunken road, flanked with an earth-covered stone wall, which was described as skirting the bottom of Marye's hill. Here Longstreet had stationed 2500 men of Cobb's division. Stooping or sitting down they were wholly hidden by the wall. Rising, they exposed only their heads, and the wall came to the exact height to serve for a rest for their muskets. The road was broad and level, and the men were formed in four lines, the first line being instructed to fall back as soon as they had delivered their volley and let the second line take their place. It was thus that the two volleys had so quickly succeeded each other and put the Federals to rout. Later in the day we shall find that even the changing of the lines was too slow for the fiery spirits behind the wall, and that the men in front kept those behind busy in loading muskets and passing them forward.

Strong though Cobb's position was, Longstreet had some doubts of his ability to hold it, and sent directions to other commanders for their guidance if Cobb fell back. "If they wait for me to fall back," said that soldier grimly, on hearing of this, "they'll wait a long time." And so it proved, for his line was the rock on which one after the other the surging lines of charging Federals broke and were dashed back in fragments.

But now another river of men comes rushing down Hanover street leading out of Fredericksburg, and crossing the canal by two bridges spreads out like a fan over the plateau. Hancock and French rally their men and join in the second assault. General Couch, some of whose troops are with Hancock, goes with General Howard to the top of a church steeple to overlook the field. It is the story of the first charge repeated. The Confederate artillery mows the gallant fellows down by scores, and when the survivors get within point-blank range of the stone wall, up rise Cobb's men and shoot them down by hundreds. "Oh, great God!" cries Howard from his lofty observatory, "see how our men, our poor fellows are falling."

General Couch thus describes the scene he saw from the steeple: "I remember that the whole plain was covered with men, prostrate and dropping, the live men running here and there, and in front closing upon each other, and the wounded coming back. The commands seemed to be mixed up. I had never before seen fighting like that,

THE STONE WALL AT FREDERICKSBURG.

nothing approaching it in terrible uproar and destruction. There was no cheering on the part of the men, but a stubborn determination to obey orders and do their duty I don't think there was much feeling of success. As they charged the artillery fire would break their formation and they would get mixed; then they would close up, go forward, receive the withering infantry fire, and those who were able would run to the houses and fight as best they could; and then the next brigade coming up in succession would do its duty and melt like snow coming down upon the warm ground."

Prominent in this second charge are the green banners that tell of the presence of Meagher's Irish brigade, and particularly savage is the fire they draw from the Confederates, who had tested the valor of the Irishmen before. The red trousers of the zouaves, too, catch the eyes of the artillerymen, and that picturesque body of men suddenly find themselves getting more than their share of the enemy's attention.

The second charge meets with no more success than the first. As before, the Union lines are fairly cut to pieces before the impregnable stone wall. Most of the survivors drift away to the rear, while some find refuge in a stout brick house that stands a little to the right of the Confederate position. From the windows of this house the Union sharpshooters can draw a bead on the men in the sunken road, and from this flanking fire alone did the defenders of the stone wall suffer during that battle. The brick house serves as a refuge for hundreds of Union soldiers who shrink from the frightful carnage of the plateau. General Couch himself rides over there. "I found the brick house packed with men," he wrote long afterwards, "and behind it the dead and the living were thick as they could be packed together. The dead were rolled out for shelter and the dead horses were used for breastworks. I know I tried to shelter myself behind the brick house, but found I could not because of the men already there."

By this time the Federals, officers and men alike, begin to think that the Confederates cannot be driven from their stronghold. "Well, Couch," says General Hooker, who is in command on the field, "things are in such a state I must go and tell Burnside it is no use trying to carry this position." And off he gallops. While he is gone word comes to General Couch that the enemy is retreating. He sends for General Humphreys, and says: "General Hancock reports that the enemy is falling back; now is the time for you to go in!" Humphreys "goes in" with two brigades. The enemy is not falling back, and the stone wall is as impregnable as ever.

Meanwhile the Confederate officers gaze from their elevated station upon the carnage below, wondering mightily that men will thus repeatedly rush upon death. They know the strength of their own position, and they marvel that Burnside should send his best brigades one after another into this trap of fire and iron. Lee, looking down upon the scene, turns to an officer standing by him and says: "It is well that war is so terrible! We should grow too fond of it."

Now Hooker comes back to the field. He reports having found Burnside deaf to all suggestions of prudence. "That crest must be carried to-night," he had said repeatedly while walking nervously up and down. Hooker bows to the will of his superior officer, and returns to hurl yet another torrent of men against the stone wall. It is almost dark when this last charge is ordered. "Take off your knapsacks," is the word. "Don't load your guns. There will be no time for loading and firing. Give them the cold steel." Thus stripped for action the men rush forward with cheers. Four thousand are in the assault. But again the Confederate artillery roars, and the musketry rattles, and the line crumbles away and is lost in the gathering darkness. Night comes on rapidly, and when under cover of its sable mantle the Confederates venture out before their stronghold, they find that the nearest dead body clad in blue lies thirty paces from the wall. There was the dead line which none might pass.

A bitter cold night follows the battle. Scores of the Union

wounded are frozen where they lie. Disappointment and chagrin prey upon the survivors. The Army of the Potomac has been beaten, cut to pieces, despoiled of its very best soldiers. Burnside is half crazed by his defeat and the slaughter. He wants to renew the assault the next day; to take seventeen regiments and placing himself at their head lead them against the foe. But from this madness his division commanders dissuade him. News of his first resolution reaches Lee, and that commander prepares to complete the discomfiture of the Federal army should it dare to attack him again in his well tested and invincible position.

There is no fighting the next day, however. Burnside wisely does not renew the attack, and Lee restrains Stonewall Jackson, who is eager to descend from the heights and try to drive Burnside into the river. As for Burnside himself, the defeat and the horrible loss of life tell fearfully upon his nerves. General Smith says that visiting Burnside at his headquarters on the day after the battle, he found the general walking up and down in great distress. "Oh, those men, those men!" he cried. "Those men over there," pointing to the battle field where the dead and most of the wounded were still lying; "I am thinking of them all the time."

Many curious incidents occurred on the day of picket skirmishing that followed the day of the great battle. A strange experience was that of the Second brigade of regulars, which was assigned to a new station at midnight, took its post quietly, bivouacked, and awoke in the morning to see dimly through the fog that it was within point-blank range of the famous stone wall. It was too slender a force to charge the Confederate stronghold. To retreat would have cost the lives of two-thirds of the men before they were out of range of the enemy's rifles. Luckily they were as yet unseen, and the whole brigade fell flat on the ground, and there remained all that cold December day. So long as the blue-coats lay absolutely motionless they were safe; to move meant a bullet from a Confederate rifle, and the men behind the wall proved themselves good marksmen. There the blue coats lay, under the guns of the enemy, with bones aching from the cold, unable to move, hungry, thirsty, and expecting every moment to be discovered. Some adventurous soldiers strove to move from one part of the line to another, to get tobacco perhaps, or to talk to a friend, but seldom did such an adventurer escape unhurt. When nightfall freed them from their long vigil, and they sprang to their feet, fired a single volley at the astonished Confederates, and fled into the darkness, the call of the roll showed that of the 1000 men present, 12 had been killed, and 114 wounded. All this had been suffered in cold blood, with no chance even to fire a gun at the enemy.

Over on the southern part of the battle field, where the lines of Stonewall Jackson confronted those of Franklin, the pickets before the day was over concluded a sort of treaty of peace and amity. During the night the firing along the picket line was constant, and as the Confederate position was such that the shots of its pickets flew as far as the bivouac of the Union army, the Federals made overtures for a truce, and it was soon agreed that the pickets of neither side should fire without due warning. But at daybreak a new detail of Union pickets came on duty, and being ignorant of the unofficial truce opened fire on the Confederates who were lounging about in full view, and many of whom were hit. Irritated by this, the Confederates kept up a constant fusilade, and a general engagement was only averted by the original suggestion of one of the Confederates, who shouted across to a Wisconsin soldier:

"Hello thar, you Yank. Let's stop this shooting, and settle this quarrel with our fists."

The Wisconsin man agreed, and the two, stripped for action, were soon boxing between the hostile lines of pickets, who put down their muskets and looked on with interest. The fight was declared a draw, but it restored good humor, and for the rest of the day an amicable exchange of tobacco, of which the Confederates had plenty, for coffee, with which the Federals were well supplied, took the place of an exchange of rifle-bullets.

FIGHTING IT OUT.

Two days thus passed away in unimportant skirmishing. On the night of the 15th of December, the Army of the Potomac, dispirited, shattered and bleeding, crossed again with lagging steps the pontoon bridges over which five days before they had marched with proudly waving banners and hearts beating fast at the thought of giving battle to the enemy. Lee remained in possession of a field won easily by him, though striven for desperately by his gallant antagonists. In the effort to take the heights Burnside had sacrificed 12,653 men, of whom 1284 were killed and 9600 wounded. Over two-thirds of these fell before the fatal stone wall. Hancock's division, which bore the brunt of the conflict there, lost 2013 out of a total strength of 5006. In eight of his regiments over half the officers and men were killed.

The Confederates on their part lost 5377 men, of whom 608 were killed and 4116 wounded. Their heaviest loss was on their right, where Meade charged through Stonewall Jackson's line. But the gallant charges against the stone wall, which cost the Union soldiers so much blood, were repelled by the Confederates with a loss of but 1555 men.

CHAPTER VII.

BURNSIDE'S ILL-FATED "MUD MARCH."— GENERAL HOOKER SUCCEEDS TO THE COMMAND OF THE ARMY OF THE POTOMAC. — REORGANIZATION OF THE ARMY. — DEVELOPMENT OF THE CAVALRY. — RAIDS OF FITZ-HUGH LEE AND AVERILL. — HOOKER TAKES THE OFFENSIVE. — HIS STRATEGY. — THE MARCH TO LEE'S REAR. — CHANCELLORSVILLE. — THE FOUR DAYS' BATTLES. — JACKSON'S FLANK MOVEMENT. — CONFEDERATE SUCCESSES. — STONEWALL JACKSON WOUNDED. — HIS DEATH. — UNION VICTORY AT MARYE'S HILL. — RETREAT OF THE UNION ARMY BEYOND THE RAPPAHANNOCK.

AFTER the disastrous failure of Burnside's attempt to drive Lee from his position at Fredericksburg, there followed a long period of inaction. Separated only by the icy Rappahannock, the hostile armies watched each other closely, but made no sign of coming again to blows. The pickets, who day after day patroled the opposite banks of the river, came to know each other by name, and to shout cheery welcomes as they came on duty. The sound of the rifle was heard no more. Though arrayed under hostile flags, the soldiers were getting to be too good friends to exchange shots unnecessarily. A lively maritime trade sprang up. The Confederates had plenty of tobacco and southern newspapers; the Federals had coffee, salt, and northern journals. Boats made of shingles, with a handkerchief for a sail, carried the commodities across the strip of running water in the middle of the half-frozen river. And so several weeks passed by, occupied by Lee in adding to the defensive works with which his position was protected, and by Burnside in resting his troops and trying to restore the morale of the army, which had been sorely shattered by the disaster at Fredericksburg.

The Union general was not long in discovering that his army, soldiers and officers alike, had lost confidence in him. To regain this confidence there was but one way possible. He must fight a battle and win it.

Midwinter is not a favorable time for offensive military movements, but Burnside felt so keenly the position in which he was placed that he determined to brave the dangers of the season and try once more to drive the foe from his stronghold. His plan was simple. From his scouts he learned that the Confederates had but a meagre force to defend Banks's Ford, some five miles up the river from Fredericksburg. Burnside determined to cross at this point in force and thus descend upon Lee's left flank. For several days the engineer officers were employed in making corduroy roads over which the attacking force might march. The preparations were conducted secretly, and no hint of the proposed attack reached the ears of the Confederates. January 20 found all preparations finished. Everything seemed propitious. The divisions of Franklin and Hooker were bivouacked within easy marching distance of the ford, which, though a ford in summer, was too deep to be fordable in winter, and required bridging. The pontoons for this purpose were on the way from Fredericksburg. The roads were frozen hard, the weather clear and bracing, so that all branches of the army found marching easy, and the outlook inspiring. The division of General Couch, which had been sent down stream to distract the attention of the enemy from the true point of attack, had made so vigorous a demonstration as to create a real panic among the Confederates, who left Banks's Ford undefended and hastened in the other direction. At sunset on the 20th, everything seemed to promise success for the

Federals, and Burnside was elated at the prospect of redeeming his waning prestige at a blow.

The night was to have been spent in getting the pontoons to the river's brink, in posting artillery to cover the crossing of the troops, in massing the infantry ready to begin the crossing as soon as the last plank should be laid. But soon after nightfall there came up a heavy storm. The rain fell in sheets. The wind swayed the trees and brought down branches on the soldiers, drearily soaking in their blankets below. Morning found the Rappahannock a raging torrent, edged by impassable swamps. Fifteen pontoons floated at the river's edge. Twenty were needed to bridge the stream, and the missing ones were a mile or more away, being dragged laboriously over muddy roads in which the wagon wheels sank to the hubs. The road was packed with trains of artillery, ammunition wagons, ambulances, and the great drags that bore the heavy pontoons. All day the soldiers and the teamsters toiled to drag the vehicles out of the mire. Horses, mules, and men pulled and tugged side by side. The air rang with shouts, curses, blows, the straining of harness and the cracking of whips. All was in vain. Deeper and deeper the wheels sunk into the road, made the more miry by the stamping of hundreds of men and animals. The rain fell incessantly. To add to the chagrin of the Federals, the Confederates had discovered their movement, and their pickets came down to the edge of the river and shouted across with fine sarcasm:

"Stick to it, Yanks. Just wait till the rain stops and we'll come over and help you build your bridges."

When that day and night had passed with no cessation of the falling torrents, Burnside knew that his plan had failed. He saw ruin come upon him through no fault of his, but he bore it like a soldier. It was useless to think of continuing the movement further. The three days' rations with which his men had been provided before starting out were almost exhausted. Lee had been fully informed of the movement, and was by this time no doubt fully prepared to dispute the passage of the river. Nothing was left but retreat, and this was accomplished over the muddy roads, with infinite toil but no loss, the swollen river preventing any pursuit.

This brief and disastrous campaign has passed into history as the "mud march." It brought down upon the head of the unfortunate Burnside a storm of ridicule and abuse, which, however undeserved, was effective, for on the 25th of January the luckless general was, at his own request, relieved of the command of the Army of the Potomac.

To Burnside succeeded General Joseph Hooker—Fighting Joe Hooker the men called him. President Lincoln felt some misgivings as to the wisdom of his choice, and expressed them in the letter which notified General Hooker of his appointment. "I have placed you at the head of the Army of the Potomac," wrote the President. "Of course I have done this upon what appear to me sufficient reasons, and yet I think it best for you to know there are somethings in regard to which I am not quite satisfied with you. I believe you to be a brave and skillful soldier, which of course I like. I also believe you do not mix politics with your profession, in which you are right. You have confidence in yourself, which is a valuable if not an indispensable quality. You are ambitious, which within reasonable bounds does good rather than harm; but I think that during General Burnside's command of the army you have taken counsel of your ambition, and thwarted him as much as you could, in which you did a great wrong to the country and to a most meritorious and honorable brother officer. I have heard in such a way as to believe it, of your recently saying that both the army and the government needed a dictator. Of course it was not for this but in spite of it that I have given you the command. Only these generals who gain successes can set up dictators. What I now ask of you is military success, and I will risk the dictatorship. The government will support you to the utmost of its ability, which is neither more nor less than it has done and will do for all commanders. I much fear that the spirit which you have aided to infuse into the army, of criticising their commander and withholding confidence from him, will now turn upon you. I shall assist you as far as I can to put it down. Neither you, nor Napoleon were he alive again, could get any good out of any army while such a spirit prevails in it. And now beware of rashness! Beware of rashness. But with energy and sleepless vigilance go forward and give us victories."

If Hooker felt piqued by this rather critical letter he made no sign, but diligently set about the task of infusing new life into the dispirited army of the Potomac. Of the methods he adopted to this end we need not speak. It is enough to say that in the course of a few weeks he had reduced to a minimum the practice of desertion which had been the bane of the army under Burnside; he had remodeled the organization of the army; finally he had increased the proportion of cavalry regiments and made strenuous efforts to bring that arm of the service up to the standard of efficiency that prevailed among the Confederates.

From the very beginning of the war the Confederate cavalry was at once the admiration and the dismay of the Union officer. The reason for this supremacy was obvious. The Confederates, coming from an agricultural country, were horsemen by habit and by early training. To join the cavalry was the highest ambition of the average Confederate recruit. The result was that the cavalry leaders had under their command the very choicest spirits of the Southern army. Stuart's cavalry was full of private soldiers who by virtue of their education, ability, and standing in the community whence they came, were qualified for and could have secured shoulder-straps in any other branch of the service, but they preferred to wear plain blouses and ride with dashing Jeb Stuart.

In the Northern army the advantage to be gained by well-drilled bodies of cavalry was under-estimated, and from the very first the War Department discouraged the formation of mounted regiments. But on his accession to the command of the Army of the Potomac Hooker insisted that more cavalry should be given him. He had possessed ample facilities for studying the tactics of his great antagonist, Stonewall Jackson, and he had observed that it was Stuart's cavalry shielding his flank and cutting off all intelligence of his movements, that enabled him to gain his enemy's rear unperceived and deliver those telling and unexpected blows that so often decided the result of a battle. As Hooker was to begin an offensive campaign he strengthened his cavalry force and put it in command of General Stoneman.

It was in the last week of January that Hooker was placed in command of the Army of the Potomac. Weeks and months passed by with no collision between the two armies that lay so near to each other beyond sharp skirmishes between the cavalry of either army. Of these skirmishes there were several. The Confederates made forays into the Union lines with their accustomed daring, and the Union troopers more than once crossed the river and rode defiantly through the enemy's country with a dash and bravado that would have done credit to Stuart or Mosby.

It was while leading a raiding party, that Fitz-Hugh Lee, nephew of the great general and one of Stuart's division commanders, fell upon a Pennsylvania regiment near Leedstown and killed, wounded or captured about a hundred men. Learning that the troops belonged to the brigade of an old West Point classmate, General Averill, the successful trooper left this note behind him:

DEAR AVERILL:—I wish you would put up your sword, leave my State, and go home. You ride a good horse. I ride a better. Yours can beat mine running. Send me over a bag of coffee.

FITZ.

General Averill disliked the reference to the speed of his horse and determined to pay his old classmate a visit. On March 17, he led a cavalry column of five regiments to the Rappahannock at

Kelley's ford, and crossed in the teeth of a vicious fire from the enemy's sharp-shooters, of whom twenty-five were captured. The remnant of the Confederate skirmishers fled, to warn Fitz-Hugh Lee of his impending danger. Averill's men followed in hot pursuit. Lee, in no wise daunted, comes out to meet them. The adversaries meet a little more than a mile from the ford, and Lee, little knowing that he is greatly outnumbered, leads a squadron against the Federals, a large number of whom have dismounted and aligned themselves behind a stone wall. This assault is easily repulsed, but is followed up by a second; the Third Virginia, a famous cavalry command, sweeps across the field and down upon the stone wall which checks its progress. Over that wall the horses cannot leap, and as the squadron halts in momentary confusion, the First Rhode Island cavalry plunges fiercely in upon its flank, throwing it into a rout. Its commander, cut off from his men and surrounded, is captured. Scarce a hundred troopers of the Virginia command return to place themselves under Lee's orders; the rest have been killed, wounded or hopelessly dispersed. The situation now becomes desperate for the Confederates. Retreating by a narrow road they are exposed to the murderous artillery fire of their assailants, who thus have added to their advantage in numbers the advantage of position. Lee determines to make one fierce effort to avert the disaster which threatens him. He has but three or four hundred men left. Of these he dismounts about two hundred and posts them behind an adjacent wall; his artillery he stations in a commanding position, and placing himself at the head of a hundred mounted men—the shattered remnant of the Third Virginia—he charges furiously upon his enemy's line. But once more failure only attends his efforts. A high wooden fence, behind which a Union regiment lies in ambush, breaks the fury of the charge, and a flank attack by a Pennsylvania regiment sends the assailants back pell-mell upon their supports. The Federals follow close, but so hot a fire is poured upon them from the Confederate artillery and foot-soldiers, that their advance is checked.

Now is Averill's opportunity. Nothing would be easier for him with his overpowering numbers than to ride over, and sweep from his path the slender body of men which disputes his further progress. But so gallant has been Lee's attitude, so fearless and dashing the repeated assaults of the Confederates, that Averill never for a moment suspects how weak, numerically, is the enemy with whom he has to do. Night is fast coming on. He is far away from Hooker's army and in a country thick with Confederates. Accordingly he begins to withdraw his forces, greatly to the delight of Lee's troopers, who had begun to see annihilation staring them in the face. Some of the Federal soldiers are too severely wounded to be moved, so these are left behind in charge of a surgeon, to whom General Averill entrusted a sack of coffee and this note for General Lee:

DEAR FITZ:—Here's your coffee. Here's your call. How do you like it? How's that horse?

AVERILL.

April came. There was stir and life in the camp of the Army of the Potomac. Quartermasters were issuing new clothing. Arms were being rigidly inspected. The ambulances and provision wagons were being overhauled. The army blacksmiths were working late into the night, shoeing horses. Fresh ammunition was issued. Everything indicated that the commanding general had determined upon his plan of campaign, and that a great battle was impending. President Lincoln came down from Washington to inspect the army in these days of busy preparation. He had long and serious interviews with General Hooker. "I want to impress one thing upon you two gentlemen," said he emphatically one day, when General Couch was present. "In your next fight put in all your men."

How the President's advice was followed we shall see when we come to read of the "next fight"—the battle of Chancellorsville.

Hooker had, indeed, decided upon a plan of attack which he

thought would enable him to oust Lee from the position he had held all winter on the heights of Fredericksburg. Over the problem he had pondered long. "My army is in a well and Lee's army is at the mouth of it," he had written to a friend at a moment when he despaired of discovering any promising plan of attack. It was Averill's raid, just described, that finally suggested to him a way out of this dilemma.

The topography of Fredericksburg—the swift-flowing, deep river that separated the hostile armies, and the line of rugged hills held by the Confederates—has already been described. At every point on the river which promised a crossing-place, from where it widened into an arm of the sea four miles below Fredericksburg up to the point where it received the current of the Rapidan River, the Confederates were posted in force. To attempt to cross between these points would be to repeat Burnside's blunder and attack the enemy where he was strongest. To go down-stream seeking a crossing was useless, for the river soon became too wide to be crossed by an army. To go up stream, beyond the enemy's left flank, was to have two rivers to cross instead of one. Nevertheless this was the plan which Hooker finally adopted. The success of Averill's expedition had shown the ease with which the Rappahannock might be crossed at Kelley's Ford, and the Rapidan was but a small stream, little likely to embarrass a marching army.

Hooker's plan, then, was to leave enough of his army before Fredericksburg to conceal his departure, send a formidable force down stream to make a show of crossing and attract the enemy's attention to that quarter, while he himself, with the main body of the army, should proceed to the northward, cross the Rappahannock at Kelley's Ford, the Rapidan at Germania Ford, and then press on and fall upon Lee's position from the left and the rear. It was an admirable plan. For its successful execution, swift, determined action alone was essential.

Part of Hooker's original plan was a cavalry raid by Stoneman, who with 10,000 men was to cross the river two weeks before the date set for the main attack, proceed to Lee's rear, cutting canals, telegraph lines and railroads, burning the Confederate depots of supplies, destroying the enemy's connections with Richmond, and spreading such general disorder and consternation in the ranks of the enemy, that Hooker's attack should fall upon a badly demoralized foe. Of this piece of projected strategy, it is enough to say that spring freshets prevented Stoneman from crossing the river until too late to accomplish anything whatsoever.

The latter part of April found the Union army ready for the projected battle, and brought weather mild enough and dry enough to make marching practicable. Without further delay Hooker began preparing for this great movement. On the 21st, Doubleday's division went about twenty miles down the Rappahannock and made a feint of building a bridge. Two days later the Twenty-fourth Michigan regiment actually did cross the river in boats a few miles below the town. The effect of these maneuvers was to somewhat distract the attention of the Confederates from the fords up-stream where Hooker actually proposed to make his crossing. Lee, however, was not entirely deceived, and looked with some suspicion upon these demonstrations below the city, as is shown by his letter to Jackson, in which he said, "I think .... the enemy's purpose is to draw our troops in that direction while he attempts a passage elsewhere. I would not, then, send down more troops than are actually necessary."

But though General Lee was not tricked into sending troops down stream, he does not seem to have divined Hooker's plan, and failed to discover that on the 28th, while a large force of Federals was building bridges under fire three miles below Fredericksburg, a still larger force was crossing the Rappahannock at Kelley's Ford. The Fifth, Eleventh and Twelfth Corps were in this flanking column, which moved with celerity toward Chancellorsville, a point in the rear of the enemy's lines which had been chosen as a point of concentration. "If you reach Chancellorsville quickly," Hooker had said to General Slocum, who commanded the flanking column, "the game is ours."

Having passed the Rappahannock on a floating bridge without molestation, the Union forces had to march about four or five miles before coming to the Rapidan, which had to be forded. On this narrow neck of land was a strong force of Confederates under the daring cavalryman, Stuart. News of this movement of the Federals reached Stuart while they were still crossing the Rappahannock. Instead of hastening toward the Rapidan to dispute the fords of that stream with the assailants, Stuart retired to Brandy Station, thinking that this force was going to follow the same route which had brought Averill into collision with Fitz-Hugh Lee at that place some weeks before. The result of this maneuver was that, after posting his force in a most advantageous position and waiting several hours for an attack that never came, Stuart discovered that the Union army had passed on toward the fords of the Rapidan. His opportunity to dispute the progress of this formidable force had vanished, and, to make matters worse, he was cut off from the remainder of the Confederate army. Only by hard riding, by outstripping and passing round the head of the Union column, could Stuart rejoin Lee, and give to his revered chief his aid in the decisive battle which the advance of so formidable a Federal force portends.

It is night by the time the Federal column reaches the fords by which the Rapidan is to be crossed. Four feet of water, still icy with the lingering chill of winter, flowed swiftly in the channel of the river. The pontoons on which the Rappahannock was crossed were coming up in the rear of the army, but to get them to the spot, and to lay the bridge, would take several hours. Full of enthusiasm over their chances of victory in the impending battle, the men plunged cheerfully into the stream and made their way across. The cavalry crossed a few yards below the infantry, and more than one foot-soldier who was swept away by the fierce current, was caught and saved from drowning by the horsemen. All night long the cross-

FORDING THE RAPIDAN.

ing went on. Huge fires were built on the banks, and cavalrymen standing in the stream held blazing torches to shed a light on the dark surface of the rushing waters. Infantry, cavalry, long trains of rumbling cannon, scores of wagons dragged by floundering mules, ambulances, and all the vast concourse of vehicles that follow in the wake of a huge army, crossed by the ford that night, while the lurid glare of the torches shone on the black bosom of the Rapidan, or flickered among the bare branches of the trees that bordered the river on either hand. Twenty-four hours later this portion of the Union army was at Chancellorsville, and was joined by Hooker, who cried out in exultation as he saw the lines of his mighty army extending on every side: "The rebel army is now the legitimate property of the Army of the Potomac. They may as well pack up their haversacks and make for Richmond, and I shall be after them."

Let us glance at the positions held by the hostile armies, and the features of the country in which the battle of Chancellorsville was about to be fought.

General Lee, of course, was still on the heights surrounding Fredericksburg, where his army had been throughout the winter. He had with him an effective force of about 60,000 men.

Beyond the Rappahannock, confronting Lee, and under orders from Hooker to cross and give him battle at a preconcerted signal, was a force of about 7000 Federals. We shall shortly see them crossing the river and winning victory on the bloody slopes of Marye's Hill, where Burnside's men fell so fast in the battle of Fredericksburg.

Behind Lee's lines, and at a point which threatened his communications with Richmond, was Hooker. In the three divisions which first reached Chancellorsville were 46,000 men. Before the day when the fiercest fighting occurred General Sickles came up with 18,000 more. Lee was thus entrapped between two hostile armies, either one of which was greater than his own.

A word about the characteristics of the country which was to witness the collision of these mighty armies: Chancellorsville, Hooker's headquarters, and the spot about which his army was concentrated, consisted of but a single house—a huge, old-fashioned southern plantation mansion, the home of the Chancellor family. It was almost directly west of Fredericksburg and about eight miles from the Confederate lines on Marye's Hill. The "plank road," which skirts the base of that famous battle-ground, runs west to Chancellorsville, splitting into two roads for the last four miles. Two churches stand by the side of the road; Salem church is three miles from Fredericksburg, and a mile or so nearer Chancellorsville is the Tabernacle church. All around the Chancellor house are open fields, bounded to the west and southwest by the dreary expanse of woods known as the "Wilderness." Two other country places are near Chancellor's. Fairview and Hazel Grove they are called; names too pretty for the ugly work that was destined to be done there.

If you go west on the road from Chancellorsville you soon find yourself in a dense forest of stunted trees. This is the "Wilderness," a spot in which the great armies of the North and South contended more than once for the mastery. May, 1863, saw Stonewall Jackson and Hooker fighting there. May, 1864, found Grant and Lee marching their regiments through its tangled recesses. A writer who had visited every part of this historic spot, says of it: "There all is wild, desolate, and lugubrious. Thicket, undergrowth, and jungle stretch for miles impenetrable and untouched. Narrow roads wind on forever between melancholy masses of stunted and gnarled oak. Little sunlight shines there—the face of nature is dreary and sad. It was so before the battle; it is not more cheerful to-day, when, as you ride along, you see fragments of shell, rotting knapsacks, rusty gun-barrels, bleached bones, and grinning skulls. Into this jungle General Hooker penetrated. It was the wolf in his den, ready to tear any one who approached. A battle there seemed impossible. Neither side could see its antagonist. Artillery could not move; cavalry could not operate; the very infantry had to flatten their bodies to glide between the stunted trees."

In the heart of this dreary waste, two miles west from Chancellorsville, is a roadside tavern called Dowdall's. A few rods away is a little meeting-house called the Wilderness church.

The campaign of Chancellorsville was short. It began and ended in the few days between April 27 and May 5. The actual battle was of four days duration, beginning on the 1st of May. All the military movements generally comprehended under the name of the battle of Chancellorsville seem to be naturally classified into three groups, viz:

The fighting about Chancellorsville and in the Wilderness.

Sedgewick's assault on the heights of Fredericksburg.

Stoneman's cavalry raid.

Let us consider the events under the first classification, which occurred under the direct personal supervision of General Hooker, until he was wounded late in the action.

On the night of the 30th of April, General Hooker had, as we have said, 46,000 men at Chancellorsville, with 18,000 more within supporting distance. No foe of any great strength barred his path to Fredericksburg. Anderson's Confederate division alone was in the way, but that puny force, unsupported and unprovided with defensive works of any sort, might have been speedily brushed aside. Jackson was in Port Royal, Lee in Fredericksburg, all his energies bent to discovering whether Sedgewick's attack in his front was formidable or only a feint. The roads were excellent; the night bright moonlight. Hooker had three or four hours of daylight, and all of a bright night in which to crown his brilliant strategy with a brilliant victory, for there is little doubt that had he, instead of halting at Chancellorsville, pressed on, he could have routed Anderson, and destroyed Lee and Jackson in detail. The logic of war is irresistible, and it is impossible to regard the positions held by the Confederates, to consider the state of uncertainty as to the exact plans of his foe which General Lee must have been in, and to remember that Hooker had over 60,000 men available, without conceding that had he pushed forward on the afternoon and night of April 30, disaster must have come upon the Confederate army.

The bright night was passed by the Confederates in active preparations for the coming battle. Anderson's men worked all night with axe and pick and shovel building breast-works and redoubts along their front. Jackson's men spent the night on the road, and together with the division of McLaws, reached Anderson's lines early in the morning. So Hooker, who the night before had had victory fairly within his grasp, now saw all of Lee's army, save one brigade and one division, thrust between him and his prize.

After a night of quietude General Hooker ordered a general advance. The army went forward by four roads, and had passed through the forest and reached the open country within a mile or two of Anderson's intrenchments, when the van of Jackson's troops was encountered. That general, in accordance with his invariable custom, had scorned to remain behind the breast-works, and had pressed forward to seek and give battle to the enemy wherever they might be found. Fighting began almost simultaneously all along the line, and the Union soldiers were going into battle full of enthusiasm, when orders arrived from General Hooker to abandon the advanced positions and retire to the vicinity of the Chancellor house. This order was received with deep disgust by officers and soldiers alike. The enthusiasm aroused by the successful march around the enemy's flank was quenched in a moment by the order for a retreat. General Couch, after withdrawing his division in accordance with the order, went to report to Hooker at Chancellorsville.

"It's all right, Couch," said Hooker as he entered, "I have got Lee just where I want him; he must fight me on my own ground."

"The retrograde movement had prepared me for something of the sort," wrote General Couch years afterward, "but to hear from his own lips that the advantages gained by the successful marches of his lieutenants were to culminate in fighting a defensive battle in that nest of thickets was too much, and I retired from his presence with the belief that my commanding general was a whipped man."

That night the Union troops spent in throwing up a circle of defensive works that surrounded the Chancellor house. Redoubts of logs blocked all the narrow roads that pierced the woods, trees were felled to obstruct the approaches, stout *chevaux des frise* were built. Everywhere the muzzles of cannon were peering out as if watching for signs of the enemy.

The Confederates for their part were not idle. There was no lack of work with the axe, the pick, and the shovel in their camp, But the work which counted most in the great battle of the next day was done by two men, sitting alone by a midnight camp-fire, with no tools save a map of the country about Chancellorsville. Seated on a pair of boxes, by the side of a flickering fire, Lee and Jackson discussed the situation, and the best plan for attacking the men in their front. Jackson wished to try his favorite maneuver— a march to the flank and rear of his antagonist. He pointed out to Lee that whatever was to be done must be done quickly. Hooker had already 90,000 men to confront their 45,000, and Sedgwick would soon cross the river, drive away the slender force left on Marye's Hill, and join Hooker. To assault the Union position in front would be futile. It was practically impregnable. But by taking a by-path through the woods, out of sight and hearing of the enemy, Jackson thought he could lead a column of 25,000 men around, and fall upon the right flank of Hooker's army at Dowdall's tavern where no attack was looked for, and no earthworks were built.

Jackson's plan was accepted, and daybreak saw his column on the road. Twenty-seven thousand men were in line, and as the country highway was narrow, the column of marching regiments, artillery trains, and ambulances stretched out for three or four miles. Every possible effort was made to follow a route secure from the observation of the Federals, who meanwhile were standing in their trenches awaiting an attack from the east. Many of the blue-coats who had been in battle with Stonewall Jackson before were worried by the seeming inactivity of the Confederates, and surmised that that much dreaded commander was up to one of his old tricks again. Despite Jackson's care, his line brushed against some of the outposts of the Union army, and the alarm was given. But the Federals did not seem to appreciate the danger that threatened them, and made no move beyond sending General Sickles, with two divisions, to attack the marching column. This Sickles did, and having cut off and captured a Georgia regiment, returned to the Union lines satisfied with his exploit, and ignorant of the threatening nature of the movement he had momentarily interrupted.

"You fellows think you've done a pretty smart thing," said one of the Confederate prisoners, "but just wait until Old Jack gets around on your flank."

Even this failed to arouse the Federals to a sense of their position, and General Hooker, though he sent word to Howard, who was on the right, to look out for a flank attack, still thought that this marching column of Confederates meant retreat, and said gleefully to General Couch, "Lee is in full retreat toward Gordonsville, and I have sent out Sickles to capture his artillery."

It was about the middle of the afternoon that Stonewall Jackson saw his troops in position to deliver an assault upon Hooker's left wing. With two or three staff officers he rode forward to a wooded knoll, whence he could look down upon his enemy. The sight he saw made the light of battle flash exultantly in his eyes. There were Howard's men, playing cards, eating, sleeping, loafing about and amusing themselves, with no thought of impending danger. There was a line of breast-works, a row of abatis, but the soldiers who should hold them were out of line and their muskets were stacked. For a moment Jackson gazed spellbound upon the scene. His lips moved in prayer. Then wheeling his horse he rode back to order the attack upon the army thus laid out at his mercy.

Meantime no word of caution had been heeded by the men in

Howard's lines. More than one warning had reached them, but all thought of danger was scoffed at. "Horseman after horseman rode into my post, and was sent to headquarters with the information that the enemy were heavily marching along our front and proceeding to our right; and last of all an officer reported the rebels massing for attack." So wrote General Noble, then a colonel commanding two companies on Howard's picket line. "Hoawrd scouted the report and insulted the informants, charging them with telling a story that was the offspring of their imaginations or their fears."

Nevertheless the story brought in by the Union pickets was correct. The woods were full of Confederates, and they came quick after the retreating pickets. The first warning the Federals had was a rush of rabbits, squirrels, game birds, and serpents driven from their haunts in the leafy recesses of the wilderness by the advance of the long line of Jackson's men. Then came the sharp reports of rifle-shots along the skirmish line, and then the rush of an overwhelming force of men in gray carrying everything before them.

"I was playing cards in the ditch, and the first thing I knew I saw the enemy looking down upon me from the crest of the parapet," writes an officer of Howard's corps.

Jackson himself must have been surprised by the effect of his charge, so completely successful was it. The troops upon whom he had so impetuously fallen were chiefly new recruits—Germans of Schurz's brigade, still untried on the field of battle. They made no attempt to stay the furious onslaught of their foes, but broke and fled. The correspondent of a northern newspaper thus described the scene:

"The flying Germans came dashing over the field in crowds, stampeded and running as only men do run when convinced that sure destruction is awaiting them. On one hand was a solid column of infantry retreating at double quick; on the other was a dense mass of human beings who were flying as fast as their legs would carry them, followed up by the rebels pouring their murderous volleys in upon us, yelling and hooting to increase the confusion; hundreds of cavalry horses left riderless at the first discharge from the rebels, dashing frantically about in all directions; scores of batteries flying from the field; battery wagons, ambulances, horses, men, cannon, caissons, all jumbled and tumbled together in one inextricable mass—and the murderous fire of the rebels still pouring in upon them! To add to the terror of the occasion there was but one means of escape from the field, and that through a little narrow neck or ravine washed out by Scott's Creek. Toward this the confused mass plunged headlong. On came the panic-stricken crowd, terrified artillery riders spurring and lashing their horses to their utmost; ambulances upsetting and being lashed to pieces against trees and stumps; horses dashing over the field; men flying and crying with alarm—a perfect torrent of passion, apparently uncontrollable."

Behind this routed disorganized mass of fugitives the Confederates pressed on, exultant, triumphant, insatiable in their thirst for conquest. Jackson himself rode in the pursuing force, and the Confederates would now and again look over to "old Jack," hear him cry, "Press forward men, press forward," and redouble their efforts. "Frequently during the fiercest of the conflict," writes one of his staff, "he would stop, raise his hand, and turn his eyes toward heaven, as if praying for a blessing on our arms. On several occasions during the fight, as he passed the dead bodies of some of our veterans, he halted and raised his hand as if to ask a blessing upon them, and pray God to save their souls."

Hearing the roar of the guns, the wild yells of the triumphant Confederates, and the inexpressible turmoil of the routed battalions of Federals, General Howard galloped to the scene of the disaster. A round shot, from one of the two cannon that Jackson had, struck his aide, killing him instantly. Then Howard's own horse reared and fell on him, pinning him to the ground. The fugitives crowding by thought him dead, but soon two faithful orderlies helped him into his saddle again. He galloped off to where his artillery reserves were stationed, as yet free from the contagion of terror. From this position he and his staff officers could see the lines in front and the panic spreading from company to regiment, and from regiment to brigade.

"Oh, General, see those men coming from that hill way off to the right, and there's the enemy after them," said Col. Dickenson, "Fire at them. You may stop the flight."

"No, Colonel," answered Howard, "I will never fire on my own men."

So for an hour or more the Confederates had it all their own way. Neither the efforts of General Howard, nor those of Hooker, who galloped in person to the scene, availed to check the panic in the ranks of the Eleventh Corps. But about six o'clock occurred an incident which saved the Army of the Potomac. This was the charge of the Eighth Pennsylvania cavalry, only 400 strong, into the very jaws of the advancing host of Confederates, checking their forward march but sacrificing most of the cavalrymen in the exploit. Accounts differ as to how this desperate charge happened to be ordered. Some of the officers that rode in the line declare that they came upon the enemy by accident, and charged because it was their sole hope of escape. Another account—supported also by the testimony of eye witnesses—declares that a battery of twenty-two guns posted on a slight eminence at Hazel Grove was the last defense standing between the Army of the Potomac and hopeless defeat. The infantry supporting the battery had fled. The guns were empty. The enemy pressing forward would be upon them before they could be loaded. Major Keenan, commanding the Eighth Pennsylvania cavalry, was on the field.

"You must charge those people, and check their advance," said General Pleasonton to him.

Keenan looked at his little band of 400 horsemen; then at the overpowering force of Confederates coming forward.

"It's the same as asking me to die," he said, "but I'll do it."

Then to his men, "Draw sabres, charge!" and away with a rattle of hoofs, a jingling of spurs, and a chorus of cheers went the squadron. With irresistible force they fell upon the enemy. Though

Keenan fell, pierced by thirteen bullets, his brave followers kept on. The sudden onslaught astonished the Confederates and checked their advance, so that when the shattered remnant of the cavalry made its way back to the Union lines, its purpose had been effected. The guns were loaded, and the charge—as gallant a one as that of the Light Brigade at Balaclava—had not been in vain. When the Confederates rallied again to the attack, the guns at Hazel Grove belched out upon them so fierce a hurricane of iron that they gave way before it. Repeated charges brought no better success to their arms, and the line of cannon at Hazel Grove continued to be the dam which held back the threatening waves of the flood of gray.

By this time it was dark. Both armies were exhausted, but rest was not for either. The Federals were hurrying forward fresh troops to strengthen the line which so precariously held the foe in check. The Confederates for their part—at least those of the divisions which had hitherto done the fighting—were unfit to continue. "Federal writers do not realize the condition of our troops after their successful charge on Howard," writes General Colston. "We had forced our way through brush so dense that the troops were nearly stripped of their uniforms. Brigades, regiments, and companies had become so mixed that they could not be handled; besides which the darkness of evening was so intensified by the shade of the dense woods that nothing could be seen a few yards off."

But General Jackson was no man to relinquish an advantage once gained. Black though the night might be, he proposed to continue the fight until the panic that had seized upon the Eleventh corps should extend to the entire Union army. To this end he was hurrying forward fresh troops to take the places of those whose tattered and demoralized condition General Colston has described. In his zeal to carry this movement to success he galloped forward on one of the side roads, and passed the front of his own army.

"General, don't you think this is the wrong place for you?" asked one of his staff.

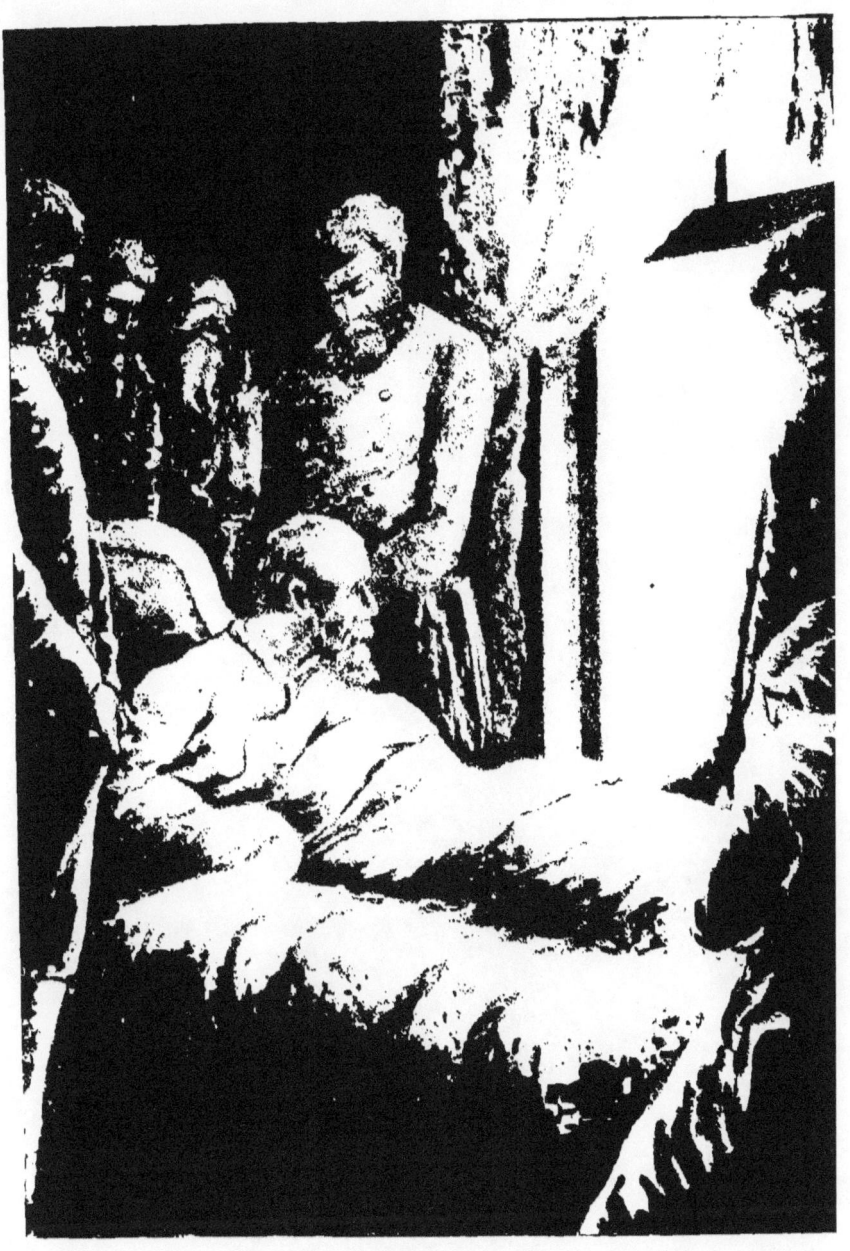

"LET US PASS OVER THE RIVER, AND REST UNDER THE SHADE OF THE TREES"
DEATH OF JACKSON

"The danger is all over—the enemy is routed! Go back and tell A. P. Hill to press right on."

And so, his mind fixed on the progress of the battle, and wholly oblivious to his own position, Jackson continued his perilous ride between the hostile lines, until suddenly there came a volley from a dark thicket; nearly all of Jackson's staff were killed, and the General himself was desperately wounded.

It was a detachment of Jackson's own troops that fired this fatal volley. They saw horsemen coming from the direction of the enemy's line and made sure it was a hostile force. Their volley wounded General Jackson with three bullets; three bones were broken, and an artery in his arm cut. With his gauntlet fast filling with blood, he reeled from his horse into the arms of an officer.

A litter was hastily improvised, and the wounded general was borne from that place, which was within a hundred yards of the Union lines and across which the shells were now sweeping. Columns of Confederate soldiers were passed going to the front. They looked with curiosity at the large group of officers escorting a litter to the rear. Who could the wounded man be? The bearers concealed Jackson's face, and gave evasive answers to all who asked.

"Tell them it is a wounded officer," said Jackson faintly.

"Great God! It is General Jackson," cried one soldier, who caught sight of his chieftain's face and was not to be deceived.

Twice the fierce fire of the Union batteries brought down one or more of the bearers of the litter, and the wounded man was thrown violently to the ground. The shock and the pain wrung a groan even from his lips. A little further on A. P. Hill's line was reached. General Pender came up and recognized Jackson.

"Ah! General," he said, "I am sorry to see you have been wounded. The lines here are so much broken that I am afraid we will have to fall back." Faint though he was with loss of blood, the martial spirit in Jackson blazed up at these words.

"You must hold your ground, General Pender! You must hold

your ground, sir!" he cried with emphasis. It was his last order on any battle field.

When the hospital was reached, the surgeons examined the wounds of the sufferer and found that the shattered arm must be amputated. The operation was soon performed, and the patient rested easily for a time. He heard the reports from the battle field, where the fight raged fiercely for three more days. But the rough usage he had met while being borne from the field, the falls he had suffered, and the long delay in getting under the care of the surgeons were too much for even Jackson's strong constitution. Pneumonia set in, and death then approached with rapid strides. At the last moment he became delirious, and thought himself on the field of battle. Orders came fast from his lips:

"Order A. P. Hill to prepare for action!"

"Pass the infantry to the front!"

"Tell Major Hawkes to send forward provisions to the men!"

After a few moments of this martial fervor, a change seemed to come over the spirit of his dream. His face became serene, his excitement vanished. With a gentle smile on his lips he murmured:

"Let us cross over the river and rest under the shade of the trees."

With this gentle and beautiful phrase on his lips the great Confederate leader passed away.

The verdict of history will rank no general, Union or Confederate, above Jackson. His was in many respects the phenomenal military genius of the war. His power as a disciplinarian fitly supplemented his skill as a tactician. His strategy, often conceived in seeming violation of all military theories, would more than once have resulted in disaster had he not at hand a body of steel-muscled, iron-hearted veterans ready to march and fight, day and night, so long as "Old Jack" led them. His death was the beginning of the Confederacy's downfall. As, while Stonewall Jackson lived, the Confederate army in Virginia was so constantly victorious as to begin to think itself invincible, so after his death there came to that army nothing but reverses and defeats.

But to return to the field of Chancellorsville. It was nine o'clock at night when Jackson was wounded. At this moment his attack on Hooker's right flank was entirely successful, and only the Union artillery at Hazel Grove was holding the Confederates in check. Jackson was leading a flank attack against this position when he was hit. His fall threw his army into confusion, and no further successes were scored by the Confederates that night.

It must be remembered that the fighting which we have thus described was that on Hooker's right flank only, and that Jackson's forces alone of the Confederates were there engaged. Lee, for his part, contented himself that day with engaging the troops at Hooker's front with just sufficient vigor to keep the Union general from disengaging troops from that part of the field to send to overwhelm Jackson.

The morning of May 3d saw the conflict renewed early on the right. In rearranging his lines Hooker had determined to abandon the position at Hazel Grove. The first steps taken to effect this attracted the attention of the vigilant Confederates, and Archer's brigade charged the retreating artillery, carrying the hill and capturing four cannon. Union batteries at Fairview opened on the victors, and by sunrise the battle was raging again all along the line. Stuart was now in command of the Confederate troops which Jackson had led, and was straining every nerve to demonstrate that he could command a division as well as he led a dashing cavalry charge. He saw at a glance the vital importance of the position at Hazel Grove and posted thirty cannon there. Then with this formidable battery hurling its missiles as far even as the headquarters of General Hooker, he put himself at the head of the Confederate regiments and led them in a series of desperate assaults on the Union lines.

"Remember Jackson!" was Stuart's war-cry as he led his troops to the assault, and the men cried "Jackson! Jackson! Remember Jackson!" as they swept up the hill of Fairview where the Union guns were fiercely flaming. For a time the assailants swept all before them. The brunt of their assault fell first upon a regiment of raw recruits which went to pieces before the shock. Drill is to an army what honest mortar is to a building; omit it and the whole military structure crumbles. But the ground lost by the weakness of these untried soldiers was regained for the Union by the veterans of the New Jersey brigade, who made a furious charge upon the advancing foe, recaptured all the Union prisoners and cannon, and took several Confederate battle-flags. For a moment this spirited charge dampened the ardor of the Confederates, but soon rallying they returned to their work. This time fortune favored them. General Berry, upon whose command their attack fell, held his men nobly in line. Wherever the serried front of his regiments seemed wavering, thither he went to cheer on his men and infuse courage into the most faint-hearted. But this gallant leader was soon laid low by a fatal bullet, and General Revere, who succeeded to the command, ordered the brigade to retreat. This movement was well under way when General Sickles appeared and countermanded the order, but it was too late. The Union lines were thrown into confusion, and the Confederates were prompt to take advantage of the opportunity. Before their furious charges, and the rapid and accurate fire of their artillery, the Federal army was rapidly wasting away.

Where was Hooker meantime? His headquarters were at the Chancellor house, which by the steady and unimpeded advance of the Confederates had now become a target for a destructive artillery fire. Here Hooker narrowly escaped death. A massive pillar against which he was leaning was struck by a solid shot, and split in twain. The shock knocked the general senseless, and his whole side was bruised in such a way as to cause him intense pain. Reviving after a few moments he mounted his horse and tried to ride away to the center of the new position of his army, but the pain overcame him, and he was forced to dismount and lie down. A little brandy renewed his strength. He rose and walked away and an instant later a round shot struck the center of the blanket on which he had been lying, and scooped a great hole in the ground beneath. "The enemy was after me with a sharp stick that day," said Hooker years after, in speaking of his two narrow escapes.

The pain of his wound unfitted Hooker for the further command of the army, and thereafter the battle was fought at hap-hazard on the part of the Federals. Once the general turned the command over to General Couch, but took it back into his own hands again before that officer had given any orders. From the time Hooker received his wound the commanders of Union divisions went into the fight or stayed out at their own discretion:—no further orders came from headquarters. And it may not be out of place to state here that many of the division commanders stayed out of the fight altogether, for, despite the injunction of President Lincoln to "put in all your men," General Hooker fought the battle of Chancellorsville with less than half his army,—a fact to which the Confederates owed their signal success.

For signal success it was that attended the Confederate arms in this battle of the 3d of May. By the middle of the forenoon the news spreads among the soldiers of Jackson's corps that General Lee himself was among their officers directing the battle. Lee with them! Then that means that their hard fighting has been crowned with triumph. That they are no longer a flanking party of 26,000 contending with a whole army, but they have formed a junction with the troops whom they left behind in beginning their long march to Hooker's right. With renewed courage they press into the battle.

Lee had indeed reunited his army. While Jackson's men were attacking the Federals on the right, Lee was pressing forward in front. The abandonment of the decisive position at Hazel Grove by Sickles left but one point—Fairview—to be captured by the Confederates in order to effect a junction of the two wings of their army. Fairview was carried after several dogged charges in which the assailants suffered severely. Then, with his army reunited, General Lee took personal command of the whole, and the lines swept forward in one grand, concentric irresistible charge which swept the Federals from their position about the Chancellor house, and away toward the river which they had crossed four days before so full of hopes of victory. As Lee sat on his horse near the blazing Chancellor mansion which at daylight that morning had been the headquarters of the Federal general, and at night was ruined and burning in the very center of the Confederate line, a courier galloped up to him bearing General Jackson's congratulations upon his victory. "Say to General Jackson," responded Lee with much feeling, "that the victory is his and that the congratulations are due to him."

One more attempt the Confederates made that day to force Hooker still further back toward the river. But the well-entrenched Union lines were more than a match for the weary, ragged, and half-starved men who had been marching and fighting for three days. The assailants were beaten back with heavy loss, and news just then came to Lee from his rear guard at Fredericksburg that convinced him that there was other and better employment for his regiments than charging an enemy who was perfectly content to rest quietly in his trenches.

It will be remembered that part of Hooker's original plan of battle had been that Sedgewick should cross the Rappahannock River before Fredericksburg and attack the Confederates in front, while Hooker fell on them from the rear. The activity of Jackson defeated Hooker's progress and the battle with that general's forces was fought some distance from Fredericksburg. Nevertheless, about 10,000 Confederates were left in the line of breastworks which had been so gallantly held against Burnside in December, and against this force Sedgewick moved on the morning of May 3. Marye's Hill was again the scene of conflict. Once more the stone wall and the sunken road sheltered the Confederate infantry. This time, however, the charge of the Federals was successful. A private soldier in a Massachusetts regiment thus tells the story:

"The assault took place Sunday, May 3, at about eleven o'clock A. M., the Seventh Massachusetts leading the left column, the Thirty-sixth

New York volunteers in support. Our company leading the Seventh, consequently caught the whole body of the first fire of the Johnnies, which they withheld until we were certainly within twenty-five yards. As some of the officers sang out 'Retreat! Retreat!' the men began to yell, 'Forward! don't go back! we sha'n't get so close up again.' Just before, and in front of the wall, facing down the street is a house, standing in a small plat, V-shaped, and inclosed by a high board fence. This wall in our front, along the base of the hill, was a rough stone wall forming the rear bank of the sunken road, while on our side, in front of the sunken road, was a good stone wall even with the level of the field. In this sunken road were two Confederate lines of battle, the front line firing on our charging lines on the left of the road, and the rear line sitting on their heels, with their backs against the terrace wall at the base of the hill and rear of the road. About opposite the right of our regiment was a depression on the hill made some time, I should think, by water from the land above, but now grassed over; at the head of this depression was a battery, placed, I suppose, to rake the ravine or depression. Some one looked through the board fence and saw the enemy's flank. In a moment the men rushed to the fence and we went through, pell-mell right upon the flank of the Confederates, at the same time giving them the contents of the muskets point blank, without aiming. The whole thing was a surprise. They were not prepared for anything from this quarter, as we were hidden from them and they from us, by the house and fence."

But the men who charged up the hill in the face of the enemy's fire suffered heavily. "A blinding rain of shot pierced the air," writes one of them. "It was more than human nature could bear. The head of the column, as it reached the lowest part of the decline near a fork in the road, seemed to melt away. Many fell; others bending low to the earth hurriedly sought shelter from the undulations of the ground and the fences and the two or three wooden structures along the road. Out of 400 comprising the Seventh

Massachusetts, 150 were killed and wounded. Col. Johns, commanding, was severely wounded. Then as if moved by a sudden impulse and nerved for a supreme effort, both columns and the line in the field simultaneously sprang forward. The stone wall was gained and the men were quickly over it. Along the wall a hand-to-hand fight took place, and the bayonet and the butt of the musket were freely used. The brilliant and successful charge occupied perhaps ten or fifteen minutes, and immediately after the wall was carried the enemy became panic-stricken. In the flight they threw away guns, knapsacks, pistols, swords, and everything that might retard their speed. One thousand prisoners were taken, besides several battle-flags and pieces of artillery. Over 600 were killed and wounded in the direct assault upon the heights, and the loss to the corps on the entire front was about 1000."

Having carried the heights Sedgewick pressed on toward Chancellorsville, thinking to fall upon the rear of Lee's army there. But Lee had learned that Sedgewick was attacking the position on Marye's Hill, and had sent part of his troops back to meet the Federals at Salem church where the Confederates had a line of intrenchments. In these trenches the men who had fled from the sunken road rallied, so that Sedgewick, on arriving at that point after a three-mile march, found a very considerable force arrayed against him. With charge and counter-charge the afternoon passed away, neither side gaining any notable advantage. Darkness put an end to the fray, just as Sedgewick was preparing for a final grand assault which he felt confident would carry the day.

Here, then, were the positions of the armies on the night of May 3, after the last charge had been made and the echoes of the last cannon shot had died away: Hooker, with the chief part of the Union army, was near Chancellorsville, holding the position to which he had been driven during the morning; confronting Hooker was Lee with some 45,000 Confederates; down the road toward Fredericksburg, in the trenches by the Salem church, was McLaws; confronting him was Sedgewick with about 15,000 blue-coats; in Fredericksburg were the wounded of Sedgewick's command with about 2000 effective men to protect them; and finally down the river below Fredericksburg was Early, with a force of 6000 Confederate infantry.

The morning's light saw some marked changes in these dispositions of the troops. Confident from Hooker's actions hitherto that he would make no attack on the morrow, Lee on the night of the 3d sent 25,000 men down the road to the aid of McLaws. Early spent the night on the road too, and when dawn broke his 6000 men were in the old position on Marye's Hill, which Sedgewick had taken and then abandoned. So, instead of being in a position to fall upon the rear of Lee's army with telling effect, General Sedgewick found himself with a force of double his number before him, and 6000 of the enemy in his rear. He saw speedily that the time for offensive action on his part was past, and that henceforth his one task was to save his army from annihilation. Had Lee attacked him early in the day this might have been impossible, but that commander spent the day in arranging his lines and it was not until 6 o'clock in the evening that he began the assault. The Confederates were gallantly repulsed, losing several hundred prisoners. That night Sedgewick's corps re-crossed the river to the north side, where they were soon joined by Hooker, who abandoned his dead and wounded on the field of Chancellorsville, and fled in the night.

So ended the battle of Chancellorsville,—ended in defeat and humiliation for Hooker; in victory and glory for Lee. The Federals had been cleanly out-generaled. An opportunity to demolish Lee's army had been lost. So far as the actual valor shown by the soldiers of the two armies is concerned there is no reason to rank either above the other. But Jackson's flanking march with its complete success, and Lee's brilliant strategy, which enabled him to beat Hooker and then lead his whole force against Sedgewick, were the two factors which determined the outcome of the battle.

The losses on each side were heavy. According to the official reports the Federals lost 17,197 men, of whom 12,197 were among the killed and wounded. The Confederates for their part reported a loss of 13,019, of whom 10,266 were among the killed and wounded. But the triumph at Chancellorsville cost the South one soldier whose loss could never be replaced, and whose death marked the beginning of the end of the Confederacy—Stonewall Jackson. Throughout the early years of the war Jackson was Lee's right arm. No jealousy existed between them. The soldier of inferior rank gave to his commander unquestioned obedience, and Lee in his turn gave to his subordinate the fullest confidence. How greatly Lee felt the loss of his able associate his utterances at the time tell. How correctly he estimated the effect of that loss we shall see when we come to read of the battle of Gettysburg.

CHAPTER VIII.

CONFEDERATE ACTIVITY. — GENERAL LEE DETERMINES TO ATTEMPT THE INVASION OF PENNSYLVANIA. — CAVALRY BATTLE AT BRANDY STATION. — LEE'S NORTHWARD MARCH. — PANIC IN NORTHERN CITIES. — HOOKER IN PURSUIT. — MEADE SUPERSEDES HOOKER. — GETTYSBURG. — THE BATTLE OF THE FIRST DAY. — OLD JOHN BURNS. — BAYARD WILKESON'S HEROISM. — INCIDENTS OF THE BATTLE.

AFTER the battle of Chancellorsville there followed a month of inaction. The North was disheartened, the Army of the Potomac dispirited. The more the soldiers and the people reflected upon the defeat, the more galling they found it. To be defeated was bad enough, but to reflect that the army had been defeated while 37,000 men stood idle, ready to be led against the enemy, but apparently forgotten by the general, added greatly to the bitterness of failure. The hostility of the Army of the Potomac to General Hooker became open. Officers and soldiers complained loudly. President Lincoln came to the camp to examine into the causes of the disaster, and received Hooker's resignation, which for the time he refused to accept. General Couch in disgust resigned, refusing to serve longer under Hooker. To add to the demoralization of the army, whole regiments were disbanding, their time of enlistment having expired.

In the Confederate camps on the south bank of the Rappahannock all was exultation. The soldiers were rapidly coming to think themselves invincible. From all parts of the South there came to the army words of encouragement and eulogy. The newspapers with one accord called upon the military authorities to abandon the policy of a defensive war and to march into the territory of the North. Political considerations, too, made some such movement imperative. The wish of the English aristocracy to recognize the Confederacy needed only some notable victory by the Southern armies to give it strength enough to overcome the opposition of the middle and lower classes of England, who were almost a unit in their friendliness to the North. Moreover an invasion which could prove that the two years of war had in no way exhausted the military resources of the South, would greatly extend the already formidable faction in the North which was resisting the war measures of the government at Washington, and called for peace at any price. It appears that General Lee himself doubted the wisdom of an invasion of Northern territory, but could not withstand the popular sentiment. The army, the people, and finally the government called upon him to lead his army to the north of the Potomac. It is even said that when Lee, shortly after the battle of Chancellorsville, sent to Richmond a requisition for rations for his army, the commissary-general returned to him the paper, endorsed "If General Lee wishes rations, let him seek them in Pennsylvania."

In deference to the public will, therefore, Lee began his preparations for the invasion of Pennsylvania. His army was strengthened and reorganized. The slender resources of the South were taxed to the utmost to supply new equipments. Engineers were busied drawing maps of the country to be invaded, and scouts and spies kept the Confederate general well informed of what was going on in his adversaries' camp and at the national capital.

On the 3d of June, the Confederate army began to move from its position at Fredericksburg. Hooker noticed a change in the appearance of the Confederate camp and sent Sedgewick across the river to investigate. But although by this time two-thirds of Lee's army were on their way northward, the one division that remained under command of D. H. Hill sallied out of its trenches and met Sedgewick with such spirit that he returned to Hooker with the report that the force in the enemy's camp was not materially decreased.

Two or three days later, as the indications of some great and decisive movement on the part of the enemy multiplied, Hooker sent Gen. Pleasonton, with all the Union cavalry, up the river toward Culpepper to reconnoitre. At the same time he sent word to Washington that he believed Lee was contemplating a movement to the north of the Rappahannock, leaving Hill at Fredericksburg. Should this surmise prove correct, Hooker asked to be permitted to cross the Rappahannock and demolish Hill, then follow after Lee and fight him wherever he could find him. But this proposition found no favor in Washington, and drew from President Lincoln a characteristic letter in which he said:

"I would not take any risk of being entangled upon the river like an ox jumped half over a fence, and liable to be torn by dogs, front and rear, without a fair chance to gore one way or kick the other."

Pleasonton's reconnoissance brought on a spirited cavalry battle, one of the few encounters in the Civil War in which two bodies of horsemen met each other in hand-to-hand fighting with the sabre. It so happened that the 8th of June saw the whole of the Confederate cavalry at Culpepper, where it was reviewed by General Lee. Stuart led his forces in the review, and the whole column of 8000 mounted men, with sabres drawn and flags flying, galloped madly past the spot where Lee stood surrounded by his staff. Then wheeling into an open field near by, the whole cavalcade charged up a slope from the crest of which the guns of Stuart's horse artillery were blazing and roaring in mimicry of war. Pleasonton's squadrons were even then on the road to Culpepper, and hearing the thunder of the cannonade wondered mightily at this sound of conflict in the enemy's lines. Next morning the Federals fell upon Stuart at Brandy Station, and a fierce battle followed. Squadrons of cavalry numbering thousands of riders were hurled against each other. Carbines and pistols, as soon as fired, were thrown away and the battle was fought out with cold steel. The ground shook beneath the tread of the thousands of galloping horses. Clouds of dust floated in air and obscured the scene of the battle. From neighboring hills the guns of Stuart's horse artillery roared and were answered by the cannon which accompanied the Union forces. For a time the advantages were with the Federals. They rode down the Confederate squadrons, fought their way to the Confederate guns, sabred the cannoneers, captured Stuart's headquarters and a box filled with valuable papers. Then fresh troops came to the aid of the Confederates. From three sides heavy battalions of horse thundered down on the front and the flanks of the Federals. The guns were recaptured and turned on their former captors. The Union gunners in their turn found themselves overwhelmed by a torrent of mounted men. The whole course of battle was changed, and a few minutes saw the Federals hastily retreating leaving three cannon behind as trophies for Stuart. The battle had been short, but it was bloody. About 600 fell on each side, and thereafter the sneering question "Who ever saw a dead cavalryman?" was not heard in either army.

This engagement in no way checked Lee's movement toward Pennsylvania, and he continued to withdraw his troops from in front of Hooker and send them north by way of the Shenandoah valley. The seemingly foolhardy manner in which he dispersed his army suggests that he must have had great confidence in the inertness of his adversary. On the 13th of June part of Ewell's division was at Martinsburg, West Virginia, and part at Winchester, Longstreet and Stuart were at Culpepper, and Hill was still in front of Hooker. It was on this day that President Lincoln wrote to Hooker.

"If the head of Lee's army is at Martinsburg, and the tail of it on the plank road between Fredericksburg and Chancellorsville, the animal must be very slim somewhere—could you not break him?"

Good military advice this, and seemingly in accordance with

CHARGE OF UNION CAVALRY, BRANDY STATION.

Hooker's already expressed ideas. But for some reason or other the general took no notice of the suggestion at this time.

It was now evident to all that the Confederates had begun a great northward march; indeed, among the papers which Pleasonton's men had captured at Stuart's headquarters, were letters and memoranda outlining the routes to be followed in the invasion of Pennsylvania. Whether it was Lee's purpose, however, to swing around and take Washington in the rear, or make a descent upon Baltimore, was still doubtful, and the Army of the Potomac was accordingly concentrated around Manassas Junction to wait there until some movement should reveal the enemy's true purpose.

The Federals were not left long in doubt. The telegraph soon began to bring to Washington the reports of Ewell's progress down the Shenandoah Valley. On the 15th of June, one portion of his troops drove the Union forces under Milroy from Winchester after a sharp fight. On the 17th Harper's Ferry was menaced, and the Union troops there, remembering the ease with which the place had been taken by Stonewall Jackson, abandoned the post and sought refuge on the other side of the river. Thus, in a campaign of but a few days, Ewell swept the Shenandoah Valley clear of Union troops, capturing in the operation 400 prisoners, 28 cannon, 11 stand of colors, 300 wagons, and an immense number of horses and mules. The total Confederate loss was 269 men.

Wholly unchecked in their advance, the Confederates pressed on to the northward. Longstreet and Hill followed close behind Ewell. A squadron of flying cavalry under Jenkins was in the van, and raided into Pennsylvania as far as Chambersburg, burning bridges and tearing up railroads, and bringing back to Hagerstown, where Lee's army was to rendezvous, hundreds of horses, great quantities of supplies, and not a few kidnapped negroes. By the 24th the whole of the Confederate army save Stuart's cavalry was north of the Potomac, while Ewell was far ahead in the outskirts of Harrisburg, and by his bold advance carrying terror to Philadelphia and even to New York. All

Pennsylvania was panic-stricken. Though the Governor issued a proclamation calling the people to arms, there was a sad dearth of volunteers. It is worth noting that the first company that marched to the defense of Harrisburg was made up of students of the Pennsylvania College—sixty mere striplings led by a theological student. All through the country which lay in the path of the invading army, the people were hurriedly sending away their horses and cattle, their grain and fruit, their household goods, money, and portable property generally. Nor was the panic confined to the people of the rural districts in Lee's immediate front. In Philadelphia many bankers hastened to send the treasures from their vaults to New York for safe-keeping. Ladies sent away their jewels and families their plate. Not even New York was considered safe, and goods were sent to Boston and to Albany. A proclamation by the Mayor closed all the manufactories, workshops, and stores of Philadelphia, and sent the people of the city out into the suburbs to build earthworks. Baltimore did likewise, and the police of the city impressed into the service over a thousand negroes, slaves and freedmen alike, and put them to work in the trenches. Even Washington was not wholly exempt from panic, though the people there enjoyed the consoling thought that the government would never allow the national capital to be entered by the enemy so long as a single regiment could be rallied to its defense.

Meantime the long, dense columns of men in gray were moving rapidly northward over the level roads and green fields of Pennsylvania. Ewell kept far in advance, having nothing to fear, as there were no troops save raw militia in his neighborhood. He made heavy demands for supplies upon the towns through which he passed. From the town of Chambersburg he required 5000 suits of clothing, ten tons of leather, five tons of horseshoes, 5000 bushels of oats, three tons of lead, one thousand currycombs, 500 barrels of flour and all the ammunition in town. At York the demands of the Confederates were equally heavy, and there was actually paid over to them $28,000 in cash, 200 barrels of flour, 40,000 pounds of fresh beef, 30,000 bushels of corn, and 1000 pairs of shoes.

But though the heavy demands made by Ewell upon the people of the captured towns were perfectly justified by the laws of war, the precedent set by him was not that which guided the Confederate army as a whole in its actions while in an enemy's country. The moderation, the humanity, the regard for the rights of property shown by these half-starved Southerners in a land overflowing with plenty must ever be memorable. "The duties exacted of us by civilization and Christianity," said Lee, in an order directing his troops to abstain from all rapine and pillage, "are not less obligatory in the country of the enemy than in our own. The commanding general therefore earnestly exhorts the troops to abstain with most scrupulous care from unnecessary or wanton injury to private property; and he enjoins upon all officers to arrest and bring to summary punishment all who shall in any way offend against his orders on this subject."

Almost universal obedience was paid both to the letter and the spirit of this order. The Southern army marched through lanes bordered on either side by fruit-trees with heavy-laden boughs, past barn-yards and pigstys that made the alert foragers yearn for an opportunity to show their peculiar skill, and by herds of cattle that brought visions of luscious steaks to the eyes of the hungry soldiers; yet seldom was any thieving committed. "By way of giving the devil his due," wrote the correspondent of a northern newspaper concerning Gen. Jenkins, who commanded Early's cavalry, "it must be said that although there were over sixty acres of wheat, and eighty acres of corn in the same field he protected it most carefully, and picketed his horses so that it could not be injured. No fences were wantonly destroyed, poultry was not disturbed, nor did he compliment our blooded cattle so much as to test the quality of their steak and roast."

On the 29th of June the Confederate army of invasion reached the limit of its northward march. Early was on the banks of the Susquehanna at Wrightsville, whither he had been sent with orders to seize and hold the magnificent bridge which spans the broad river at that point. In this purpose he was balked, for the Federal commander at the place set the torch to the structure, and when Early arrived it was a bridge of flame. The rest of Ewell's corps marched upon Harrisburg, and Jenkins's cavalry, which led the advance, was already skirmishing in the suburbs of the Pennsylvania capital, when orders arrived from Lee directing all the troops to form a junction at Cashtown. At this moment Longstreet and Hill were near Chambersburg, while Stuart was some thirty miles from Baltimore engaged in a third ride round the Army of the Potomac, an exploit which he performed, but which cost the Confederacy dear.

What was it, then, that led Lee to thus suddenly check his northward march and call back his advance corps? Let us consider the course of the Army of the Potomac since the last of Hill's regiments disappeared in the Shenandoah Valley, and we shall find an explanation.

Hooker had kept a vigilant watch upon the movements of the Confederate army. Almost at the same moment when Longstreet and Hill were crossing the Potomac, the Union army was crossing further down stream. Once north of the river Hooker proposed immediate measures to check Lee's movement. The chief of these was an expedition of the Twelfth corps along the north bank of the river, picking up the garrison of Harper's Ferry from its camp on Maryland Heights, cutting Lee's communications with Virginia and attacking him in the rear. This plan, an excellent one, as the sequel will show, met no favor with General Halleck, and he curtly refused to allow Hooker to move the Harper's Ferry garrison from its place. As Hooker had but a few days before been invested with the command of the troops at Harper's Ferry, he considered that he "was not allowed to maneuver his own army in the presence of the enemy," and asked to be relieved of his command. His request was granted, and on the 27th of June General Hooker with great and unfeigned emotion bade farewell to the Army of the Potomac. That his resignation was forced upon him by deliberate and willful persecution by General Halleck there can be no doubt. When, after a short stay in Baltimore, the deposed soldier visited Washington, the War Department subjected him to a final indignity by putting him under arrest for having visited the city without permission.

To Hooker there succeeded Major-General George C. Meade. That he sought the promotion does not appear, and indeed he must have accepted it with some hesitancy, knowing that a great battle was impending. Nevertheless he quickly familiarized himself with Hooker's plans, and as the Army of the Potomac had changed commanders too often to be seriously disturbed by missing a familiar face at headquarters, it soon appeared that in this instance President Lincoln's homely maxim, "It's a bad time to swap horses when you're crossing a stream," did not apply.

Meade therefore became commander of the Army of the Potomac. The enemy, exultant, with full ranks, with the memory of two notable victories still fresh, buoyant with the enthusiasm of invasion, was in his front. He had to overtake that enemy; bring him to bay, fight him, and beat him. A victory was essential for the preservation of the Union. Even to-day, knowing as we do the wonderful resources of the North in that hour of civil combat, and the marvelous willingness with which those resources were expended, we still believe that had Lee won a victory at Gettysburg the Union must almost infallibly have gone to pieces. In 1863 people North and South alike were sure that one more defeat for the Army of the Potomac meant the complete triumph of the Confederacy.

General Meade felt the heavy responsibility that rested upon his shoulders, and went about his work as one who had determined to leave no means unemployed to win a victory. It is worthy of note that his very first act was to withdraw the Harper's Ferry garrison and order it to Frederick, where on the 28th of June his army concentrated. For this act, the suggestion of which a few days before had cost Hooker his command, no word of censure came to Meade from the War Department.

On the 29th the Army of the Potomac marched from Frederick

into Pennsylvania, moving almost due north by several parallel roads. It was not long before the enemy was encountered.

Incredible as it may seem, it is none the less true that up to this moment General Lee was ignorant of the advance of his adversaries, and supposed the Army of the Potomac to be still resting quietly in its camp south of the Potomac River. The absence of Stuart on his ill-timed raid deprived the Confederate general of the use of the "eyes of the army," as the cavalry has been termed, and he was completely in the dark as to his enemy's position. A spy whom Longstreet had sent out before leaving Virginia first brought the news that the Federals were concentrating at Frederick. The news alarmed Lee, for he saw his communications with Virginia endangered. So far as subsistence for his men was concerned this danger gave him no uneasiness, for he was in the midst of a rich country, off of which his army could well live. But with his line of communication with Richmond cut, he could get no more powder and shot. One great battle would exhaust the store he had on hand, and his army would then be helpless in a hostile country. It was for this that Lee in haste recalled Ewell from the banks of the Susquehanna, and concentrating his army at Cashtown, set about investigating the reports of danger in his rear.

On the 30th of June, Pettigrew's brigade of Hill's corps, being very ill-shod, was sent to the little town of Gettysburg to make requisition upon the inhabitants for a sufficient supply of shoes. After a few hours Pettigrew returned reporting that he had found Gettysburg occupied by a heavy force of Federals. On receipt of this news Hill notified Lee that on the morrow he would take his corps to Gettysburg, and give battle to the enemy's force there. From this accidental turn of affairs the little village of Gettysburg became the scene of a great battle, one of the decisive conflicts that have marked epochs in the history of the world.

Let us consider for a moment the topography of the region in which the two great armies, each made up of the flower of the section that it represents, are to clinch in mortal combat. Gettysburg, the village which gives its name to the battle, is a little country town, quiet, dull, far from the great highways of trade and commerce. Some military importance it had, because of the many good roads concentrating there, and this fact had led General Meade to send General Buford to take possession of the place. It was Buford's outposts that Pettigrew had seen on the day before. Two streams flowing almost parallel in a north and south course drain the fertile fields about Gettysburg. The one to the west of the town is called Willoughby Run; that to the east is Rock Creek. Chains of hills—ridges they called them—also cluster about the town extending north and south. Directly west of the village, lying between its outskirts and the banks of Willoughby Run, is Seminary Ridge, so called from the dome-crowned building of the Lutheran seminary that stood upon its crest. Directly south of the city is Cemetery Ridge, on the grassy slopes of which the town burial-ground is situated. A ponderous gateway in the style of a triumphal arch formed the entrance to the cemetery and was a prominent feature in the landscape. West of the southern end of Cemetery Ridge was the peach orchard of Farmer Sherfy. At the very southern end of Cemetery Ridge two bold hillocks rise above the level of the surrounding hills. Round Top, the southernmost and larger of the two is called; Little Round Top the other. Just east of the town sloping down to Rock Creek is Culp's Hill.

With the situation of these landmarks well fixed in the mind it becomes comparatively easy to understand just how the two armies moved, and where they clashed on those three bloody days that ushered in July, 1863.

The night of the 30th of June saw the crest of Seminary Ridge held by Buford's troops. Reynolds's division was on its way to Buford's support, but still a few miles away. Hill's Confederate division meanwhile was moving upon Gettysburg with the intention of driving away the militia force which it was supposed was holding the place, for at that time none of the Confederate commanders thought the

Army of the Potomac was hanging so closely upon the flank of the Army of Northern Virginia.

At eight o'clock in the morning the crack of a musket down the road, in the direction of the pickets, set the drums rolling in Buford's camp. Another shot followed, then a volley, and the pickets began pouring in with the report that the enemy was advancing in force. Buford sent off couriers to Reynolds begging him to hasten his advance, and in the mean time posted his dismounted troopers wherever the ground gave promise of success against an enemy of overpowering numbers. The Confederates for their part were sluggish. They expected nothing but a skirmish. It was no part of General Lee's plan to fight an offensive battle.' So Hill's men planted a famous Virginia battery to shell the woods in which Buford's lines were arrayed, and set themselves leisurely to the task of driving from the crest of the ridge the few Yankee militiamen whom they expected to meet.

Meantime Buford himself mounted into the cupola of the seminary and scanned the country anxiously for signs of coming aid. He had not long to wait. Scarce an hour had elapsed from the moment the first shot was fired, when Reynolds's division began to come up, and its commander, having galloped on in advance, clambered up the seminary stairs to join Buford in his observations. The newly arrived troops deployed and pushed on into the thick of the fight. It so happened that a clump of woods which filled the triangular space between two converging roads was the position which both armies strove most fiercely to gain and hold. Archer's Confederate brigade, and Meredith's brigade, known as the "Iron Brigade," rushed at each other. The contest was sharp but the blue-coats carried the position, captured Archer himself and a large part of his brigade and swept the rest away on the run. The astonished Confederates, who had expected to meet only militia, shouted in dismay: " 'Taint no militia. It's the —— black-hatted fellows again. It's the Army of the Potomac." The chagrin of the rank and file of Archer's brigade, on finding themselves opposed by veterans, extended to their commander.

After being captured he was taken to General Doubleday, who had been his classmate at West Point. "Good-morning, Archer," said Doubleday blandly, "I am glad to see you."

"Well I'm not glad to see you," responded the prisoner in high dudgeon. "Not by a —— sight."

But while the gallant charge of the Iron Brigade had won much for the Union army, it cost the army dear in one respect. General Reynolds, who accompanied the brigade, was shot through the head by a Confederate sharpshooter and instantly killed. General Doubleday succeeded to the command. He found that, on the left of the line of battle, the brilliant charge had made everything favorable for the Union arms, but on the right disaster was impending. Two New York regiments posted there had been outflanked, surrounded, and nearly cut to pieces. Hall's battery had narrowly escaped capture, and had fled with a loss of one gun. The triumphant yells of the Confederates, no less than the reports brought to him by excited aides, convinced Doubleday that the situation was rapidly becoming serious. He sent over to that part of the field his reserve force, which arrived in the very nick of time to catch the enemy on the flank. The Confederates, who had been hotly pursuing their disorganized adversaries, were seized with panic at this attack from an unsuspected quarter, and rushed into a railway cut which seemed to promise shelter. But their refuge proved their destruction, for the blue-coats seized both ends of the cut, and the unhappy Mississippians, caught like rats in a trap, were forced to surrender at discretion. The few that escaped drifted back to the banks of Willoughby Run, where Heth was re-forming.

Then for a time a calm succeeded the storm of battle. The struggle of the morning was over, and the two gladiators were tightening their harness and sharpening their weapons for the fiercer combat of the afternoon. Thus far the advantage rested with the Federals, but General Howard, who came galloping up about eleven o'clock to take command of the field, had ample reason to look forward to the afternoon's fight with anxiety. He had only the First and Eleventh corps with him—about 20,000 men in all. The Confederates on the field outnumbered him, and additional forces were coming up to their aid. In position alone did the Army of the Potomac hold any advantage. Meredith held the triangular patch of woods which had been so gallantly won. Steinwehr, with two batteries, was posted on Cemetery Hill, a superb position whence the cannon could sweep all the country round about. This spot Howard designated as the rallying point in case of disaster. Seminary Ridge was held by the First Corps, now under Doubleday's command, while the Eleventh Corps under General Carl Schurz was on the plain north of the town, aligned at a right angle to Doubleday's troops and facing north.

It was while these troops were marching along the roads and through the fields to their designated stations, that a little old man, wearing a swallow-tailed coat with smooth, bright, brass buttons, came up alongside of the Seventh Wisconsin regiment, and fell in step with the men of Company N. The men in the ranks began to make fun of him.

"Better quit this crowd, old fellow," said one. "The fighting will be hot where we are going."

"I know how to fight," responded the old man earnestly; "I have fit before."

"Where's your cartridge box?" sung out one of the company wits. "You'll need something to put in your gun when you get down yonder."

"I've got plenty of cartridges in here," was the answer, as the old fellow slapped his trousers pocket. "I can get my hands in here quicker than in a box. I'm not used to them new-fangled things."

By a little questioning the soldiers found out that their strange companion was John Burns, a Gettysburg farmer. The rebels had driven away his cows, he said, and he proposed to seek vengeance on the battle field. When the first volley came the soldiers looked around to see their civilian friend run away, but he stood his ground bravely and fought until three wounds gave him ample excuse for seeking the rear.

The battle was reopened by the Confederates about two o'clock by a general assault on the Union First Corps. The batteries thundered from all the adjacent hill-tops, and an especially destructive fire which a hitherto unsuspected battery opened upon the right flank of Doubleday's line from Oak Hill, told the Federals that Ewell, whose arrival had been momentarily expected, had come at last, and was advancing upon them from the north. Rodes's division was in the van of Ewell's corps, and swung around to join the left flank of Hill's line. In so doing it clashed with the right of Doubleday's line, and he did not get away without some deep scars. There was bitter fighting in the farmyard and garden of Farmer McLain, and the stone walls and fences sheltered swarms of skirmishers whose bullets whizzed through the air like angry bees.

It was not far from this farmhouse that Iverson's brigade of South Carolinians made its way into a trap whence scarcely a quarter of it came out again. While gallantly advancing against a stone wall which sheltered a heavy Union force the Carolinians failed to notice the stealthy advance of a formidable body of blue-coats on their flank. All unsuspecting of danger from that quarter, the assailants pressed on gallantly breasting the storm of bullets, all eyes fixed on the wall they seek to carry, all hearts intent on setting the Stars and Bars where the general has ordered them established. Suddenly from the flank comes a thunderous volley and the men fall in rows. The Union brigade behind the stone wall rises and pours in its volley with deadly aim. The cross-fire does its work well. When the smoke blows away, only disorganized groups and squads of Confederates are seen standing where a moment before were well drilled and disciplined battalions pressing forward eagerly and confident of victory. It needed then no order for the Union troops to understand what to do. On the spur of the moment the soldiers leap the stone wall and rush down upon the bewildered men who stand amid the rows of dead. There is no resistance. White handkerchiefs appear all along the Confederate line, and what is left of Iverson's brigade is very soon disarmed and on its way to the Union rear. "The enemy charged," said Iverson in his official report, "in overwhelming force and captured nearly all that were left unhurt of the three regiments of my brigade. When I saw white handkerchiefs raised and my line of battle still lying down in position, I characterized the surrender as disgraceful; but when afterward I found that five hundred of my men were left lying dead and wounded, and in a line as straight as a dress parade, I exonerated the survivors and claim that they nobly fought and died without a man running to the rear."

But save for this notable bit of success, little triumph came to the Union arms that day. Everywhere the Confederates attacked in irresistible force. Ewell's troops went into the fight as fast as they arrived, and each fresh battalion added to the telling superiority of the Confederates in numbers. On the right of the Union line, the fighing was fiercest, for it was against that point that Ewell's rapidly arriving battalions were hurled as fast as they came up. It was there that one of the noblest types of the American soldier—Lieutenant Bayard Wilkeson—met his death in gallantly withstanding the persistent Confederate advance. Lieutenant Wilkeson was but a lad in years. When but seventeen years old he had received his commission. Two years he had spent in active service on the field. At Fredericksburg and at Chancellorsville he had smelt gunpowder and learned to look with calmness on wounds and death. He had long been the ranking officer in his battery, and had brought the soldiers under his command to so high a degree of proficiency and discipline that men forgot his youth in admiration of his soldierly ability.

So it happened that on this first day of the great battle, which was to prove the turning point in the war for the Union, the task of holding one of the most critical and decisive positions was left to this nineteen-year-old soldier. Four guns he had—light twelve-pound field pieces. With these he plunged gallantly into the conflict and for a

WILKESON AT GETTYSBURG.

time held in check the advancing troops of General Gordon. But the Confederate commander, soon discovering that his infantry was making no headway against Wilkeson's telling fire, brought up two batteries and posting them on a commanding hill ordered the cannoneers to silence or to drive away the spiteful little Union battery that was working such havoc in his ranks. Twelve guns were turned on Wilkeson's four cannon, and as the Confederate battery was posted on a hill which towered above the knoll on which his guns were posted the advantage of position, as well as in weight of metal, rested with the enemy. But though the solid shot and shell fell thick and fast among his guns and artillerymen, Wilkeson never faltered. Bestriding his well-trained horse, he rode about among the guns, speaking a word of encouragement here, giving an order there, never once losing his complete self-possession, and everywhere cheering his men up by his display of calm courage. Finally, seeing that the situation was becoming desperate, he spurred his horse to the front and sat there immovable and statuesque, seeking by this means to inspire his men with confidence. Animated by their commander's daring example, the men of the battery worked their guns with such rapidity and precision that the utmost efforts of the Confederate infantry failed to force the battery from its position. Through their field-glasses the officers of the Confederate artillery could clearly see that it was Wilkeson who was thus doggedly holding the Union cannoneers to their work. General Gordon himself pressed forward to discover what it was that thus delayed the advance of his lines. It needed but a glance to convince him that if the officer who so defiantly rode about among the Union guns could be disabled, the battery would soon be silenced.

"Turn your guns on that fellow on horseback," he said to the Confederate artillerymen. "When he is out of the way we can silence his cannon."

With twelve guns turned upon him Wilkeson could not long go unscathed. A rifle-shot struck his leg, cutting and tearing the flesh and shattering the bone. His horse fell to the ground with him. His comrades picked him up and started to bear him to the rear, but he ordered them to lay him on the ground where he could watch the progress of the conflict. No surgeon was on the field, and with his own hand the wounded youth twisted a handkerchief about his mangled limb to serve for a tourniquet, and with a jack-knife cut away the lacerated flesh and shattered bones of the leg. Fever came upon him and parching thirst took possession of him. An artilleryman went back to the well at the Almshouse, a few rods to the rear, and brought thence a canteen of cool water. Wilkeson's eyes brightened as he saw the messenger return with the water, but just as he took the canteen and was raising it eagerly to his lips, a wounded soldier lying near cried. "For God's sake give me some." Unmindful of his own suffering the young officer handed the canteen to his wounded neighbor, who drank greedily every drop it contained. Wilkeson smiled on the man, turned slightly, and was dead in a few minutes.

It was not long after Wilkeson was disabled when his battery was swept away, and soon thereafter it was evident that the Confederates were carrying all before them. On the right of the Union line, at the corner where the Eleventh and First corps joined in a right angle, everywhere save at one point where the blue-coats were stubbornly holding a position on Seminary Ridge, the Union lines were crumbling away, and stragglers in squads, and companies and regiments in fairly good order were marching away from the foe through the streets of Gettysburg. It looked at the moment as though the history of Fredericksburg and of Chancellorsville was to be repeated on the soil of Pennsylvania.

The First Corps, driven from its advanced position, had secured a strong position on Seminary Ridge, where behind a breastwork of rails the soldiers set their faces firmly toward the foe and for a time stayed his further progress. The corps had suffered dreadfully during the day's battle. In Wadsworth and Rowley's divisions full half the men were either killed or wounded. The Twenty-fourth Michigan had six color-bearers killed, among them the colonel of the regiment himself. General Paul was desperately wounded, a Confederate bullet passing through both of his eyes. But despite its losses the corps maintained its organization, and held its slender breastwork of rails against all comers for some time. Scales and Pender assaulted the position several times only to be driven back. In his report Scales declares that one time his line came within seventy-five feet of the Union works, and adds: "Here the fire was most severe. Every field-officer but one was killed or wounded." Not until the increasing numbers of the Confederates enabled them to stretch out and envelope the Union line on both flanks, did the gallant defenders of Seminary Ridge abandon their position, and retreat sullenly through the town toward Cemetery Ridge, whither all the shattered remnants of the Eleventh Corps were already proceeding. "As we passed through the town," writes General Doubleday, "pale and frightened women came out and offered us coffee and food, and implored us not to abandon them."

This, then, was the situation at sundown of July 1. The Federals had been driven from all their positions, to the position on the crest of Cemetery Ridge, where their reserves had been stationed throughout the battle, and which had been designated as the point at which the army should concentrate in case of defeat. General Hancock had arrived upon the field, with orders from Meade to take supreme command. He was well known to the Union troops, and his arrival inspired them with confidence, for they knew that if Hancock was on the field his division could not be far away. In fact the whole Union army was by this time within a few miles of the battle field. The Twelfth Corps under Slocum arrived about sundown and took up its position on Culp's Hill. The second corps arrived before midnight. The Third Corps was on the march all night and reached the field by eight o'clock the next morning. The Fifth and Sixth corps were still far away.

On the Confederate side the divisions of Hill and Ewell were up before sundown of the first day, while Longstreet reached the field during the night.

When on the afternoon of the first day the Union troops began their retreat to Cemetery Hill, the Confederates were in overwhelming numbers. General Lee, who had then just reached the field, saw clearly the advantage of numbers that his men then enjoyed, and discerned with equal certainty the vast advantage of position that the Federals would possess were they allowed to retain possession of Cemetery Hill. Accordingly he sent a courier to General Ewell directing him to assault the Union position if in his estimation a successful attack was practicable. But Ewell concluded that the assault would be hazardous, and accordingly failed to order it. Whether the attack could have been made successfully is indeed doubtful, but the fact remains that the retention of the position on the crest of Cemetery Hill enabled the Army of the Potomac during the next two days, not only to hold its ground against the most determined assaults of its enemies, but also to inflict upon Lee's army such prodigious damages as weakened that organization forever after. The power of the Confederacy was hopelessly crippled by the losses sustained in the vain attempts to carry Cemetery Hill in the battles of the second and third of July.

Therefore it is that though we find that during the first day's conflict the Confederates finally drove the Federals from every position which they actually tried to carry, and though the loss inflicted upon the Union forces was far in excess of that suffered by the men of the South, yet we cannot look upon the result of the day's fighting as a triumph for the Confederacy. The one commanding, decisive position on the field of battle remained in the hands of the Federals, and the history of the battles of the next two days will show that the posession of that position alone was worth all of the successes won by the Confederates on the first day of the battle of Gettysburg.

The story of the first day's battle is replete with exciting and romantic incidents. To tell of all the notable displays of personal courage on both sides would alone require a volume. Some few anecdotes, however, may be interesting.

Three such stories we quote upon the authority of General Doubleday. "Colonel Wheelock of the Ninty-seventh New York was cut off during the retreat of Robinson's divisions, and took refuge in a house," writes Doubleday. "A rebel lieutenant entered and called upon him to deliver his sword. This he declined to do, whereupon the lieutenant called in several of his men, formed them in line, took out his watch and said to the colonel: 'You are an old, gray-headed man and I dislike to kill you, but if you don't give up that sword in five minutes I shall order these men to blow your brains out.' When the time was up the colonel still refused to surrender. A sudden tumult at the door, caused by some prisoners attempting to escape, called the lieutenant off for a moment. When he returned the colonel had given up his sword to a girl in the house who had asked him for it, and she secreted it between two mattresses. He was then marched to the rear, but, being negligently guarded, escaped the same night and returned to his regiment."

Another incident which fell under General Doubleday's personal observation was the death of a mounted officer who came galloping up to Colonel Dawes of the Sixth Wisconsin regiment. From the man's firm carriage and composed demeanor the colonel thought that he came for orders, but the next moment was undeceived, for tearing open his vest the officer showed a gaping wound in his breast, and gasping out: "Tell them at home that I died like a man and a soldier," fell dead at the colonel's feet.

General A. P. Hill in his report bears testimony to the gallantry of some of the Union men who fought against him on that day. "A Yankee color-bearer floated his standard in the field," he writes, "and the regiment fought around it; and when at last it was obliged to retreat, the color-bearer went last of all, turning round now and then to shake his fist in the face of the advancing rebels. I was sorry when I saw him meet his doom." And General Doubleday tells of an artilleryman who was driving off with one of the guns of Stewart's battery just as the Confederates swooped down upon him. A Confederate officer, with his hand on the cannon, and his pistol within five feet of the driver's back, ordered him not to attempt to escape, but the gallant fellow lashed his horses into a gallop, and though he received his enemy's ball in his back, managed to carry the gun out of danger, falling lifeless from his saddle as soon as the Union lines were reached.

But full of exciting incidents as the first day's battle was, it was but the prelude to a still more exciting drama, and a still more bitter struggle for supremacy on the field of Gettysburg.

CHAPTER IX.

BATTLE OF GETTYSBURG. — LEE DETERMINES TO ATTACK. — LONGSTREET'S PROTEST. — THE BATTLEFIELD. — THE STUGGLE FOR LITTLE ROUND TOP. — THE ATTACK ON THE PEACH ORCHARD. — THE SACRIFICE OF BIGELOW'S BATTERY. — THE CHARGE OF WILCOX AND WRIGHT. — THE NIGHT ASSAULT ON THE UNION RIGHT. — CHARGE OF THE LOUISIANA TIGERS. — BATTLE OF THE THIRD DAY. — PICKETT'S GREAT CHARGE. — ITS REPULSE. — CLOSE OF THE BATTLE. — RETREAT OF THE CONFEDERATES.

ALL the country roads leading into Gettysburg were choked that July night with marching men, galloping horsemen, rumbling trains of cannon, ambulances and ammunition wagons. From the south and east the Federals; from the north and west the Confederates, were pressing on to Gettysburg. Accident had brought the foes into collision there, but the gauntlet had been thrown down and picked up. On a field of neither army's choosing, the destiny of the nation was to be fought out.

In the gray dawn of the 2d of July, Generals Lee and Longstreet rode to the crest of Seminary Ridge, and, through their fieldglasses scanned the Union position on Cemetery Hill. They saw the rows of cannon on the brow of the hill, the smoke of innumerable camp fires marking the situation of the Union troops already on the ground, the clouds of dust rising above the tree-tops everywhere betokening the rapid concentration of a great army.

Lee's blood was up. The successes of the day before, added to the almost uninterrupted series of victories won by his army when opposed to the Army of the Potomac, inspired him with confidence. He forgot that he had come into Pennsylvania with the determination to fight none but defensive battles. The tactical superiority of Meade's position daunted him not a whit.

"The enemy is there, and I am going to attack him there," he said with cool decision.

Longstreet demurred. "Why not swing around to his left," said he, "and interpose between Meade and Washington? Then we can force him to give us battle on grounds of our own choosing."

"No; they are there in position, and I am going to whip them or they are going to whip me."

Lee spoke with determination, and the colloquy was ended.

Meantime there had been some doubt in the mind of General Meade as to the wisdom of continuing the battle on the field of Gettysburg. Behind Pipe Creek, a small stream a few miles south of Gettysburg, the engineers of the Army of the Potomac had laid out a line of defense, and all Meade's strategy had been planned with the view of inducing Lee to fight him at that point. When Hancock was sent forward about the close of the first day's fighting to take the command, it was with orders from Meade to withdraw the army to the Pipe Creek line. But a staff officer who was present on Hancock's arrival declares that that officer said to General Howard that he had been ordered to choose the Pipe Creek line, but that he thought the line then occupied, extending from Culp's Hill along Cemetery Ridge to Round Top, was "the strongest position by nature upon which to fight a battle" that he had ever seen, and accordingly determined to stay and fight it out there. To this decision Meade, upon his arrival a little after midnight, agreed.

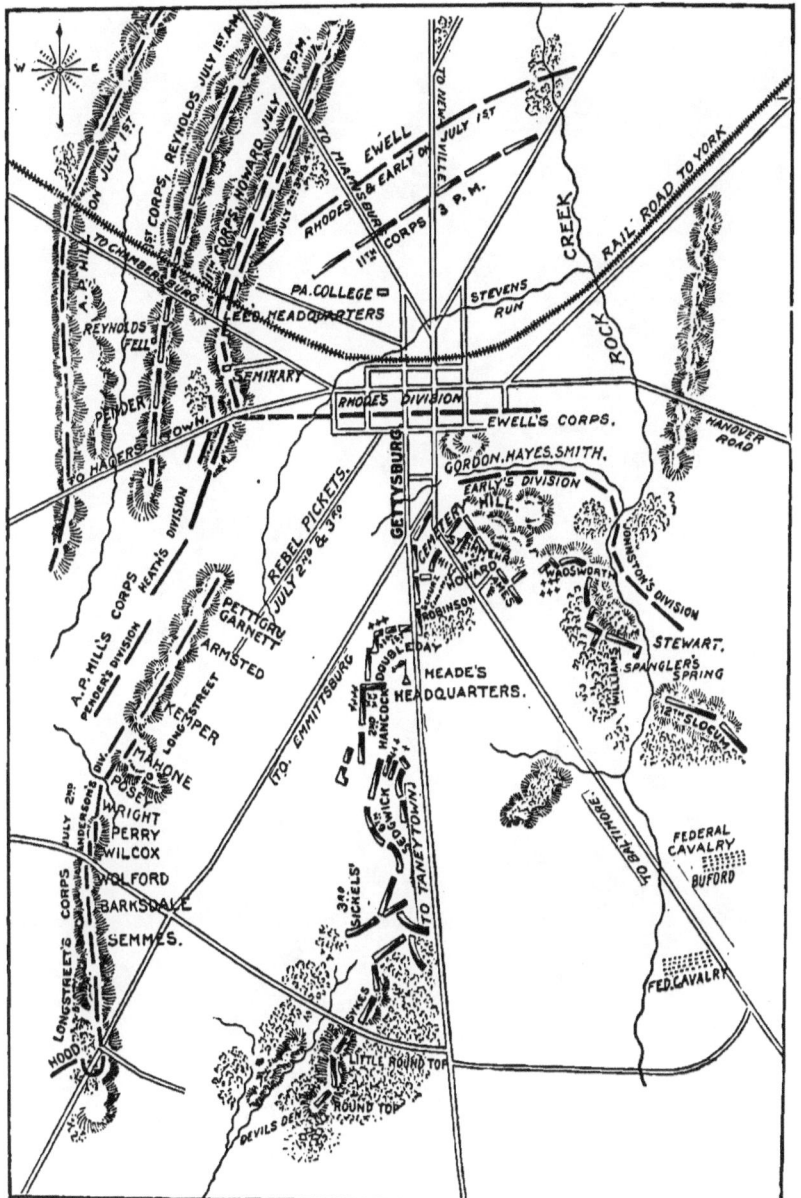

PLAN OF THE BATTLE OF GETTYSBURG.

The field of battle on the second and third days of the battle then lay wholly south of the town. A glance at the map opposite will make clear the positions held by the antagonists on the morning of the 2d of July. All along the crest of Seminary Ridge between the Emmitsburg and the Fairfield roads extended the Confederate line. Longstreet was farthest south; A. P. Hill joining him on the north. At Hill's right the line made a sharp bend to the east, Ewell's corps holding the streets of Gettysburg and extending eastward on the Hanover road. The Confederate lines faced east and south. Before them stretched away a fertile plain for the space of a half a mile. Wheat-fields, pastures, peach orchards, cosy farm-houses nestling among the trees, spacious farms well filled with garnered crops all told how the valley had prospered before the blight of war fell upon it. At its farther edge the plain sloped gently up to the petty acclivity called Culp's Hill, the high land which took its name from the cemetery which made its green crest glisten with white gravestones, and the two bolder hills called Round Top and Little Round Top. Along this series of hills extended the Union line. Its general contour was something like that of a horseshoe with unequal arms.

It was on the extreme left of the Union line that the fiercest fighting of the second day's battle occurred. As the battle of the first day was chiefly for the possession of Missionary Ridge, so on the second day Little Round Top was the point for which the warring hosts did battle. Two considerations led Lee to choose the Union left for his point of attack. Could he but once establish his batteries on Little Round Top he would hold all the Union lines at his mercy. Moreover General Sickles, who was stationed on the Union left, had been forced by the configuration of the country to arrange his lines in the form of a right angle—a formation that always invites attack.

It was against this angle that General Lee ordered Longstreet to hurl his corps. Meantime Ewell and Hill were to attack the Federals in their immediate front to prevent Meade from sending troops from other parts of his line to Sickles's aid. The order was given at night on the first of July, but Longstreet's attack did not come until four o'clock next day. We shall see that had it been made early in the morning Gettysburg might have been a field of sorrow for the Union.

Here then is the battle field on which Longstreet and Sickles are to contend for the mastery. A straight road—the Emmitsburg pike—extended up the valley northeast toward Gettysburg. At a point about opposite Little Round Top another road intersects it, and in the corner thus formed was a peach orchard—a celebrated spot that little grove of fruit trees was destined to become, for right there was Sickles's angle; the right wing of his corps extended up the Emmitsburg road toward Gettysburg, while the left wing extended down the cross road toward Little Round Top. South of this road is a wheat-field, and south of the wheat-field and at the base of Little Round Top is a craggy heap of boulders called Devil's Den.

All day the roads were choked with Longstreet's men moving over toward the Union left flank. Great pains were taken to conceal the movement from the Federals, and in this effort much time was lost by choosing circuitous routes, narrow lanes, and rugged byways. Notwithstanding this caution the vigilant signal officers on the crest of Round Top signaled to General Meade that large bodies of the enemy's infantry were moving toward the Union left flank. Doubtless this intelligence did much to dissuade Meade from his already half formed purpose of taking the offensive himself and assaulting Lee.

Four o'clock found Longstreet's corps in position; Hood on the right, McLaws on the left. The men were in good spirits and eager for action. Outnumbering their immediate adversaries and greatly outflanking Sickles, the prospects of the Confederates for victory were excellent.

Fifty-four guns now begin to play upon Sickles's unfortunate angle in the peach orchard. The whizzing cannon-shot enfilade both lines. From the orchard itself and from the crests held by the Federals the Union guns respond with spirit. The Confederate artillerymen looked for an easy time of it, but soon discover that the rapidity and precision with which the Union guns are served come near making amends for the disadvantages of the Federal position. "The fight was longer and hotter than I expected," writes General Alexander, Lee's chief of artillery. "So accurate was the enemy's fire that two of my guns were fairly dismounted, and the loss of men was so great that I had to ask General Barksdale, whose brigade was lying down close behind in the wood, for help to handle the heavy 24-pounder howitzers of Moody's battery. He gave me permission to call for volunteers, and in a minute I had eight good fellows, of whom, alas! we buried two that night and sent to the hospital three others mortally or severely wounded."

While the guns were roaring on both sides, and before the Confederate infantry had advanced from the shelter of the woods to make the grand assault which all knew was coming, General Warren rode over from Meade's headquarters to examine Sickles's line. "I rode on until I came to Little Round Top," he writes. "There were no troops on it, and it was used as a signal station. I saw that this was the key to the whole position, and that our troops in the woods in front of it could not see the ground in front of them, so that the enemy would come upon them before they would be aware of it. The long line of woods on the west side of the Emmitsburg road (which road was on a ridge) furnished an excellent place for the enemy to form out of sight, so I requested the captain of a rifle battery just in front of Little Round Top to fire a shot into these woods. He did so, and as the shot went whistling through the air the sound of it reached the enemy's troops and caused every one to look in the direction of it This motion revealed to me the glistening of gun-barrels and bayonets of the enemy's line of battle already formed and far outflanking the position of any of our own troops, so that the line of his advance from his right to Little Round Top was unopposed."

Startled by this discovery, Warren sent a courier galloping to General Meade with an earnest request that a division at least be sent to hold Little Round Top. Meantime he tried to hold the hill-top by strategy. He saw a large part of Hood's division advancing upon him—for Hood was aware of the defenseless condition of Little Round Top and was anxious to seize upon it—and he knew that his time for preparation was short. So telling the signal officer, who alone occupied the crest of the hill, to keep waving his flags as though signaling to a heavy force in the rear, Warren picked his way down the steep hillside covered with stones, to where he saw a body of Union troops marching along the road toward the peach orchard. The troops proved to be Warren's old brigade. General Weed, who then commanded it, had gone on ahead, but Warren convinced Colonel O'Rorke of the vital importance of Little Round Top, and took upon himself the responsibility of detaching O'Rorke's regiment from the marching column and hurrying it to the crest of the hill.

Meantime, unknown to Warren, Colonel Vincent with a brigade of the Fifth Corps was hastening to the defense of Little Round Top. Making no attempt to scale the hill, he posted his brigade on the southern slope toward which the Confederates were rapidly advancing. Michigan, New York, Maine and Pennsylvania troops were in Vincent's command. The boulders and outcropping ledges of rock with which the field is plentifully besprinkled greatly impeded the Confederate advance and afforded shelter for the defenders. Nevertheless the men in gray trudged boldly forward, passing through the zone of fire of a battery posted so as to enfilade their lines, breasting the pelting storm of bullets that came singing in their faces, sheltering themselves behind boulders whenever occasion offered long enough to load and fire a hasty shot, but all the time pressing onward and upward toward the thin line that stood between them and the crest of Little Round Top. "Sometimes the Federals would hold one side of the large boulders on the slope until the Confederates occupied the other," writes General Law, whose troops were engaged in the assault. In some cases my men, with reckless daring, mounted to the top of

CLIMBING LITTLE ROUND TOP.

the large rocks in order to get a better view and to deliver their fire with better effect. One of these, Sergeant Barbee of the Texas brigade, having reached a rock a little in advance of the line, stood erect on the top of it loading and firing as coolly as if unconscious of danger, while the air around him was fairly swarming with bullets. He soon fell helpless from several wounds; but he held his rock, lying upon the top of it until the litter-bearers carried him off."

So fighting their way from stone to stone the men of Law's division gradually made their way toward the top of the hill, forcing Vincent back before them. Near the crest the Federals made a determined stand. They met and repelled charges with the point of the bayonet; muskets were clubbed; pistols fired at point-blank range; jagged stones even were used as weapons of war. Once the Twentieth Maine with a superb charge swept the enemy from the hill, but the ground thus gained for the Union was soon lost again, for the Texans returned with dogged pertinacity to the assault.

There was a reason for the stubbornness with which Vincent's men clung to their position. As they were forced back higher up the hillside the commanding features of the position became evident to the least skilled soldier in the ranks. All knew that with a Confederate force established on the crest of the hill, the whole Union position would be indefensible. They knew too that reënforcements were coming to their aid. Up the northern slope of the hill even at the moment O'Rorke's infantry was marching, followed by Hazlitt's battery. Seldom were guns ever dragged over so difficult a route. The steep hillside, cut up with gullies and obstructed everywhere with huge rocks, seemed impassable for heavy cannon. But the artillerymen put their shoulders to the wheels, levers wielded by a score of men at a time were brought into play, long ropes were fastened to the gun-carriages at which whole companies tugged, the straining horses were skillfully guided, and so after long and strenuous effort the battery swung into place on the crest of the hill.

It was none too soon. With triumphant yells the Confederates were breaking through Vincent's line at half a dozen points. A few minutes more and they would have been in undisputed possession of the crest. But O'Rorke's regiment gave them a volley, and Hazlitt's guns opened with canister. The assailants, already sorely weakened by their struggle up the slope, were dazed by this sudden and unexpected addition to their enemy's ranks. They wavered but only for a moment, then returned to their work with renewed spirit. A contest at short range followed. Hazlitt's battery, which had so gallantly made its way to the crest of the hill, soon found that it could do but little execution owing to the steep slope of the hillside. Still the guns were kept flashing and roaring, for the knowledge that they had artillery with them while the enemy had none gave added courage to the Union soldiers. Soon the short range fighting began to tell. Men fell fast on both sides. The gallant O'Rorke—only two years out of West Point—was shot dead. General Weed was struck to the ground with a mortal wound, and groaned as he lay dying on the stony ground, "I would rather die here than that the rebels should gain an inch of this ground." Lieutenant Hazlitt bent over his dying commander to catch his last words, and he too fell a victim to a flying bullet and was stretched dead across the body of his chief. Vincent too was quickly laid low. Though the losses of the Federals were heavy, it soon became evident that the fight was going against the Confederates. Reënforcements were necessary to enable them to hold the position they had won on the hill, but no reënforcements came. The Federals saw the signs of weakness spreading in the Confederate ranks, and redoubled their efforts. Faster the cannon roared; the rattle of the musketry grew louder. It became the turn of the Federals to advance, and they pressed the foe before them down the hill, until a final grand charge by the Twentieth Maine swept the last Texan and the last fluttering Confederate flag from the slope of Little Round Top. Near the foot of the hill, amid the heaped-up boulders and crags that formed the rocky fastness called by the country folk "Devil's Den," the disappointed men of the South rallied, and from that position could not be dislodged. We shall see them on the morrow renewing, from that point of attack, the fierce and fruitless struggle for Little Round Top.

While the men with muskets and cold steel had thus been struggling for the mastery on the hill-side, the battle field about the peach orchard was shrouded in the smoke of the cannon, and the shouts of the soldiers and the rattle of the musketry were lost in the thunderous roar of the artillery. Eleven Confederate batteries were pouring a rapid and effective fire into the peach orchard, where seven Union batteries together with Graham's brigade of infantry were posted. Other Union batteries on the road by the orchard added their chorus to the general din. The air was full of sulphur fumes and flying missiles. Trees were stripped of their leaves; fences demolished. There seemed no chance for a living creature to pass unscathed through that rushing hurricane of lead and iron.

Nevertheless in the main positions must be carried and battles won by the infantry. However effective a cannonade may be, its result are trivial unless promptly followed up by an infantry attack. Accordingly while the Confederate guns were pounding away at the Union line, the brigades of Barksdale and Kershaw moved forward to the assault; the former directing its attacks against the angle in the peach orchard, the latter advancing toward the road leading east, along which the Union divisions of De Trobriand and Graham were arrayed with a cannon at almost every spot where a gun could be made effective.

With a tempest of missiles beating in their faces the Union soldiers gallantly held their ground. Stone walls gave a partial shelter to the infantry, for crouched behind them the soldiers could load and fire their muskets while exposing but a small portion of their bodies to the bullets of the foe. But the cannoneers working with sponge and with rammer, carrying cartridges and shells, or laboriously shifting the position of their guns, were wholly unprotected, and upon them the fire of the enemy's guns, which were roaring and flaming on two commanding ridges, fell with fearful effect. Sturdily the blue-coats held to their work. More than once, when Barksdale and Kershaw were on the very verge of success, did the hurtling grape-shot from the flaming muzzles of the guns of Bigelow, Phillip, Ricketts, Hart, and other noted artillerists check them and send them sullenly back to cover. The precision with which the guns were served, no less than the rapidity of their fire, was remarkable. General McLaws declares that he knew of a single shell from one of these guns which burst in the center of a company of thirty-seven Confederates and killed or wounded thirty of them.

But human flesh and blood, and for that matter the wood and iron of the cannon too, could not long withstand the enfilading of the Confederate batteries. The men began to fall fast among the guns. The batteries were soon short-handed, but the round shot from the enemy's cannon dismounted a gun or two and left their crews free to aid in working the other guns. Soon the heavy losses began to tell. The Union fire slackened, and Barksdale's men seized on the opportunity to make a rush and carry the peach orchard. Before them the Federals retreated slowly, firing as they went. In the withdrawal of the Union artillery Bigelow's battery, the Ninth Massachusetts, was particularly conspicuous. So persistently was this battery held to its place that, when it became evident that it must be withdrawn, there was no longer time to limber up for flight. "We can retire by prolonge," said Bigelow, and the order was soon given. Long ropes were stretched from the limbers to the gun-carriages, while the gunners all the time kept up their deadly work and the cannon belched out their spiteful messages of death. So with the horses harnessed to the limbers, and the limbers attached to the gun carriages by long cables, the men fought their guns until the enemy was near enough to threaten their capture. Then a word of command, a cracking of whips and a rumble and rush of hoofs, and away went the battery a hundred yards or more. Then a halt, and the storm of canister was again launched full in the faces of the pursuing foe.

So with the angle at the peach orchard broken by the concentrating attack of the Confederates, the infantry, sharpshooters, and the battery all fall back from the orchard and the road to a new position around the farm-house of Mr. Trostle, north of the road and east of the orchard. Here a furious encounter took place. The guns were planted in Trostle's dooryard. The few infantry supports that remained to the devoted batteries were aligned in the garden and barnyard. The Confederates thought they had an easy prey before them and pressed on boldly.

But the position at Trostle's was a mere outpost of the main Union line which was rapidly forming on the ridge behind. Still it was an outpost which must be held tenaciously until that line could be formed.

"There is no one to support you," said McGilvery to Bigelow, "but you must remain and hold this ground. Sacrifice your battery if need be, but keep them back until I get some guns on the ridge back there."

Then he galloped away, and was soon hurrying twenty-five guns into position. Before they could be put in place, however, the foe swept up in front of Bigelow's position and was not to be kept back by grape or shrapnel. A narrow brook—Plum Run the people thereabouts called it—flowed between Bigelow and the advancing enemy, and for a time the artillerymen with fierce energy were able to keep their assailants on the further side of this natural barrier. But when the cannoneers began to fall fast around their guns so that the fire of the battery slackened, one gray regiment—the Twenty-first Mississippi—pushed its way across the run and pressed on to where the few cannon that had not been silenced were still hoarsely booming. Right bravely the men of Bigelow's battery stood to their guns, while from the ridge behind the cannon brought up by McGilvery opened fire. Still the Confederates advanced. They made their way in among the guns, which Bigelow's men were by this time trying to drag from the field. Hand-to-hand fighting followed. One Confederate was killed while trying to spike a gun. Another was knocked down with a handspike. Rammers, sponge staffs, the butts of muskets were all used as weapons, and the struggling crowd surged about the guns dealing fierce and cruel blows. Outnumbered from the start, the artillerists nevertheless fought desperately to save their pieces, but all was of no avail. The battery was sacrificed, as McGilvery had foreseen it might be when he posted it in that exposed position. Bigelow was severely wounded, and lay under one of the gun-carriages while the fighting went on around him. Of the other three commissioned officers one was killed and one mortally wounded. Of the 104 men who went into the fight 28 were killed or wounded. Eighty horses drew the battery to the field; 65 of them were shot. But the bitter resistance the battery had opposed to the Confederate advance had had its effect, and when the victors swept on expecting to seize the ridge behind Bigelow's guns they were met with so fierce a reception from the row of cannon that McGilvery had by that time posted there, that all recoiled and drifted in confusion back to the further side of Plum Run. That point on the Union line was not again seriously menaced that day.

Meantime there had been bitter fighting at all parts of the field. Barksdale, intrepidly leading his men, had been struck down with a mortal wound. He was brought into the Union lines and there died, says General Doubleday, "like a brave man, with dignity and resignation." The Union troops too suffered the loss of one of their general officers, for General Sickles, while hurrying toward the peach orchard, was struck by a bullet which shattered his leg. The injured limb was afterward amputated.

From this time forward until the day's conflict ended the Confederates pushed the Union troops back steadily before them. But it was from no very commanding position that the men in blue were thus dislodged. Driven slowly from their outposts, they clung stubbornly to the ridge that formed the connecting line between Cemetery Hill and Little Round Top. That ridge was the key to the whole field; it was the key to the whole situation. Let the Confederates once gain possession of it and the Union army would be dismembered, cut in twain, and its communications would be in the hands of the enemy. This the Federals knew, and right doggedly did they set their teeth and oppose an unflinching front to the advancing foe. In the work of beating back the Confederates General Hancock won golden laurels. He had succeeded to General Sickles's command when that officer was wounded, and set himself about the task of strengthening his line, patching the weak places, and encouraging the officers with such zeal, that his activity and success on this day, coupled with his determined resistance of the fierce Confederate charges of the day following, earned for him the sobriquet of "Hancock the Superb." General Meade too was on the field in person, exposing himself fearlessly, and while so doing had his horse shot beneath him by a bullet which narrowly missed the rider.

Once only was the Union control of the ridge put in serious jeopardy. The Confederate brigades of Wilcox and Wright, late in the evening when the twilight was deepening into night, pushed up the slope in the teeth of the Union fire, captured several Union guns, and for the moment drove the Federal defenders from their position. It was a moment fraught with intense peril to the Union cause. The center of the Federal line was pierced. The Confederates were established on the crest of the ridge—that ridge the possession of which was of vital importance to the success of Meade's plans. The victors, elated with triumph, began to turn upon the retreating Federals their captured cannon. Fleet messengers galloped away to bear to Meade the dire tidings that the center had been pierced.

But the Confederate triumph was destined to be short-lived. Had Wright and Wilcox been supported the battle of Gettysburg would have been won for the South then and there. But though they held to their hard-won position with despairing tenacity there came no fresh regiments to their aid. And so when Webb's brigade, seconded by Doubleday's division, fell furiously upon them there was nothing to do but to fall back, sacrificing the captured guns and the precious position on the ridge.

General Doubleday thus relates an incident of Wright's charge: "As they approached the ridge a Union battery limbered up and galloped off. The last gun was delayed, and the cannoneer, with a long line of muskets pointing at him within a few feet, deliberately drove off the field. The Georgians manifested their admiration for his bravery by crying out 'Don't shoot,' and not a musket was fired at him."

After Wright was thus driven from his hard-won foothold in the very center of the Union position, the fury of the Confederate assaults in that part of the field abated greatly. Night was now fairly upon the field. The soldiers saw that no decisive movement could be accomplished before the next rising of the sun, and so the cannons' hoarse voices and the sharp reports of the muskets, the shrill yells of the Confederates and the sturdy cheers of the Union troops died gradually away. A sort of peace—a peace only less terrible than active war—reigned over the bloody slope of Little Round Top and the ensanguined fields about the peach orchard and the Trostle farmhouse.

But to other points of the field, which throughout the day had seen no fiercer fighting than the noisy but almost harmless long range artillery duel, the setting of the sun brought the fury of the charge and the mad turmoil of the hand-to-hand struggles of heavy detachments of infantry.

It was late in the evening when the blue-coated defenders of the trenches on the northern slope of Cemetery Hill saw the Confederate line of battle emerge from the outskirts of Gettysburg and push forward up the slope. It was the attack which Lee had ordered should be made simultaneously with Longstreet's assault upon the Union right. But so far from being made simultaneously, Longstreet's attack was almost over and his columns had been repulsed from most of the decisive positions they strove to carry, before the advance against Cemetery Hill was begun.

The Confederate cannon had been pounding away at the slender earthworks that crested the hill all the afternoon, and when at sundown their fire ceased, the defenders thought for a time that the close of day had brought a welcome truce. But soon a long line of men clad in butternut gray appeared from the grove whence the guns had a few moments before been roaring. The troops of Early and of Johnson were in that line of battle,—prominent among the former that body of dashing soldiers known as the Louisiana Tigers. It fell to the lot of the Tigers to charge straight up the hill into the very center of the Union line. Right gallantly did the dashing fellows discharge their perilous duty. As with a shrill yell they started up the hill the batteries behind them, that had ceased firing to let the "Tigers" pass, now opened again and were soon throwing solid shot and shell into the Union position. But the Federal batteries were now in full cry. Disregarding altogether the enemy's artillery, the blue-clad cannoneers turned their pieces on that swiftly advancing line of gray. More than a score of guns were flaming and smoking and thundering on the brow of that green hill. Though sorely stricken by the pelting storm of bullets, the charging line swept swiftly onward. The "Tigers" were born soldiers and veterans of half a dozen fields; encouraging each other and closing up the gaps in their lines, they pressed forward until, sorely shattered but still formidable in numbers and full of fight, they rushed right in among the Union guns. Weidrich's battery was overrun in an instant, but the men of Ricketts's battery were veterans and stood manfully by their pieces. Muskets, sponge-staffs, rammers, fence-rails, and stones, were all used by the artillerists with good effect. "The batteries were penetrated," says Doubleday, "but would not surrender. Dearer than life itself to the cannoneer is the gun he serves, and these brave men fought hand-to-hand with handspikes, rammers, staves, and even stones. They shouted 'Death on the soil of our native State rather than lose our guns!'"

With all their gallantry the Union artillerists could not long have maintained themselves against the furious onslaught of their foes, who came on in overwelming numbers. But the Louisiana men were not destined to reap the full reward of their dashing charge. The noise of the conflict coming to the ears of Hancock, he sent a fresh brigade to the scene, which arrived just as the Federal resistance began to grow feeble. At the same moment Stevens's battery opened fire with canister upon the unprotected Confederate left. While the Federal resistance thus gained in vigor and effectiveness, there came no reënforcements to the aid of the Confederates. Disheartened, maimed, and bleeding they fell back over the ground they had so dashingly carried. Of the 1750 "Louisiana Tigers" who went with brave hearts and tense nerves into the fight only 150 returned.

On the extreme right of the Union line, meanwhile, the Confederates advanced against the Union works on Culp's Hill. They made some progress there but were held in check by a small Federal force until nightfall, when hostilities ceased. But had the Confederate attack at that part of the field been vigorously pressed, disaster might have come upon the whole Union army, for at no point was the Federal line so weak, and with that line once pierced Meade's whole army would have been thrown into confusion and irretrievably wrecked.

Such were the chief features of the fighting on the second day, sketched in brief. It was dark when the battle ended. Nearly 40,000 men were then lying dead or wounded upon the battle field. The survivors were huddling about their flickering camp fires, pacing their lonely picket lines, or eating with scanty relish their frugal rations. All knew that in but a few hours the fighting would begin again. No decisive advantage had come to either Meade or Lee from the day's battle. The Confederates had gained much, but the Federals still held the positions the continued possession of which meant victory. The two Round Tops and Cemetery Ridge were still in the hands of the men in blue. Until Lee could wrest from them the mastery of this line of defense, all his successes on the field of Gettysburg were worthless.

There was little chance for sleep that night. In General Meade's

AROUND THE CAMP FIRE.

headquarters were gathered all the corps commanders of the Army of the Potomac. To retreat or to stay and fight it out was the question there presented for their consideration. All voted that the ground should be held.

General Lee for his part held no council of war. He knew wherein he had been successful during the day, and his successes encouraged him. He saw wherein he had been unsuccessful, and his failures only stimulated him to prepare for renewing the combat with still greater determination on the morrow. All night he was busy issuing orders for the concentration of the Confederate artillery where it could bear directly upon the point against which he proposed to direct a charge which has become one of the most famous of all the great exploits of war. Toward morning Longstreet came to urge again that the direct attack should be abandoned and an attempt made to move around Meade's left flank.

"No," said Lee, "I am going to take them where they are on Cemetery Hill. I want you to take Pickett's division and make the attack. I will reënforce you by two divisions of the Third Corps."

"That will give me fifteen thousand men," responded Longstreet. "I have been a soldier, I may say, from the ranks up to the position I now hold. I have been in pretty much all kinds of skirmishes from those of two or three soldiers up to those of an army corps, and I think I can safely say there never was a body of fifteen thousand men who could make that attack successfully."

But Longstreet's counsel went unheeded. Lee had determined to assault Meade in his stronghold. Strategy he discarded. The fighting of the two first days had redounded to the advantage of the Confederates. The great Virginia general now proposed to deal one ponderous blow that should settle the conflict.

If the tactics and the operations of the first two days which saw the great armies grappling on the field of Gettysburg were confused and complicated, the plan of the third day's battle was simple enough.

General Lee's plan contemplated simply a furious cannonade of the Federal position on Cemetery Hill, to be followed by a desperate charge of 15,000 men against that position. The divisions of Pickett, Pettigrew, and Trimble, composed largely of fresh troops, were chosen to form the charging body. All night the Confederate chief of artillery was busy posting the artillery where it could most effectively support the charge. Morning saw every hill crowned with a Confederate battery. For two miles—from the town to the peach orchard—the long line of cannon extended, plainly visible from the Union lines across the plain. When Meade's general officers gazed through their field-glasses upon the spectacle, they fathomed Lee's purpose at once. All knew that it meant a pounding cannonade followed by a charge.

One hundred and thirty-eight cannon the Confederates had in position to bear upon Cemetery Hill and the connecting ridge. To respond to this fire there were seventy-seven cannon. These are the orders General Hunt, Meade's chief of artillery, issued for the direction of the Union artillerists in the impending battle: "Beginning at the right I instructed the chiefs of artillery and battery commanders to withhold their fire for fifteen or twenty minutes after the cannonade commenced, then to concentrate their fire, with all possible accuracy, on those batteries which were most destructive to us, but slowly, so that when the enemy's ammunition was exhausted, we should have sufficient left to meet the assault."

All through the morning there was skirmishing and sharp fighting between the lines of the two armies. At one point a large brick barn attracted the attention of the hostile pickets, each of whom wished to take advantage of its shelter. The Confederates gained it first, and the bullets that came flying from their rifles soon stung the Federals into action. Some Union cannon were turned upon the barn, but as the Confederates held their ground manfully a Connecticut regiment was sent down to drive them out. Other Confederates came to the aid of their comrades. There was fighting around the barn, and under the spreading trees of the orchard that adjoined it. But at last the Connecticut men gained entrance to the building, set it afire, and retreated, leaving the Confederates in possession of the surroundings of the blazing structure.

On the extreme right of the Union line, too, the fighting began at an early hour. It will be remembered that the Confederates under Johnson had won a position on the slope of Culp's Hill. From this position it was essential that they should be dislodged, and that task was undertaken by Geary's division. As Johnson had no artillery, and was prevented by the nature of the ground from bringing any up, Geary had easy work of it. Despite the strenuous efforts of the Confederates—among whom the members of the famous "Stonewall Brigade" were conspicuous—they were soon driven away, and by eleven o'clock the Union line was again established on Culp's Hill.

But all this was but the preliminary mutterings of the great storm that was to make the 3d of July, 1863, memorable in the annals of war. Pickett's men were being massed opposite the ridge. Pettigrew and Trimble were getting their troops into position to follow closely in Pickett's rear. Batteries were galloping along the road and across the fields seeking positions whence they could turn upon the Union lines a flood of deadly missiles before which no living thing could stand. Two guns fired by the Washington Artillery were to give the signal for opening fire. It was 1:30 P.M. when a courier from General Longstreet came galloping to where the Washington Artillery was stationed in the famous peach orchard, with a note: "Let the batteries open," it said; "order great care and precision in firing." Instantly the word was passed to the gunners, and the two signal guns boomed out. Both pieces had been carefully trained on a Union battery some thousand yards away, and the shot from each exploded a caisson in that battery. The echoes had scarcely time to die away before all the Confederate guns burst into full cry. The din was deafening. The concussions shook the earth as though the hidden forces of nature were struggling beneath its surface. The air was full of flying missiles. "Every size and form of shell known to British and to American gunnery shrieked, whirled, moaned, and whistled and wrathfully fluttered over our ground," wrote Samuel Wilkeson, father of the young artilleryman who died so bravely upon the first day of the battle. "As many as six in a second, constantly two in a second, bursting and screaming over and around headquarters, made a very hell of fire that amazed the oldest officers. They burst in the yard—burst next to the fence, on both sides garnished as usual with hitched horses of aides and orderlies. The fastened animals reared and plunged with terror. Then one fell and then another—sixteen lay dead and mangled before the firing ceased, still fastened by their halters. These brute victims of a cruel war touched all hearts. . . . A shell tore up the little step at the headquarters cottage and ripped bags of oats as with a knife. Another carried off one of its two pillars. Soon a spherical case burst opposite the open door. Another ripped through the low garret. Shells through the two lower rooms. A shell in the chimney that fortunately did not explode. Shells in the yard; the air thicker and fuller with the howling and whirring of these infernal missiles."

From this heavy fire the Union batteries suffered severely. No less than eleven caissons were blown up, and the explosions cost many lives. General Meade, too, was forced to abandon his headquarters and seek a more protected spot. But the Union infantry was all well sheltered, and though the Confederate guns maintained a rapid fire, the Union line of defense was not seriously weakened.

While the cannonade was progressing the Confederates were making ready for the charge. General Lee remained at headquarters. He had issued his orders for the direction of the battle. There now remained nothing for him to do but to stay where he could be found readily by couriers bringing reports of the progress of the battle. General Longstreet, to whom the immediate direction of the charge fell, did not like the plan. Ever since the battle opened, two days earlier, he had opposed Lee's ideas, and urged fighting a defensive battle only. Now that the time had come to order a desperate charge—to send

15,000 men across a broad plain and up a slope raked by the crossfire of a long line of hostile cannon — he was fearful and apprehensive of disaster. He strove to shift the responsibility, and sent a note to General Alexander, the Confederate chief of artillery, directing that officer to use his judgment to determine the most advantageous moment for Pickett to charge.

"If, as I infer from your note," responded General Alexander, "there is any alternative to this attack it should be carefully considered before opening our fire, for it will take all the artillery ammunition we have left to test this one thoroughly, and if the result is unfavorable we will have none left for another effort. And even if this is entirely successful it can only be so at a very bloody cost."

But Longstreet's answer was a curt note directing Alexander to order Pickett forward as soon as the enemy's artillery should show signs of distress before the continuous fire of the Confederate guns.

But while Longstreet and Alexander doubted the possibility of a successful charge across that shot-swept valley, other Confederate officers were more sanguine. "Pickett seemed glad to have the chance," writes a soldier who was with him that day. And General Wright, whose mettle was tested on the second day of the battle, responded to General Alexander's doubts as to whether the ridge could be won: "It is not so hard to *go* there as it looks; I was nearly there with my brigade yesterday. The trouble is to *stay* there. The whole Yankee army is there in a bunch."

Alexander was somewhat encouraged. "When our artillery fire is at its best I shall order Pickett to charge," he wrote to Longstreet.

Let us allow General Alexander himself to tell the story of what followed: "Before the cannonade opened I had made up my mind to give Pickett the order to advance within fifteen or twenty minutes after it began," he writes. "But when I looked at the full development of the enemy's batteries and knew that his infantry was generally protected from our fire by stone walls and swells of the ground, I could not bring myself to give the word. It seemed madness to launch infantry into that fire, with nearly three-quarters of a mile to go at mid-day under a July sun. I let the fifteen minutes pass, and twenty and twenty-five, hoping vainly for something to turn up. Then I wrote to Pickett: 'If you are coming at all you must come at once, or I cannot give you proper support; but the enemy's fire has not slackened at all; at least eighteen guns are still firing from the cemetery itself.' Five minutes after sending that message the enemy's fire suddenly began to slacken, and the guns in the cemetery limbered up and vacated the position.

"We Confederates often did such things as that to save our ammunition for use against infantry, but I had never before seen the Federals withdraw their guns simply to save them up for the infantry fight. So I said, 'If he does not run fresh batteries in there in five minutes this is our fight.' I looked anxiously with my glass, and the five minutes passed without a sign of life on the deserted position, still swept by our fire and littered with dead men and horses, and fragments of disabled carriages. Then I wrote Pickett urgently: 'For God's sake come quick. The eighteen guns are gone; come quick or my ammunition wont let me support you properly.'"

We, who have read General Hunt's instructions to the Union artillerymen, know that the eighteen guns were withdrawn merely to save them for the more important work of repelling the charge that all knew was coming. But the Confederates did not suspect this and thought the guns were silenced and a gap made through which their regiments could press on to victory. Pickett carried Alexander's note to Longstreet, who read it and said nothing.

"Shall I advance, sir?" asked Pickett.

Still dreading to order so desperate a charge, still convinced of its futility, Longstreet made no verbal answer, but merely bowed in token of assent.

"I am going to move forward, sir," said Pickett proudly, and then rode back to his troops, that were soon put in motion. Longstreet rode after him and was soon at General Alexander's side. "I don't want to make this attack," he said. "I would stop it now but that General Lee ordered it and expects that it should go on. I don't see how it can succeed."

While the two officers were speaking, the long line of gray-clad men swept grandly out from the shelter of the trees and pushed out upon the open hillside. "There they come! There comes the infantry!" cried the soldiers in the Union lines opposite. The magnificence of the spectacle impressed all beholders. Even those who were about to feel the shock of those advancing gray lines were thrilled with admiration for the valor which animated the men who marched with Pickett. This is how the scene is described by a lieutenant-colonel of Ohio volunteers:

"They moved up splendidly, deploying into column as they crossed the long sloping interval between the Second Corps and their base. At first it looked as though their line of march would sweep our position, but as they advanced their direction lay considerably to our left; but soon a strong line with flags directed its march immediately upon us. . . . . We changed our front, and taking position by a fence facing the left flank of the advancing column of rebels, the men were ordered to fire into their flank at will. Hardly a musket had been fired at this time. The front of the column was nearly up the slope and within a few yards of the line of the Second Corps' front and its batteries, when suddenly a terrific fire from every available gun from the Cemetery to Round Top Mountain burst upon them. The distinct, graceful lines of the rebels underwent an instantaneous transformation. They were at once enveloped in a dense cloud of smoke and dust. Arms, heads, blankets, guns and knapsacks were thrown and tossed into the clear air. Their track as they advanced was strewn with dead and wounded. A moan went up from the field, distinctly to be heard amid the storm of battle; but on they went, too much enveloped in smoke and dust now to permit us to distinguish their lines or movements, for the mass appeared more like a cloud of moving smoke and dust, than a column of troops. Still it advanced amid the now deafening roar of artillery and storm of battle. Suddenly the column gave way; the sloping landscape appeared covered all at once with the scattered and retreating foe. A withering sheet of missiles swept after them, and they were torn and tossed and prostrated as they ran. It seemed as if not one would escape. Of all the mounted officers who rode so grandly in the advance, not one was to be seen on the field; all had gone down."

Meantime from the Confederate lines General Longstreet was watching the charge. "That day at Gettysburg was one of the saddest of my life," he writes. "I foresaw what my men would meet, and would gladly have given up my position rather than share in the responsibilities of that day. It was thus I felt when Pickett at the head of 4900 brave men marched over the crest of Seminary Ridge and began his descent of the slope. As he passed me he rode gracefully with his jaunty cap raked well over his right ear and his long auburn locks, nicely dressed, hanging almost to his shoulders. He seemed rather a holiday soldier than a general at the head of a column which was about to make one of the grandest, most desperate assaults recorded in the annals of wars. Armistead and Garnett, two of his brigadiers, were veterans of nearly a quarter of a century's service. Their minds seemed absorbed in the men behind and in the bloody work before them. Kemper, the other brigadier, was younger, but had experienced many severe battles. He was leading my old brigade that I had drilled on Manassas plains before the first battle on that noted field. The troops advanced in well-closed ranks, and with elastic step, their faces lighted with hope. Before them lay the ground over which they were to pass to the point of attack. Intervening were several fences, a field of corn, a little swale running through it, and then a rise from that point to the Federal stronghold. As soon as Pickett passed the crest of the hill, the Federals had a clear view and opened their batteries, and as he descended the slope of the ridge his troops received a fearful fire from the batteries in front and from Round Top. The troops marched steadily, taking the fire with great coolness. As soon as they passed my batteries I ordered my artillery to turn their fire against the batteries on our right, then raking our lines. They did so, but did not force the Federals to change the direction of their fire and relieve our infantry. As the troops were about to cross the swale I noticed a considerable force of Federal infantry moving down as though to flank the left of our line. I sent an officer to caution the division commanders to guard against that move, at the same time sending another staff officer with similar orders, so as to feel assured the orders would be delivered. Both officers came back bringing their saddles, their horses having been shot under them. After crossing the swale, the troops kept up the same steady step, but met a dreadful fire at the hands of the Federal sharpshooters; and as soon as the field was open the Federal infantry poured down a terrific fire, which was kept up during the entire assault. The slaughter was terrible, the enfilade fire of the batteries on Round Top being very destructive. At times one shell would knock down five or six men. I dismounted to relieve my horse, and was sitting on a rail fence watching very closely the movements of the troops. Col. Freemantle, who had taken a position behind the Third Corps, where he would be out of reach of fire and at the same time have a clear view of the field, became so interested that he left his position and came with speed to join me. Just as he came up behind me, Pickett had reached a point near the Federal lines. A pause was made to close ranks and mass for the final plunge. The troops on Pickett's left, though advancing, were evidently a little shaky. Col. Freemantle, only observing the troops of Pickett's command, said to me, 'General, I would not have missed this for anything in the world.' He believed it to be a complete success. I was watching the troops supporting Pickett, and saw plainly they could not hold together ten minutes longer. I called his attention to the wavering condition of the two divisions of the Third Corps, and said they would not hold, that Pickett would strike and be crushed, and the attack would be a failure. As Pickett's division concentrated in making the final assault, Kemper fell severely wounded. As the division threw itself against the Federal line, Garnett fell and expired. The Confederate flag was planted in the Federal line, and immediately Armistead fell, mortally wounded, at the feet of the Federal soldiers. The wavering divisions then seemed appalled, broke their ranks, and retired. Immediately the Federals swarmed around Pickett, attacking on all sides, enveloped and broke up his command, having killed and wounded more than two thousand men in about thirty minutes. They then drove the fragments back upon our lines. As they came back I fully expected to see Meade ride to the front and lead his forces to an immense counter-charge. Sending my staff officers to assist in collecting the fragments of my command, I rode to my line of batteries, knowing they were all I had in front of the impending attack, resolved to drive it back or sacrifice my last gun and man. The Federals were advancing a line of skirmishers which I thought was the advance of their charge. As soon as the line of skirmishers came within reach of our guns the batteries opened again, and their fire seemed to check at once the threatened advance. After keeping it up a few minutes, the line of skirmishers disappeared, and my mind was relieved of the apprehension that Meade was going to follow us."

Col. Fremantle, of whom Longstreet speaks, was an officer of the British army who had attached himself to Lee's headquarters with a view to seeing some fighting. He has recorded in entertaining fashion some incidents of the great charge.

"When I got close up to General Longstreet," he writes, "I saw one of his regiments advancing through the woods in good order; so, thinking I was just in time to see the attack, I remarked to the General that I wouldn't have missed this for anything. Longstreet was seated at the top of a snake fence and looking perfectly calm and unperturbed. He replied, laughing: 'The devil you wouldn't! I would like to have missed it very much. We have attacked and been repulsed. Look there.' For the first time I then had a view of the open space between the two positions, and saw it covered with Confederates slowly and sulkily returning toward us under a heavy fire of artillery.

"The General was making the best arrangements in his power to resist the threatened advance, by advancing some artillery, rallying some stragglers, etc. I remember seeing a general (Pettigrew I think it was) come up to him and report that he was unable to bring his men up again. Longstreet turned upon him and replied with some sarcasm: 'Very well; never mind then, General; just let them remain where they are; the enemy's going to advance and will spare you the trouble.'

"Soon afterward I joined General Lee, who had in the mean time come to the front on becoming aware of the disaster. If Longstreet's conduct was admirable, that of General Lee was perfectly sublime. He was engaged in rallying and encouraging the broken troops, and was riding about a little in front of the wood, quite alone, the whole of his staff being engaged in a similar manner further to the rear. His face, which is always placid and cheerful, did not show signs of the slightest disappointment, care, or annoyance, and he was addressing to every soldier he met a few words of encouragement, such as 'All this will come right in the end; we'll talk it over afterward; but in the mean time all good men must rally. We want all good and true men just now.' He spoke to all the wounded men that passed him, and the slightly wounded he exhorted to bind up their hurts and take up a musket in this emergency. Very few failed to answer his appeal; and I saw many badly wounded men take off their hats and cheer him.

"He said to me: 'This has been a sad day for us, Colonel—a sad day; but we can't expect to always gain victories.'

"Nothwithstanding the misfortune which had so suddenly befallen him, General Lee seemed to observe everything, however trivial. When a mounted officer began beating his horse for shying at the bursting of a shell, he called out: 'Don't whip him, Captain; don't whip him. I've got just such another foolish horse myself, and whipping does no good.'

"I saw General Wilcox (an officer who wears a short round jacket and battered straw hat) come up to him and explain, almost crying, the state of his brigade. General Lee immediately shook hands with him, and said cheerfully: 'Never mind, General,—all this has been my fault; it is I that have lost this fight, and you must help me out of it in the best way you can.'"

There was no more fighting in the valley before Cemetery Ridge after the hurricane of death had swept away the men who charged with Pickett. Meade made no counter-attack. "An advance of 20,000 men from Cemetery Ridge in the face of the 140 guns then in position would have been stark madness," is the opinion of General Hunt on this seeming failure of the Union commander to follow up his advantage. But on both flanks of the warring armies the fighting still continued. On the right of the Union line the cavalry commands of Stuart and Gregg contended fiercely for the mastery, and with furious charges and sharp artillery combats scattered the fields about the Rummel house with dead and wounded. On the Union left Farnsworth's cavalry made a desperate charge against the Confederate artillery and infantry. The charge was repulsed, but it served its purpose in holding the Confederate left wing in check. General Farnsworth himself fell at the head of his troops, struck down with five mortal wounds. He knew when he rode out into the field that he had been sent on a mission from which there was scarce one chance in ten of his returning, but he did his duty like a man and died like a hero. "I was near Kilpatrick when he impetuously gave the order to Farnsworth to make the last charge," writes one of the Union troopers. "Farnsworth spoke with emotion: 'General, do you mean it? Shall I throw my handful of men over rough ground, through timber, against a brigade of infantry? The First Vermont has already been fought half to pieces; these are too good men to kill.' Kilpatrick said: 'Do you refuse to obey my orders? If you are afraid to lead this charge, I will lead it.' Farnsworth rose in his stirrups—he looked magnificent in his passion—and cried, 'Take that back!' Kilpatrick returned his defiance, but soon repenting, said, 'I did not mean it. Forget it.' For a moment there was silence, when Farnsworth spoke calmly: 'General, if you order the charge I will lead it; but you must take the responsibility.' I did not hear the low conversation that followed, but as Farnsworth turned away he said, 'I will obey your order.' Kilpatrick said earnestly, 'I take the responsibility.'

But though the cavalry combats on the flanks afforded opportunity for the display of daring and gallantry on both sides, they had little or no bearing on the fortunes of the day. Pickett's charge was the sledge-hammer blow with which Lee had planned to crush the Union army. When it failed the whole plan of invasion fell to pieces, and one unprejudiced foreign historian has said that when Pickett's line crumbled away, Lee must have foreseen Appomatox. Whole volumes have been written to show just why Pickett failed. Whether Lee erred in refusing to entertain Longstreet's suggestion that the Confederates should move around the Union flank and force Meade to take the offensive; whether Longstreet carried out Lee's orders with zeal and celerity, or whether it was to his indifference and dilatoriness that the failure of the great charge was due; whether the right troops were chosen to support Pickett—all these things have been the subject of endless controversy. Doubtless it is true that the charge was not ordered as early in the day as General Lee had intended. Some reason there is to believe that Longstreet was lacking in zeal both on the second and third days of the battle, and it was really on the second day that the Confederates lost the battle. An hour then would have decided the fate of the nation at Gettysburg. The key to the whole Federal position was Little Round Top, and it will be remembered that the Union troops secured that vitally important hilltop scarce five minutes before the Confederates reached it. In a reply to General Longstreet's criticisms upon General Lee's conduct of the battle, published in "Battles and Leaders of the Civil War," Colonel William Allan of the Confederate army says: "Had Longstreet attacked not later than 9 or 10 A.M., as Lee certainly expected, Sickles's and Hancock's Corps would have been defeated before part of the Fifth and Sixth Corps arrived. Little Round Top (which, as it was, the Fifth Corps barely managed to seize in time) would have fallen into Confederate possession; and even if nothing more had been done, this would have given the field to the Confederates, since the Federal line all the way to Cemetery Hill was untenable with Round Top in hostile hands."

It is also urged, with some reason, that the disaster to the Confederate arms at Gettysburg was due in part to the absence of Stuart and his cavalry. The army was robbed of its eyes; it was deprived too of its oft-employed means for deceiving the enemy and cloaking its own movements. Without the cavalry to interpose a screen before Meade's pickets that flank movement which Longstreet so strenuously urged could never have been accomplished without attracting the attention and encountering the opposition of the Union army. Nor were the results of Stuart's circuitous expedition such as to offset in any way the disadvantages suffered by Lee because of his absence. Beyond spreading panic in Baltimore and Philadelphia, capturing a Union baggage train rich in provisions and ammunition, and fighting a sharp battle with Kilpatrick at Hanover, Stuart accomplished nothing. He did not appear upon the battle field at Gettysburg until late in the afternoon of the second day, and his men were then so exhausted with long continued riding and fighting as scarcely to be worth reckoning as effective troops.

So ended in complete defeat for the Confederates, the battle of Gettysburg. With it ended Lee's hope for a successful invasion of Northern territory. It was more than a mere battle lost for the Confederacy. It was a more serious disaster than the mere failure of a campaign. Far away beyond the Atlantic, England and France were waiting for some notable triumph of the Southern armies to afford

RAID UPON A BAGGAGE TRAIN.

them an excuse to recognize the Confederacy as one among the family of independent nations. Success at Gettysburg would have meant much for the Confederacy. Failure meant the postponement of any possible European intervention, and perhaps meant that all hope of such intervention must be abandoned. Doubtless this thought came to General Lee when he saw Pickett's men driven from the lodgement they had effected in the center of the Union line. From General Imboden we learn of the heavy sadness that came upon the great Virginian when night brought time to reflect upon the disaster of the day.

"When he arrived there was not even a sentinel on duty at his tent," writes General Imboden, telling of General Lee's return to headquarters at midnight, "and not one of his staff was awake. The moon was high in the clear sky, and the silent scene was unusually vivid. As he approached and saw us lying on the grass under a tree, he spoke, reined in his jaded horse, and essayed to dismount. The effort to do so betrayed so much physical exhaustion that I hurriedly rose and stepped forward to assist him, but before I reached his side he had succeeded in alighting, and threw his arm across the saddle to rest, and fixing his eyes upon the ground leaned in silence and almost motionless upon his equally weary horse—the two forming a striking and never-to-be-forgotten group. The moon shone full upon his massive features and revealed an expression of sadness I had never before seen upon his face. Awed by his appearance, I waited for him to speak, until the silence became embarrassing, when, to break it and change the silent current of his thoughts, I ventured to remark in a sympathetic tone and in allusion to his great fatigue:

"'General, this has been a hard day upon you.'

"He looked up and replied mournfully:

"'Yes, it has been a sad, sad day to us,' and immediately relapsed into his thoughtful mood and attitude. Being unwilling again to intrude upon his reflections I said no more. After perhaps a minute or two he suddenly straightened up to his full height, and turning to me with more animation and excitement of manner than I had ever seen in him before, for he was a man of wonderful equanimity, he said in a voice tremulous with emotion:

"'I never saw troops behave more magnificently than Pickett's division of Virginians did to-day in that grand charge upon the enemy. And if they had been supported as they were to have been,—but for some reason not yet fully explained to me, were not,—we would have held the position and the day would have been ours.' After a moment's pause he added in a loud voice, in a tone almost of agony: 'Too bad! *Too bad!* OH! TOO BAD!'"

The story of Gettysburg is replete with incidents of personal valor, romance, and interest. It was the seventeen-year-old grandson of President Tyler who carried the Confederate colors in Armistead's brigade of Pickett's division. "I will plant these colors on yonder breastworks, or die," he had promised his General before the charge began. He kept his word. For a moment the colors flaunted gallantly above the Union line. Then they were fairly shot to pieces, and the young color-bearer was struck down with a mortal wound.

Behind the stone wall on which Robert Tyler planted his colors was a battery commanded by Lieutenant Alonzo Cushing. On it the heavy fire of the Confederate artillery fell fiercely during the cannonade preceding the Confederate charge. Horses and men were struck down, guns dismounted. Cushing himself fell mortally wounded. When the great charge was begun General Webb, who commanded that part of the Union line, stood near the dying artillerist. But one gun of the battery was fit for use. Seeing the advancing line of gray, Cushing sprang to his feet. "Webb, I'll give them one more shot!" he cried. Running his cannon forward to the wall he discharged it, and crying out, "Good-by!" fell dead by the side of his last gun.

After the Confederates had been beaten back, the men in blue left their trenches and went out on the field to care for the enemy's wounded. "Tell Hancock I have wronged him and wronged my country," said a dying Confederate officer over whom they bent. And another officer, whose brilliant uniform had led General Doubleday to send to inquire his name and rank, responded grimly: "Tell General Doubleday, in a few minutes I shall be where there is no rank."

Though the ultimate results of the battle of Gettysburg were greatly to the advantage of the Union, and though the battle was in every sense a notable defeat for the Confederates, the losses of the opposing armies were about equal. The official reports of the losses of Meade's army show that 3072 men were killed, 14,497 wounded, and 5434 captured; a total loss of 23,003. Lee's reports, which are somewhat fragmentary, show 2592 killed, 12,709 wounded and 5150 captured; a total of 20,451. There is much reason to believe, however, that the actual Confederate loss was largely in excess of that reported, and that it really exceeded the Union loss to no small degree.

It is unnecessary for us to follow the course of Lee's army after the thunders of the battle about Cemetery Ridge were stilled. The Southern general recognized his defeat. He knew that the resources of his country would not justify him in any attempt to snatch victory from the jaws of defeat by any desperate renewal of a hopeless contest. For him there was nothing left but retreat, and the night was scarcely half over before preparations for a movement back toward the Potomac were well under way. By the fifth of July his whole army was in full retreat.

Meade pursued, but over-cautiously. He was satisfied with his victory, and dreaded to press too closely his retreating foe. Despite urgent messages from Washington directing him to push the pursuit with more energy, and to seize his opportunity to end the rebellion by annihilating the chief army of the Confederacy, he still lagged in Lee's rear. And so the Confederate army, beaten and sorely crippled, but a powerful and dangerous army still, escaped into Virginia.

Here we shall take leave for a time of the Army of Northern Virginia, and its persistent enemy, the Army of the Potomac. The last and the greatest effort of the Confederates to carry the war into

Northern territory had failed. The period of Southern aggressiveness had come to an end. When we again—in another volume—take up the fortunes of General Lee and his army of tried veterans, we shall see them no longer in conscious strength and with high ambitions invading the territory of their foe. Henceforth their part was to defend their own country desperately and with rapidly dwindling forces, against the persistent and stubborn attacks of a foe vastly their superior in resources and in numbers.

CHAPTER X.

OPENING THE MISSISSIPPI. — SHERMAN'S EXPEDITION. — BATTLE OF CHICKASAW BAYOU. — EXPEDITIONS UP THE YAZOO AND THROUGH THE BAYOUS. — GRANT'S MOVEMENTS WEST OF THE RIVER. — CROSSING THE RIVER. — BATTLE OF PORT GIBSON. — BATTLE AT JACKSON. — BATTLE OF CHAMPION HILL. — BATTLE AT BIG BLACK RIVER BRIDGE. — VICKSBURG INVESTED. — THE SIEGE. — PEMBERTON'S SURRENDER. — FALL OF PORT HUDSON.

"THE men of the Northwest," said John A. Logan in the early days of the war, "will hew their way to the Gulf." From the day when General Grant went down the Mississippi River to attack the Confederate camp at Belmont, the military authorities of the Union never withdrew their attention from the great river that flowed from the cool lakes of Minnesota to the turquoise waters of the Gulf of Mexico. When once that river should be cleared of hostile batteries so that a vessel flying the stars and stripes might go unmolested from St. Louis to New Orleans, the Confederacy would be split in twain. To accomplish this end vast armies were raised, roads built, canals dug, fleets of ironclads and rams set afloat, the waters of the river were turned into the bordering forests, new engines of war were devised, and all the complex machinery of modern military science was employed upon a scale hitherto unparalleled.

Of the earlier campaigns and naval expeditions looking toward the opening of the Mississippi we have already spoken. The Union forces gradually worked their way southward from Cairo, ousting the Confederates in rapid succession from Columbus, New Madrid and Island No. 10, Fort Pillow and Memphis, so that the autumn of 1862 saw the banks of the great river north of Vicksburg unoccupied by a single hostile cannon. The army and navy of the Union were pushing northward too from the mouth of the Mississippi. After passing Fort St. Philip and Fort Jackson and capturing New Orleans in April, Farragut pushed on up-stream, captured Baton Rouge and Natchez, and flaunted the flag before the batteries of Vicksburg, which were then but pigmy fortifications in comparison with their proportions of later days. Nothing was done at this time, but some weeks later he returned, and with a fleet of three men-of-war, seven gunboats and sixteen mortar-boats, together with a land force of about 3000 men, made an attempt to carry the town. In this the Federals were unsuccessful, and soon left the field and retired down the river, the land forces stopping at Baton Rouge, where on the 4th of August they fought a victorious battle against an attacking force of Confederates under General Breckinridge.

Soon after the battle of Baton Rouge the Confederates began the construction of formidable batteries at Port Hudson, a few miles above that town. Here the bluffs rose steep from the water's edge, and the batteries built by Breckinridge effectually closed the river against the passage of any save the most formidable ironclads. The purpose of the Confederates in choosing this spot for their batteries is obvious. Between Port Hudson and Vicksburg there empties into the Mississippi the Red River, which winds away in great curves through the heart of Louisiana. Down this river came floating steamers and barges freighted heavily with food products for the famishing people in the eastern part of the South, where the armies tramping backward and forward had ruined the crops and converted the cattle into rations. It was of vital importance to the Confederacy that the Red River and the Mississippi about its mouth should be kept free from Union gunboats, and to this end the frowning batteries at Port Hudson were built to cut off marauders from the south, while the rows of cannon on the bluff at Vicksburg seemed to bid defiance to any Union vessels that might seek to come down from the north.

As the works on the river bluffs at Vicksburg and Port Hudson grew more formidable it became evident that no naval force alone could carry them. Vicksburg was the chief point to which the attention of the War Department was directed, and soon another movement for the Confederate stronghold was under way.

In December, 1862, Grant's army was in northern Mississippi and southern Tennessee, on the line of railroad between Iuka and Memphis. From this point a land and water expedition against Vicksburg was begun. Grant was in command of the land forces, and had made considerable progress in his advance, when a raiding party of Confederate cavalry under Forrest fell upon his rear, cut his communications, and destroyed his depot of supplies at Holly. This proved fatal to the issue of the campaign, for Grant was forced to retreat, and was unable to co-operate in the attack which Sherman was about to make.

Sherman meantime, with some 30,000 men, had gone down the river upon transports and landed near the mouth of the Yazoo River just north of Vicksburg. No news had come to him of the disaster that had befallen Grant, and he pushed on in the full belief that the Confederates were already engaged by Grant and would be able to offer at best only a slight resistance to his advance.

It was a difficult country through which Sherman's line of march lay. The roads were narrow and muddy, flanked on either side by gloomy morasses, swamps in which the water stood two feet deep, while huge cypress trees towered high above and shut out the light of day. Through this desolate region, harassed continually by Confederate pickets and sharpshooters, the Union forces painfully made their way, a part of them overland and some in transports by way of the Yazoo River, until all had finally secured a position on the bottom lands beneath the lofty bluffs known as the Walnut Hills.

Sherman's campaign had been planned upon the theory that the greater part of the Confederate forces would be engaged by Grant and that he would find but a meagre force opposing his march to Vicksburg. But the disaster at Holly Springs had turned Grant back and left Pemberton free to hurry his troops to the defense of the Confederate stronghold. And so it happened that on the crest of the towering bluffs that overlooked Sherman's lines there were not less than 12,000 men in a well-fortified position. One thousand men should have been able to hold that line against the assaults of Sherman's entire force. "Our troops," wrote a Union officer, "had not only to advance from the narrow apex of a triangle, whose short base of about four hundred yards and short sides bristled with the enemy's artillery and small arms, but had to wade the bayou and tug through the mucky and tangled swamp under a withering fire of grape, canister, shells and minie balls before reaching dry ground. Such was the point chosen for the assault by General Sherman. What more could be desired by an enemy about to be assailed in his trenches!"

It is unlikely that General Sherman under-estimated the desperate character of the assault he was about to order. But he had gone too far to retreat without striking a blow. "Tell General Morgan," said he to an aide who came from that officer to advise against the assault—"Tell General Morgan to give the signal for the assault; that we will lose 5000 men before we take Vicksburg, and that we may as well lose them here as anywhere else."

General Morgan had no choice but to obey, though he returned word to his chief that it would be easy to sacrifice the 5000 men but impossible to carry the enemy's position. The brigades of De Courcey and Blair and a part of Thayer's brigade—6000 men in all—were chosen to make the assault. As they were forming, Col. De Courcey rode up to General Morgan and asked gravely:

"General, do I understand that you are about to order an assault?"

"Yes, form your brigade," was the response.

"My poor brigade!" answered De Courcey sadly; "your orders will be obeyed, General."

Soon the drums beat fiercely, the opening volley crashed out, and the troops moved forward to the assault. Across the bayou, through the bristling abatis, over the marshy ground they advanced doggedly, losing all vestige of orderly formation, crowded together in one confused but determined mob, leaving scores of brave fellows on the ground behind them, but still pressing onward in the teeth of the furious storm of missiles that rained down from the bluffs above. It was a gallant but a hopeless charge. Though they swept the Confederates from two lines of rifle-pits at the base of the bluffs, the batteries on the crests tore great rents in the ranks of the assailants. Blair's brigade began to scale the hills, but found itself unsupported and was forced to retreat, leaving 500 men behind. The Sixth Missouri Regiment marched straight to the foot of the bluff and were there protected from the enemy's cannon. But the Confederates came out to the brow of the hill, held out their muskets at arm's-length, and fired straight down upon the cowering, helpless crowd. It took scarcely half an hour to prove that the Confederate position was impregnable, though in demonstrating this fact hundreds of gallant soldiers had shed their blood.

So ended in a complete but not ignominious defeat for the Union forces the battle of Chickasaw Bayou, fought on the 29th of December, 1862. The loss to the Union army was heavy. No less than 191 men were killed in the assault and the supporting attack at other portions of the line. The wounded and missing numbered 1738. The Confederates from their secure entrenchments repelled the attack with a total loss of only 207 men.

The failure of the attack at Chickasaw Bayou ended for a time the operations against Vicksburg. General Sherman at first determined to re-embark his troops and proceed up the Yazoo to Haines's Bluff and there make another attempt to pierce the enemy's lines. But a heavy fog settled down upon the water-soaked country. Then came a rain-storm and the rivers and bayous began to rise. Sherman saw by the water-marks on the trees that the water sometimes covered the low ground on which his troops were then encamped to the depth of ten feet. Moreover his scouts reported that reënforcements were constantly entering the enemy's lines. With the elements thus against him, and with all signs indicating that Grant had met with some disaster, Sherman concluded that his wisest course was to abandon for the present his operations against Vicksburg. Accordingly he loaded his troops upon the transports, and soon landed them upon the bank of the Mississippi at the mouth of the Yazoo.

We may pass hastily over the events which took place before the advance upon Vicksburg was taken up again. Soon after establishing his army at the mouth of the Yazoo, General Sherman was superseded in his command by General McClernand, a "political soldier," whose experience in the field was as yet limited. However, McClernand's first undertaking was successful, for he took his forces up the Arkansas River, and with the aid of the gunboats reduced the Confederate works at Fort Hindman. By this victory the national forces captured nearly 5000 prisoners and a great quantity of stores. McClernand would have proceeded farther up the river, but was recalled by peremptory commands from General Grant, who now took command of all the Union armies on the Mississippi. These forces Grant divided into four corps, with McClernand, Sherman, Hurlbut, and McPherson as their respective commanders.

The troops available for the movement against Vicksburg were now on the west bank of the river a few miles above the city. The winter had been unusually rainy, and the country bordering the great river was fairly waterlogged. Scarcely enough dry land could be found to afford a camping place for the Union troops. Strung out along the levees they extended for nearly seventy miles up the river.

The problem which now confronted Grant was peculiarly perplexing. It was two-fold in its character. His duty, his one purpose was to reduce Vicksburg. The first step toward the accomplishment of this object must be to find a dry, safe landing-place for his troops on the eastern bank of the river. But his armies were all above the city. To cross and make the assault from the north would be to encounter again that ridge of precipitous bluffs, those lines of impregnable earthworks before which Sherman's gallant brigades had fallen back torn and bleeding. South of the city the land lay favorably for an attacking force. But how was Grant to get his troops below the town? Not by the river surely, for long lines of frowning earthworks, crowded with cannon, promised speedy destruction to any unarmored vessels that should strive to pass them, and on the ironclads no troops could be carried. To march down the west side of the river, out of range of the Confederate batteries, and cross the river below the town would have been the natural way out of the difficulty, but the nature of the country made this impracticable at this season. "The country," writes General Grant in his Memoirs, "is cut up by bayous filled from the river in high water—many of them navigable for steamers. All of them would be, except for overhanging trees, narrowness, and tortuous courses, making it impossible to turn the bends with vessels of any considerable length. Marching across this country in the face of an enemy was impossible; navigating it proved equally impracticable."

Had military considerations alone been allowed to dictate Grant's action he would have taken his army up the river to Memphis again, and recommenced his advance against Vicksburg by way of Holly Springs and Jackson. But this would have been a retrograde movement, and would have been construed by the people as a retreat. The North was then in no humor to look with philosophy upon a retreat, and political considerations determined the General to remain where he was, and wait until the warm sun of spring should dry up the mud and water that held him captive and enable him to move his army.

Meanwhile he tested several projects which seemed to promise him a way of getting to the position below the city that he coveted. He tells us in his Memoirs that he regarded most of these experiments as rather hopeless, but pushed them forward, partially to give employment to his troops, and partly to let the people of the North see that his army was not idle. Nevertheless he was ever ready to take advantage of the success of any one of these expedients, should success be won.

Engineering more than fighting finally won Vicksburg for the Union cause. Throughout the six months during which Grant plodded stubbornly on, closing relentlessly in upon the doomed city, the pickaxe and shovel, the sap-roller, gabions, and fascines were the true weapons which the men in blue wielded to the discomfiture of their antagonists. Accordingly the first attempt made by Grant to get his army past the enemy's batteries was by means of a vast piece of engineering.

Before Vicksburg the Mississippi River makes—or did make in 1863—one of those mighty bends for which it is famous. For three miles its current flows straight toward the city, then bending suddenly flows straight away in a directly opposite direction. The peninsula inclosed between the almost parallel lines of the river is scarce a mile wide, and is lower than the river at high-water time, and protected by levees. For the whole six miles of river included in this bend, a vessel going up or down stream was exposed to the fire of batteries which no transport could ever pass. The idea was suggested to Grant that by cutting a canal across this peninsula, the current of the river might pour into it and make a channel through which the boats might pass. Though not wholly out of range of the hostile batteries, this route would leave the boats exposed to fire for only a mile, and on a dark night so short a gauntlet might safely be run.

Accordingly the work was begun. Four thousand men threw down sword and musket to take up the shovel. Steam dredges were set to work. The canal grew apace. But the enemy was not idle. He brought up his heaviest guns and turned them upon the toilers in the big ditch. His shells drove the workmen away and knocked the dredges to pieces. Finally a bursting shell cut the levee. The water quickly enlarged the gap so made, and rushing in flooded the whole peninsula so that Sherman's men came near being drowned by regiments. Thereafter that field of operations was abandoned.

A new idea now came to Grant. The whole country just west of Vicksburg was a maze of bayous, most of which were of sufficient depth to float a transport steamer. Might there not be then some connecting waterways which, with a little dredging, and a few canals cut, would give a continuous channel from a point above Vicksburg to the Red River, which in turn empties into the Mississippi River below the city?

This experiment too was tried. Surveying parties explored the bayous with care. A possible route was discovered and carefully mapped. It was thought that by cutting the levee at Lake Providence, some seventy miles above Vicksburg, a water communication with the Red River might be had. This was accordingly done and the country was soon flooded. But the labor of sawing off the trunks of trees ten feet under water, and of dredging, was so great that Grant soon saw that there was no hope of completing this work with sufficient speed. So, although he allowed his soldiers to continue the work, he set about devising some other plan.

It was to the eastern side of the river that the Union officers now directed their attention. It was useless to think of getting below Vicksburg on that bank, but the Yazoo River and the bayous connecting with it seemed to offer a route whereby a body of troops might be landed back of the city. Again levees were blown up and the current of the great river turned into the swamps and bayous. It was to the navy that the task of exploring this network of waterways fell, and the work was undertaken by Commodore Porter with great intrepidity. The unusual spectacle of ironclads afloat in the forest; running at full speed into bridges and knocking them down; crawling through ditches with scarce a foot of leeway on either side, and generally deporting themselves like amphibious rather than purely marine monsters, was presented to the astonished Confederates. But these in their turn were not wanting in activity. They threw up forts at commanding positions. They swept the decks of the gunboats with a constant storm of bullets. They felled trees before and behind the boats, filled the bayous with obstructions, and once had Porter so completely entrapped that only the timely and unexpected arrival of Sherman with a small body of troops saved that gallant officer from the necessity of blowing up his whole flotilla. After the happy termination of that adventure, the gunboats sought deep water again and the search for Vicksburg's back door was abandoned.*

But by this time the early Southern Spring was well advanced, and the roads which a month before had been impassable were now in fairly good condition. So abandoning his encampments, Grant marched his army southward by a road several miles from the river, returning to the river's bank opposite Grand Gulf. Here he was joined by Porter, who had run the batteries with his fleet. The Confederates knew of his coming and had built huge fires on the bank to light up the river, but though all the guns on the Vicksburg bluffs roared and flamed, the ironclads passed in safety, and one transport only was sunk. But though the actual casualties were thus trivial, the exploit seemed so hazardous when first proposed that none of the regular officers or crews of the river steamers that were pressed into service for transports dared to undertake it. Volunteers were called for, and among the regiments enlisted along the banks of the great rivers were found men enough, who were well versed in the art of river navigation, to man all the vessels.

Having established his army on the western bank of the river opposite Grand Gulf, Grant requested Porter to attack the Confederate batteries on the bluffs, intending to send a force across the river as soon as the Confederate fire showed signs of weakening. But by this

---

* For an account of the part taken by the navy in the siege of Vicksburg, see "Blue Jackets of 61," by Willis J. Abbot. New York: Dodd, Mead & Company, 1886.

RUNNING THE VICKSBURG BATTERIES.

time the Confederates had made of Grand Gulf a stronghold scarcely second to Vicksburg, and though Porter's eight gunboats hurled shells against their solid earthworks for five hours and a half, the guns on the hill-tops still responded spitefully, and the 10,000 men whom Grant had put on board the transports to be ready to cross the river as soon as an opportunity offered, were forced to march ashore again. Seventy-four men were lost by the navy in this engagement. General Grant now concluded that it was hopeless to attempt to gain a foothold on the eastern bank of the river at Grand Gulf, and accordingly marched his troops three miles further down the river, while the transports slipped past the Grand Gulf batteries at night, under cover of a heavy bombardment by the fleet, and made their way to the same point. One of the "intelligent contrabands" who were always on hand to help the Union Generals in moments of perplexity, came to Grant's tent during the night, and told him that Bruinsburg, a few miles farther down-stream, afforded a good landing-place, with fair roads leading thence to the country back of Vicksburg which Grant sought to reach.

To Bruinsburg accordingly the Federals turned their steps, and soon all the troops were safely ferried across the river. The Confederates were scarcely aware of the fact that their enemy had gained a foothold in their country, for Sherman, who had been left behind to cover Grant's movements, made such vigorous demonstrations against the northern side of Vicksburg as to lead its defenders to look for danger from that quarter only.

Masterly, rapid and daring were the movements by which Grant, leaving Bruinsburg, marched straight into the enemy's country and thrust his army between the wings of the Confederate army, which, if they could but have effected a junction, would have crushed him; beating Johnston and Pemberton in detail, and cooping the latter up in Vicksburg; doing all this with his line of communication wholly abandoned, and doing much of it in direct defiance of orders from Washington. From the strategy of the campaign which ended with Pemberton locked up in Vicksburg and Grant holding the key, did the people of the North, civilians and soldiers alike, first learn to appreciate the military genius of the quiet volunteer soldier who ranks to-day with the great captains of history. Nevertheless, over the events of the campaign preliminary to the siege of Vicksburg we must pass hurriedly.

No time was lost by Grant at Bruinsburg, but the very night of his arrival McClernand's division was pushed forward to Port Gibson in the hope of saving a bridge there before the Confederates could burn it. But the enemy was first on the ground, and to the number of 8000 opposed McClernand's advance. All day the battle raged, and at nightfall the Confederates made an orderly retreat, burning the bridge behind them. The bridge was rebuilt on floating rafts made of fence rails and lumber stripped from barns and houses in the neighborhood, and over this frail structure the men of Grant's army strode toward Vicksburg,—Crocker's division first, in hot pursuit of the Confederates, who were now fast retreating to the northward. Grand Gulf was evacuated by its defenders and seized by Grant for a base of supplies. Blue-clad soldiers now looked down upon the river from the frowning ramparts that had so long resisted the stoutest assaults of Porter's ironclads.

Grant waited at Grand Gulf a day or two for Sherman to come up, then pushed onward. He had about 45,000 men under his command; his enemy, General Pemberton, had 50,000, but Grant's forces were concentrated while Pemberton's were widely scattered. The Union commander therefore determined to press hotly upon his enemies, fight them wherever found, prevent their concentrating, and beat them in detail. This was a more than ordinarily perilous plan of campaign. One road only led from Grand Gulf into the territory whither the Union army was going. It was useless to hope that all the supplies necessary for the sustenance of that army could be transported over that narrow highway. Sherman besought the general to abandon his plan, declaring that "this road will be jammed as sure as life," but Grant adhered to his purpose, believing that all the supplies that failed to get over the road could be obtained from the rich country through which the troops were to march. Events proved that he was right, for, except for a scarcity of bread, the troops endured no privations during the ensuing campaign.

On the 12th of May, McPherson's division encountered the enemy, about 5000 strong, at Raymond. A battle followed in which the United States forces were easily victorious. The Confederate loss was 100 killed and 720 wounded and captured. McPherson's loss amounted to 442 men, of whom 66 were killed.

The result of this battle was to put Grant squarely between the wings of the Confederate army. Pemberton was on his left with nearly 50,000 men. On his right, at Jackson, were 12,000 men with reënforcements constantly coming up. General Joseph E. Johnston was hastening from Tennessee to take command of the forces at Jackson. He had seen long before the dangers to which Pemberton remained blind. "If Grant crosses, unite all your troops to beat him," he had telegraphed to Pemberton on the day Grant landed at Bruinsburg. "Success will give back what was abandoned to win it." But Pemberton failed to take the action suggested and now saw his army dismembered.

Quick to take advantage of his favorable situation, Grant determined to turn his back upon Pemberton and his 50,000 men, march to Jackson, demolish the Confederate force there, and then return and give battle to the larger force. To do this meant to relinquish even the narrow road that bound him to Grand Gulf. It meant the abandonment of his base of supplies, and his line of communication with the outside world. Nevertheless the hazardous step was taken and the army was speedily put on the march for Jackson. When General Johnston reached that place he was told that all communication with Pemberton was cut off, and that Grant's legions were even then moving upon the slender force at Jackson. He foresaw disaster at once, and though he at once set about preparing to resist the coming attack, he sent off to the military authorities at Richmond the ominous dispatch, "I am too late."

In the forenoon of May 14, the divisions of Sherman and McPherson, whom Grant had sent forward to the attack upon Jackson, were approaching the town. A heavy spring rain was falling in sheets. The roads were ankle-deep with mud and the fields like soaked sponges. Johnston sent two brigades two miles out from the city to meet his assailants. Walker's brigade, which opposed McPherson, made a desperate stand, and the soldiers fought for hours in the driving rain with damp cartridges. But the Confederates were only fighting to gain time, for Johnston was evacuating the town, and by noon McPherson had swept all impediments out of his path and was in the city.

There was little time for the Federals to enjoy the fruits of this victory. In their rear Pemberton was marshaling his men to offer battle. Johnston was making strenuous efforts to effect a junction with Pemberton and take command of the combined armies. Unfortunately for Johnston's plans he had a traitor in his employ, for one of the couriers engaged in carrying his dispatches to Pemberton stopped by the way to give copies to Grant, who was thus kept fully informed of his enemy's plans, and enabled to defeat them.

Leaving Sherman to destroy the railroads and whatever public property there was in Jackson, Grant turned his face westward, seeking the Confederate army. This was soon found aligned on the slope of Champion Hills. The Confederate commander had 23,000 men, well posted so as to cover all the roads leading to Vicksburg. The Federals rushed into battle without delay and pressed the enemy hotly on every side. Logan's division even worked its way around on Pemberton's left flank and secured a position in the Confederate rear, covering the only road over which a retreat was practicable. But unfortunately the Federals did not appreciate the importance of the position thus gained, and when Hovey called for reënforcements Logan was sent to his aid. The road was thus uncovered and the Confederate retreat speedily began. It was a narrow escape for Pemberton. "Had McClernand come up with reasonable promptness," writes

General Grant, "or had I known the ground as I did afterward, I cannot see how Pemberton could have escaped with any organized force. As it was he lost over three thousand killed and wounded, and about three thousand captured in battle and in pursuit." Grant's total loss in the battle was 2048, of whom 397 were killed. Among other trophies the Union forces captured twenty-four Confederate cannon.

Pemberton's army by this time was thoroughly demoralized. The soldiers had lost confidence in their commanding officer, and Pemberton had lost confidence in himself. He had disobeyed the orders of Johnston, his superior officer. He had called a council of war to determine what course to adopt, and then disregarded the recommendation of a majority of the council. He had committed the blunder of trying to harass Grant by cutting his communications, when Grant was living on the country and cared nothing at all for his communications. Finally, after his complete defeat at Champion Hills, Pemberton sought at once to shift the blame on some one else, and as he led the retreat said bitterly to those about him, "I call upon you, gentlemen, to witness that I am not responsible for this battle—I am but obeying the orders of General Johnston." He did not add that he had delayed giving obedience to these orders until too late for obedience to be a virtue.

Downhearted, weary, and sullen the Confederates trudged away from the field of Champion Hills through the dreary country toward Vicksburg. Loud was the grumbling in the ranks. The soldiers openly declared that they would serve no longer under Pemberton. Many deserted the ranks. But the persuasions of their officers kept most of them in line until they reached the Big Black River where Pemberton determined to make another stand. The Big Black is a deep, sluggish stream, bordered by steep bluffs on the west, and a level expanse of low bottom land on the east. Through the bottom land there flowed a bayou with a foot of water in its channel. Along this bayou the Confederates had built ramparts of cotton bales covered with earth. To defend this position Pemberton left a large detachment of troops, while the greater part of his army crossed the

Big Black on a single bridge and was posted on the high bluffs on the western side.

On the 17th of May, Grant's advance encountered the resistance of the gray-coats behind the bayou. The Union soldiers were flushed with victory, the Confederates depressed and demoralized. Without delay the Federals advanced to the attack, plodding through the muddy bayou, and threading their way through the thick vegetation which bordered it. In the midst of the battle came an order to Grant from Halleck, directing him to abandon his advance upon Vicksburg, return to Grand Gulf, and co-operate with General Banks, who was then trying to capture Port Hudson. "I told the officer who brought it," writes Grant, "that the order came too late, and that Halleck would not give it now if he knew our position. The bearer of the dispatch insisted that I ought to obey the order, and was giving arguments to support his position, when I heard great cheering to the right of our line, and, looking in that direction, saw Lawler in his shirt-sleeves leading a charge upon the enemy. I immediately mounted my horse and rode in the direction of the charge, and saw no more of the officer who delivered the dispatch—I think not even to this day."

The charge that General Lawler led in his shirt-sleeves decided the fortunes of the day. He had secured a position whence he could fall upon the flank of the Confederates. They made little resistance to his attack, but fled in the wildest confusion. The narrow bridge across the Big Black was soon thronged with fugitives, but Pemberton, fearing that Grant's army would cross in pursuit, set fire to it, leaving thousands of men, hundreds of his wounded, and a score of guns in the hands of the Federals. Many of the Confederates plunged into the river to swim across, and not a few were drowned. Others disappeared in the surrounding woods and made their way to their homes in different parts of the South, to serve no longer in the Southern army. Nearly 1800 prisoners were taken by the victorious Federals.

Grant's advance was now checked by the Big Black River, spanned by no bridge. Pemberton marched straight into Vicksburg and shut himself and his army up there. This is the way that army looked to a woman who saw the weary and disheartened troops march in: "I never shall forget that woful sight of a beaten, demoralized army that came rushing back. Wan, hollow-eyed, ragged, footsore, bloody, the men limped along, unarmed, but followed by siege-guns, ambulances, gun-carriages, and wagons in endless confusion."

General Pemberton, too, was sorely depressed. "Just thirty years ago I began my military career by receiving my appointment to a cadetship in the United States Military Academy," he said to a staff officer who rode into Vicksburg with him, "and to-day—the same date—that career is ended in disaster and disgrace." But he soon shook off his depression sufficiently to give active supervision to the work on the fortifications surrounding the city, which was immediately begun. To this work every one in the city lent a hand. The "Yankees" were coming, and Vicksburg must be protected against their assaults, so civilian and soldier, slave and freeman worked side by side in the trenches. Pickaxes were lacking, but bayonets served instead; there were not shovels enough to go round, but the soldiers made wooden ones. And so, with thousands of willing hands at work, a chain of earthworks soon surrounded all the landward side of the city, and 102 guns, great and small, peered over the ramparts and bade Grant's army defiance. But to man these works he had but about 30,000 men. The few days in which he had been vainly striving to check Grant's advance had cost the Confederate commander no less than 14,000 men.

On his arrival in Vicksburg Pemberton had sent off a courier to Johnston, thirty miles away, with the news of the disasters at Champion Hills and Big Black River. This is the answer that came speeding back:

"If you are invested in Vicksburg you must ultimately surrender. Under such circumstances, instead of losing both troops and place we must, if possible, save the troops. If it is not too late, evacuate Vicksburg and its dependencies and march to the northeast."

"Give up Vicksburg! Never!" exclaimed Pemberton when he received this order. It was then probably too late for him to undertake the movement ordered by Johnston, for Grant was by this time closing in upon him. But Pemberton estimated the value of Vicksburg to the Confederacy too high to think for a moment of evacuating the town. So he replied to Johnston:

"I intend to hold Vicksburg to the last. I conceive it to be the most important point in the Confederacy."

Twenty-four hours later the last gap in the Union lines was filled up, and the Confederates were caught in a trap from which there was no escape, and into which no aid, no provisions, no munitions of war could find an entrance.

It was the delay caused by the burning of the bridge across the Big Black River that gave the Confederates time to re-form their shattered ranks and build up their earthworks about Vicksburg. "But for the successful and complete destruction of the bridge," writes Grant, "I have but little doubt that we should have followed the enemy so closely as to prevent his occupying his defenses around Vicksburg." With the bridge destroyed, however, there was nothing to do but to devise other means for crossing the stream. Sherman had all the pontoons with him, and straightway built a pontoon bridge for his division. General Ransom contrived a unique structure by felling trees on opposite sides of the river, cutting the trunks only half through and throwing the trees so that they would fall with their tops interlacing without being wholly separated from their stumps. On these trees the bridge platform was built. Another bridge was built on floating rafts made of the timbers of a neighboring cotton gin. Yet another bridge was made by using great numbers of floating cotton bales for pontoons. All the bridges were completed with about twenty-four hours' work, and the long columns of infantry and the rumbling artillery trains passed safely over them and pressed relentlessly onward toward Vicksburg.

On the 19th, all of Grant's troops were aligned before the defenses of Vicksburg. Commander and soldiers alike were exultant. They had achieved nothing but victories. The enemy had been both outgeneraled and outfought. Flushed with victory, Grant thought that he needed but to put forward one more effort and Vicksburg would be his. He saw before him long lines of massive earthworks well garnished with cannon, but he thought those works were manned by a demoralized and beaten army which could not repel a vigorous assault. Events proved, however, that Grant had underestimated the task before him. Demoralized though the Confederates had been, their spirits, always buoyant, rose when they reached the shelter of their breastworks, and they felt themselves strong enough to withstand any attack. So it happened that Grant's attack on the afternoon of the 19th failed. McPherson and McClernand could not bring their men to the attack because of obstacles in their front. Only Sherman made an attack. He sent forward a body of regulars under Captain Washington. They charged gallantly across a ravine, picked their way through a tangled abatis in the teeth of a pitiless fire, and rushed upon the intrenchments. Though men fell fast the parapet was reached. Captain Washington scaled it and waved the flag he carried in his hand as a signal for his men to follow him, but at that moment a bullet struck him and he fell mortally wounded. The flag was captured by the Confederates. Though other assaults were made by other troops, none came so near success as the gallant Washington and his regulars.

Grant concluded that the Confederates were not quite so demoralized as he had supposed, and concluded to wait a few days before renewing the assault. This time he occupied in establishing a base of supplies on the Yazoo River and revictualing his army. This work, by this time, had become necessary. Since landing at Bruinsburg the soldiers had been marching and fighting for eighteen days with but five days' rations. The neighboring farms provided pork and poultry, potatoes and corn meal, but bread was scarce. The day after the ineffectual assault upon Vicksburg, General Grant was passing along the lines when a hungry soldier near him said in a low voice, "Hard tack!"

Soon the cry was taken up all along the line, and shouts of "Hard tack! Hard tack!" were heard on every side. "We are building a road now to the river," said the General, "and you soon will have full rations again." The outcry was stilled at once.

After two days Grant determined to make another attempt to carry the enemy's works by assault. His troops were still flushed with victory and eager to put an immediate end to the campaign which had been thus far so successful. Moreover he knew that Johnston was in his rear with an army of no contemptible size, and it was to be expected an attack on the Union rear would soon be made with a view of raising the siege.

Accordingly, on the morning of the 22d, the Union army in three columns pressed forward to the assault. From the river came the roar of great guns as Porter's gunboats flung their huge shells into the city, where they burst, tearing up streets, wrecking houses, and carrying terror to defenseless women and children. On the right of the Union line was Sherman's corps—tried veterans all. A desperate task is before them. High on a ridge in their front looms up the "Graveyard Bastion," so called from its proximity to a cemetery. Before it the ground is rugged, rising into hillocks, sinking into gullies. A deep ditch is between the bastion and the Union troops. It must be bridged, but how? Volunteers are called for. One hundred and fifty men step out, and provided with timbers, boards, and tools, will dash forward under the enemy's fire, and lay the bridge if the work can be done before the last of the builders shall be shot dead. Ewing's division stands ready to cross the bridge first. Then the divisions of Giles Smith and Kirby Smith will follow. Four Union batteries—twenty-four guns in all—are posted so as to sweep the Confederate works and cover the advance of the storming party.

Ten o'clock has been set as the hour for the assault to begin all along the line. All the watches of the division commanders have been compared, that there may be no delay at any point. The hour draws near. The fury of the bombardment from the river, and the roar of the cannonade from all the field-guns on Grant's lines have given Pemberton warning that an assault is to be made. Yet from all his works no gun speaks out in answer. He is hemmed in in Vicksburg with a scarcity of percussion caps. When he can get more he cannot tell, so the order has been given prohibiting firing on the skirmish line and directing all artillerists to save their fire for moments of the direst need.

So the Graveyard Bastion stands sullenly silent, seemingly empty, while the Federals form before it for the assault. Ten o'clock has come. The Union batteries are pouring a rapid and concentrated fire upon the fort. The volunteers of the forlorn hope are running forward with timbers and boards in their hands. For a moment more there is no sign of the force and fury that is held pent behind those impassive walls of clay. Then suddenly the whole bastion is ablaze. Fire and smoke leap from the black muzzles of the cannon that peer from the embrasures. The parapet is black with riflemen, whose bullets whistle among the devoted soldiers below. There is no cessation in the Confederate fire. The rattle of the musketry and the deep boom of the cannon are united in one continuous roar. Before this withering blast the assaulting column halts irresolute. Some of the men fall back. Others press on and throw themselves into the ditch before the rampart, where they are safe from that terrible fire. A few daring ones scale the bastion and plant the flag upon it, but are quickly shot down. There on the Confederate ramparts the Stars and Stripes wave grandly. The Confederates strive to seize the flag, but are shot down by the Union men in the ditch. Throughout the day the flag waves proudly, riddled by the bullets of friend and foe alike, and surrounded by a heap of bodies clad in blue and gray. But it is only an empty sign of conquest, those colors floating over a hostile battlement, for the works cannot be carried, and night leaves the Confederates in safe possession.

On Sherman's left was McPherson's corps. Here the Confederate position was no less strong and held the assailants at bay. Before the divisions of McArthur and Quimby the configuration of the enemy's works was such that to attempt to storm them would have been madness, and these troops were forced to content themselves with standing aloof, and pouring in their fire at long range. But Logan's division saw a chance of success and made a gallant charge. Though a deadly fire was turned upon them, the well-disciplined regiments pressed forward until two regiments reached the ditch before the earthworks, and the colors of the Seventh Missouri were raised above the rampart. Instantly the man who held the colors was shot down. A second soldier seized them and met the same fate. Six color-bearers were shot down in as many minutes, and the handful of men who had gained the shelter of the ditch were forced to retreat without having been able to scale the counterscarp.

McClernand's corps was on the extreme left of the Union line. Here the experience of the other corps was repeated. Two Iowa regiments charged boldly up a steep hill and reached the ditch of a fort on its summit. Here the greater part of the assailants were forced to halt, but a handful of them, headed by Sergeant Joseph Griffith, scaled the counterscarp, entered the work, and by desperate hand-to-hand fighting drove the defenders out. A second Confederate work on higher ground, one hundred yards in the rear, commanded the interior of this fort, so that the victorious Federals could not long hold possession of it. Planting their colors on the parapet the Iowans sought shelter in the ditch, where they were soon joined by the Seventy-seventh Illinois, whose colors were placed beside those of the Iowa troops.

General Grant meanwhile had posted himself on the crest of a hill overlooking the field. McPherson was a few hundred yards in his front, McClernand a mile and a half to his left, Sherman about a mile to his right. He could hear the cheers of the men as they rushed forward to the charge, and through his field-glasses could watch the results. All along the lines he witnessed the same sights. The

A SHELL IN THE STREETS OF VICKSBURG.

charges were desperate, the resistance stubborn. At several points the Union colors were floating above the enemy's works, but nowhere had the blue-coats gained a lodgement within the Confederate lines. Everywhere they were crowded in the ditches, safe from musketry or cannon shot, but suffering severely from the hand grenades which the enemy tossed into their midst.

Grant had concluded that the assault was a failure, and was about to give orders for its abandonment, when a courier came galloping up. He brought a dispatch from McClernand. "We are hotly engaged with the enemy," it read. "We have part possession of two forts and the Stars and Stripes are floating over them. A vigorous push ought to be made all along the line." From his position Grant could see nothing of the successes reported by McClernand, but his doubts were set at rest when a second dispatch arrived from that commander, saying: "We have gained the enemy's intrenchments at many points, but are brought to a stand. I have sent word to McArthur to reënforce me if he can. Would it not be best to concentrate the whole or a part of his command at this point?"

Convinced by these reports that McClernand had won some notable successes, and that it only needed the coöperation of the rest of the troops to win a victory, General Grant ordered another assault all along the line. Nobly the soldiers responded to the call of their leaders. Gallantly they marched up to the earthworks only to be beaten back again by the pitiless hail of lead and iron. The assault was a failure, like those that had preceded it, and General Grant found out too late that McClernand's reported successes were purely imaginary. In his official report the general severely censured McClernand for making the incorrect statements which led to a renewal of the attack, and "resulted in the increase of our mortality list fully 50 per cent without advancing our position or giving us other advantages."

The two assaults on the 19th and 22d of May cost the Union army no less than 4075 men. The Confederates, sheltered by their breastworks, had beaten them back with a loss of scarce 500. After the failure of the second assault on the 22d, there lay on the ground before the Confederate works a great number of the Union dead and wounded. The sufferings of the wounded were fearful to witness. Unsheltered from the broiling sun, with no water to quench their burning thirst, with no surgeons to attend to their hurts, they lay there in agony between the two armies and their moans were borne on the breeze to their comrades. There were no Confederate wounded on the field. They had fallen within the breastworks and were speedily cared for. The men that lay on the bloody field before the redoubts all wore the blue, and it was the duty of the Union commander to ask for an armistice that all might be gathered up and carried tenderly to the field hospitals. But for some inexplicable reason Grant chose not to ask for a truce, and his wounded lay uncared for for two days, until the more humane Pemberton suggested a cessation of hostilities long enough to enable the Union wounded to be removed from the field. By this time many poor fellows were dead who, had they received prompt care, would have easily recovered from their hurts.

While the truce was in force General Sherman went to Pemberton's chief engineer, who was walking about before the works, and handed him a package of letters which some Northern friends of the Confederate officer had given him for delivery.

"I thought this would be a good opportunity to deliver this mail before it got too old," said Sherman.

"Yes, General," was the response, "it would have been very old indeed, if you had kept it until you brought it into Vicksburg yourself."

"So you think, then, I am a very slow mail route?"

"Well, rather," was the reply, alluding to the preparations making for a siege, "when you have to travel by regular approaches, parallels and zig-zags."

"Yes, that is a slow way of getting into a place," admitted Sherman, "but it is a very sure way, and I was determined to deliver those letters sooner or later."

The Union army now settled down to the task of reducing Vicksburg by the slow and tedious operations of a regular siege. The navy held the river and no aid could come to the imprisoned Confederates that way. On the landward side the whole town was invested by Grant's forces, which were within two hundred yards of the Confederate lines. Through the zone of iron that Grant drew so closely about the beleaguered Confederates, no wagon loads of provisions could force their way. A few alert, fleet-footed backwoodsmen, heavy laden with percussion caps, did pick their way through the swamps and past the Union pickets, carrying their precious burden safely to Pemberton. But save for this no assistance from the outside world could reach Vicksburg, and as there were 30,000 soldiers besides the normal population shut up in the city, Grant knew that he had only to be patient and his foes would be brought to terms by starvation.

But Grant was too active a man to sit down and wait for hunger to do his work for him. He pressed his siege with as much energy as if there were danger of his foe escaping him. He gathered reënforcements from all parts of the West until his army numbered over 70,000 men. He pressed the negroes of the surrounding country into service and set them to digging. The engineers laid out a system of regular approaches and diagonals, and the soldiers with pickaxes and shovels were set to work. It was hard work and tedious. Many hundred yards had to be dug in order to get ten yards nearer the enemy's line. But the soldiers were confident of victory and accepted the drudgery cheerfully. On top of the earth thrown from the trenches were piled sandbags with a little space between them. On the sandbags were laid logs. This made a wall higher than the soldiers' heads, pierced with loopholes for the sharpshooters to fire through. Behind this wall the sappers and miners worked in perfect safety, wheeling loads of dirt to the rear and carrying sap rollers, gabions and fascines to the front, while all the time the Union sharpshooters kept a steady stream of lead whistling over the enemy's earthworks.

The Confederates were sorely harassed by this continual fusilade, to which they could make no adequate response owing to the scarcity of caps. "The enemy's sharpshooters were all splendid marksmen," wrote one of Pemberton's men, "and effectually prevented any of our men from rising above the parapet on pain of certain death, while it was an utter impossibility for our cannoneers to load the guns remaining in position on our line without being exposed to the aim of a dense line of sharpshooters." One of these sharpshooters, called "Coonskin" by the soldiers because he wore a cap made of that fur, was particularly active in his work. At night he would steal out from the Union lines and dig himself a pit near the Confederate works, where he would lie all day, picking off with his unerring rifle any rash Confederate who dared show himself within range. Finally he built a tall tower of railway ties, from the top of which he could look down into the enemy's trenches. Protected by the ties from the Confederate bullets he would stay in his tower for hours at a time, and became a veritable terror to the Confederates.

Working day and night the Federals soon brought their lines close to the Confederate breastworks. At some points, scarce thirty feet separated them; at others, the same wall of clay that protected the gray against the blue, protected equally the blue against the gray. The Confederates were not idle. They impeded the Federal advance by all means in their power. Flaming wads of tow were fired from large-bore muskets into the Union sap rollers and set them afire. The Federals promptly made new ones and kept them wet while in use. Hand grenades and shells were tossed into the nearest of the Union trenches and did great damage, though sometimes the Federal soldiers deftly caught them and tossed them back to explode within the Confederate lines. At one point the Federals had a screen of heavy timbers which resisted the shock of 13-inch shells. A barrel containing 125 pounds of gunpowder was rolled down upon it by the Confederates and touched off. The screen flew in all directions, and the air was filled with flying timbers. Then Grant's men began digging mines under the enemy's works intending to blow them up. Pemberton sank counter-mines to intercept them. The first mine touched off by the Federals buried six of the enemy alive in their counter-mine. The second mine was loaded with a ton of powder. When it exploded, it blew to pieces a whole corner of a Confederate fort, sending timbers, guns, and men flying into the air. One negro was thrown over into the Union lines alive, literally blown out of slavery. Some one asked him how high he had been thrown. "Dunno, massa; 'bout tree miles I think," was his answer. When the mine exploded, the Federal storming party rushed into the crater only to find that the Confederates had a second line of defense in the rear, and that as yet no breach had been made in Pemberton's impenetrable breastworks.

But other messages than shells and bullets passed between the soldiers in the hostile trenches. Sometimes in the evening an informal truce would be declared. The tobacco which was plentiful in Vicksburg would be tossed into the Union trenches, and bits of hard bread or paper parcels of coffee given in exchange. In exchange for Northern newspapers the Southerners would pass out the Vicksburg paper, reduced to sore straits now because of the siege and printed on the blank side of wall paper. It was this paper that, by way of comment on the "Yankee boast" that Grant would eat his dinner in Vicksburg on the Fourth of July, remarked that the best rule for cooking a rabbit was, "First ketch your rabbit."

The printing of its newspaper on wall paper was not the only evidence that the siege was bringing sore distress upon Vicksburg. The rations of Pemberton's soldiers had been cut down 75 per cent. "How do you like mule meat, Johnnie?" was the cheery way in which the blue-coats used to notify their gray-clad foes that they knew an unusual article of food was being served in Vicksburg. The citizens were starving, mule steaks and dressed rats hung in the markets. The scarcity of provisions and the depreciation of Confederate money made prices enormously high. The shells from the gunboats kept dropping in the streets of the city, driving the people to live in caves. With starvation in their homes and death in the streets, the plight of the people of Vicksburg was indeed gloomy.

It became evident to all in the city that the time was fast coming when surrender would become inevitable. The army had done nobly. It had beaten back every attempt of the Federals to pierce its lines. It had driven away Porter's gunboats, and sent the *Cincinnati* to the bottom. But the constant strain and the lack of food were telling upon the soldiers. Johnston had made no sign of coming to their aid, and they saw no chance of relief from the persistent cannonade of their relentless antagonist, no hope of relieving their famished stomachs with full rations once more. A letter which Pemberton received on June 28, signed "Many Soldiers," gave him a hint of the sentiments which prevailed among his men. We quote a few sentences:

"Everybody admits that we have covered ourselves with glory, but alas! alas! General, a crisis has arrived in the midst of our siege.

"Our rations have been cut down to one biscuit and a small piece of bacon a day—not enough scarcely to keep body and soul together, much less to stand the hardships we are called upon to stand.

"Men don't want to starve and don't intend to, but they call upon you for justice, if the Commissary Department can give it, but if it can't you must adopt some means to relieve us very soon. The emergency of the case demands prompt and decisive action on your part.

"If you can't feed us you had better surrender us, horrible as the idea is, rather than suffer this noble army to disgrace themselves by desertion. I tell you plainly, men are not going to lie here and perish; if they do love their country, self-preservation is the first law of nature, and hunger will compel a man to do almost anything. You had better heed a warning voice though it is the voice of a private soldier.

"This army is now ripe for mutiny unless it can be fed."

How much effect this remarkable document had upon Pemberton, it is impossible to say. But he would have been more than blind had he failed to see that an early surrender was the only course open to him. For a time he cast about seeking some desperate expedient for escaping from his plight. He thought of trying to escape across the river, and actually began the construction of some hundreds of heavy boats. Then he considered the feasibility of making a bold dash and cutting his way through Grant's lines. Concerning the advisability of this maneuver he consulted his division commanders on the 2d of July, and received an almost unanimous report that the men were too much exhausted and enfeebled to make the effort. Thereupon Pemberton determined to surrender.

On the morning of the 3d of July work was going on as usual along the Union lines. Another assault had been planned for the 6th, and many of the men were at work filling bags with cotton to be used in filling the ditches, and making scaling ladders. Suddenly there appeared over the Confederate works a white flag, then another, and another, until over each of the chief Confederate batteries a white flag was floating. The blue-coats knew it meant surrender, and cheered until all the hills around rung with the echoes.

Grant and Pemberton met under an oak tree between the lines to formulate the terms of surrender. Grant would hear of nothing but an unconditional surrender. "Men who have shown so much endurance and courage as those now in Vicksburg," said Grant, "will always challenge the respect of an adversary, and I can assure you will be treated with all the respect due to prisoners of war." But Pemberton would not agree to surrender unconditionally. He declared himself able to hold Vicksburg for some time longer, and would only surrender if liberal terms were allowed him. The conference broke up without any conclusion having been reached, Grant agreeing to send Pemberton a letter that night. It was agreed further, that hostilities should be discontinued until the negotiations were ended. So an unwonted quiet hung over the lines, while everybody was wondering what would be the result of the conference between the two generals commanding.

There could be but one result to that conference. Pemberton was beaten and he knew it. He knew that his troops could not and would not resist the assault which Grant threatened to make on the next day. He knew that the people of Vicksburg were crying aloud for the siege to be raised. And so after an interchange of letters the Confederate general declared his willingness to surrender. By a strange coincidence the surrender was made on the Fourth of July, which redoubled the enthusiasm of the victorious Federals. Yet there was little exultation on the part of the Union troops. They felt for their defeated foe, and were careful not to triumph over him openly. When the Federals marched into the town, the first thing the men in blue did was to open their knapsacks and give their half-famished foes a part of their plentiful rations. One bit of boasting over the victory was mightily enjoyed by the victors, for a soldier brought up in a printing office went to the office of the Vicksburg newspaper and soon had out an edition announcing that the Yankees had caught their rabbit.

On the afternoon of the 4th, the formal ceremonies of the surrender were completed. "They marched out of their intrenchments by regiments upon the grassy declivity immediately outside their fort," writes a Union man who saw Pemberton's army lay down its arms. "They stacked their arms, hung their colors upon the center, laid off their knapsacks, belts, cartridge boxes and cap pouches, and thus shorn of the accoutrements of the soldier returned inside their works and thence down the Jackson road into the city. The men went through the ceremony with that downcast look so touching on a soldier's face; not a word was spoken; there was none of that gay badinage we are so much accustomed to hear from the ranks of regiments marching through the streets; the few words of command necessary were given by their own officers in that low tone of voice we hear used at funerals. Their arms were mostly muskets and rifles of superior excellence, and I saw but very few shotguns or indiscriminate weapons of any kind; it was plain that Pemberton had a splendidly appointed army."

More than anything else, except perhaps the battle of Gettysburg, the fall of Vicksburg discouraged and disheartened the people of the Confederacy. It was a notable triumph for the North. It made the military reputation of America's greatest soldier. Only in the campaigns of Napoleon can the student of military science find equally brilliant results accomplished with an equal force. Nor had it been a costly campaign for the Federals. Scarce 10,000 men had been lost, and of this number many were but slightly wounded and soon resumed their places in the ranks. At such light cost Grant had wholly destroyed an army of 46,000 men, captured 60,000 small arms and 260 cannon, taken Vicksburg, and re-opened the Mississippi River to navigation.

For though Vicksburg was not the only Confederate stronghold on the banks of the great river, yet its fall ended Confederate domination over the stream. At Port Hudson the enemy had batteries scarcely less powerful than those which had so long held Grant in check at Vicksburg. Here a garrison of 6000 men was besieged by General Banks. The same tactics as those in force at Vicksburg were followed by Banks. Ever tightening his lines about the beleaguered town he drew his forces nearer and nearer to the Confederate works, threatening an assault and rapidly bringing the besieged soldiers to the verge of starvation. When Vicksburg fell Banks caused salutes to be fired all along the line. The Confederate pickets asked what it meant, and were told the reason. As soon as he had satisfied himself of the truth of the report, General Gardner, who was in command, hoisted the white flag and surrendered upon the same terms as those granted at Vicksburg.

Thus was the Mississippi opened and the Confederacy cut in two. The men of the Northwest had hewn their way to the Gulf.

CHAPTER XI.

MANEUVERING BRAGG OUT OF TENNESSEE. — THE CHATTANOOGA CAMPAIGN. — ROSECRANS'S ARMY IN PERIL. — BATTLE OF CHICKAMAUGA. — THOMAS TO THE RESCUE. — BRAGG'S PLANS FOILED. — STARVING IN CHATTANOOGA. — OPENING THE CRACKER LINE. — GRANT IN COMMAND. — BATTLE OF WAUHATCHIE. — BATTLE OF LOOKOUT MOUNTAIN. — MISSIONARY RIDGE. — BRAGG'S FINAL DEFEAT.

WHILE Grant's guns were thundering away before Vicksburg, and while Lee and Meade were making those moves on the chessboard of war that ended in the decisive battle of Gettysburg, two other great armies were confronting each other in Tennessee, neither being anxious to move first. After the battle of Stone's River, which may fairly be called a drawn battle, the Confederate Army of Tennessee under General Bragg, and the Union Army of the Cumberland under General Rosecrans, remained intrenched near Murfreesboro for some time watching each other. Rosecrans thought that by keeping his army always ready to attack Bragg he would keep the Confederate commander from sending any troops to the assistance of Pemberton at Vicksburg. Bragg for his part had concluded to adopt precisely similar tactics to prevent Rosecrans from sending any troops to Grant, and the two armies accordingly remained inactive until after Vicksburg had fallen, though they were but a few miles apart. Throughout the summer they marched and countermarched, threatened, made demonstrations, skirmished and did everything except to meet in battle. There was a great deal of strategy, but, except for a few cavalry raids, very little fighting, so that Lee's trusty lieutenant, General D. H. Hill, who had been sent to take command of a corps in Bragg's army, was moved to say to a fellow-officer, "When two armies confront each other in the East, they get to work very soon, but here you look at one another for days and weeks at a time."

"Oh, we out here have to crow and peck straws awhile before we use our spurs," was the laughing response.

The battle of Stone's River was fought on the 1st and 2d of January, 1863, and though the two armies were almost within sight of each other for the next eight months they did not again come to blows until the middle of September. In the meantime by a series of rapid marches and demonstrations, Rosecrans had succeeded in forcing his antagonist back step by step until September found Bragg's army quartered in Chattanooga in the extreme southeast corner of the State. The Federal campaign was a brilliant one, and rightly won for General Rosecrans the favorable attention of students of military science, for, with but a trivial loss to his own army, he had pushed a powerful adversary backward for hundreds of miles and had freed the greater part of the State of Tennessee from Confederate domination. Burnside had led an expedition into the mountainous regions of eastern Tennessee, driving Buckner away from Knoxville, and his successes with those of Rosecrans resulted in the disappearance of gray uniforms and barred flags from all parts of Tennessee save the region surrounding Chattanooga.

But of all places in Tennessee, Chattanooga was the one which the national authorities least desired to see occupied by a Confederate force. Its geographical position is commanding. It is the chief southern gateway between the East and the West, and owing to that fact bears to-day the name "The Gate City." Through Chattanooga passed the railroads that led from Vicksburg and Mobile to the chief towns of northern Mississippi, Tennessee, and Kentucky. With Chattanooga once in the hands of the Federals the Confederacy would be split in twain. No longer could the rich spoils of Tennessee farms be sent to feed the armies about Richmond. No longer could a brigade be put on the cars at Richmond and sent rumbling away to reënforce some threatened Confederate post in the West. Federal occupation of Chattanooga meant the shutting off of all communication between the East and West.

Accordingly, having driven Bragg into Chattanooga, Rosecrans immediately set about devising a way of driving him out. The problem was greatly complicated by the physical configuration of the country about the town. The Tennessee River flows broad and deep before the city, which lies in a little valley between two rugged ridges of lofty hills. To cross the river directly in front of the city meant for Rosecrans to ferry his troops over in the teeth of the enemy's fire. To cross either above or below the town was to have added to the peril of crossing a broad, swift stream, the labor of scaling mountain ridges or the hazard of leading a column of troops through narrow and tortuous passes in which an enemy might lie ambushed.

After duly considering the situation, Rosecrans determined to cross the river below the city and advance against Bragg from the south. His first care was to deceive his enemy as to the plan of campaign he had adopted. General Hazen with four brigades was entrusted with this task and sent up-stream to appear on the bank at every bridge and ford above the town threatening to cross. Hazen's work was well done. A myriad of camp fires marked the nightly halts of his fifteen regiments. His days' marches were slow as though he had a huge army to handle. His scouts and small detachments of his forces were seen by the enemy's pickets and scouts at every crossing place for a hundred miles above the city. Bragg was worked into a fever of apprehension, and exerted all his energies toward meeting an attack upon Chattanooga from the north.

Under cover of this diversion Rosecrans rapidly pushed his army across the stream below Chattanooga. By three different roads the divisions of Thomas, McCook, and Crittenden marched toward Chattanooga. The news of their advance was carried by swift scouts to Bragg. He saw himself threatened from a hitherto unsuspected quarter. Moreover he at once recognized the fact that unless he instantly evacuated Chattanooga, Rosecrans would place his army between him and his communications, cutting off the reënforcements he was hourly expecting from Richmond, and blocking up the only path by which he could retreat, should the impending battle go against him. Bragg was not one of the great generals of the South, but he was quick to recognize the necessity which had been forced upon him by the able strategy of Rosecrans. Not underestimating for a moment the value of Chattanooga, he concluded that he could best defend the city by evacuating it and giving battle to the enemy elsewhere.

Meantime the Union army was closing in upon Chattanooga by slow and toilsome marches. Crittenden's division, which marched by the bank of the Tennessee, made the most rapid progress, having no mountains to climb. His vanguard entered the town just as the last regiments of the Confederate army were marching out. But the other divisions of the Union army were having a weary and a laborious time of it. Sand and Raccoon mountains had to be passed, and the steep slopes of Lookout Mountain to be scaled. The narrow, rugged, precipitous country roads were wholly insufficient for the needs of the marching column. With axes, spades, and picks the soldiers labored to prepare the road for the passage of the ponderous artillery and the ammunition and supply trains. The regular artillery teams were powerless to drag the heavy guns up the steep incline. Though doubled they were still unequal to the task. Soldiers tugged at long ropes; soldiers put their shoulders to the wheels, pushing, hauling, forcing the heavy field-pieces along through ruts and over rocks until the summit was reached. Nor was the descent of the mountain-side accomplished with much greater ease. The task then was to hold back and check the heavy guns and wagons lest their too rapid descent should end in disaster.

In order to utilize the roads that cross the Lookout range it became necessary for Rosecrans to permit his army to become widely scattered. Thus when on September 9, Crittenden entered Chattanooga, McCook was on the crest of the Lookout range forty-six miles south, while Thomas was twenty miles below McCook on the same range. This was a situation which would have given the Union commander much uneasiness had he not confidently believed that Bragg was retreating in all possible haste without intending to strike a blow. This belief was carefully fostered by Bragg, who sent into Rosecrans's lines soldiers, pretending to be deserters, who told doleful tales of the panic in Bragg's army and the disorderly haste with which the retreat was being conducted. Moreover the Union war authorities at Washington were in complete ignorance of the movements of Bragg's army, and were sending to Rosecrans dispatches which increased his confidence in the theory that his adversary was in full retreat. As late as September 11, General Halleck telegraphed, "It is reported here by deserters that a part of Bragg's army is reënforcing Lee." Instead of this being the case, however, a part of Lee's army was reënforcing Bragg, for at that very moment a large portion of Longstreet's famous corps was on the cars and speeding away toward Chattanooga.

In fact Bragg was not retreating. He had shifted his position just enough to inspire Rosecrans with a dangerous confidence, and was now rapidly concentrating his army again with a view to falling upon the scattered Union divisions and crushing them one by one. Though in this purpose he failed completely, it cannot be said that his ill success was due to any failure on the part of Rosecrans to afford him the wished-for opportunities. More than once victory was placed within his very grasp and he failed to clutch it. He himself lays the responsibility for this failure upon his subordinates—notably upon General Polk, whom he charges with disobedience of orders—but there are not wanting military critics who declare that Bragg himself was the author of his own misfortunes. An undue haste to attack caused him to miss his first opportunity to seriously cripple Rosecrans's army. Repeated and most inexplicable delays robbed him of his final chance to win on the borders of the Chickamauga Creek a complete and decisive victory.

On the 10th of the month the advance division under General Negley, of Thomas's corps, had crossed Lookout Mountain by way of Stevens's Gap and passed into the narrow valley known as McLemore's Cove. Continuing his march eastward, Negley came to Dug Gap which opened a way through Missionary Ridge. Here he found his way blocked, for the Confederates had felled trees across the road in such numbers that it was impossible for an artillery train to pass, and even the progress of a column of infantry was greatly impeded. While Negley was hesitating before these obstructions Bragg saw an opportunity to fall upon him and cut him off. Orders to that effect were accordingly issued to Cleburne and Hindman, but the obstructions which had embarrassed the Federals in their advance now proved their salvation, for by them the march of the Confederates was so greatly impeded that Negley had time to fall back to Stevens's Gap and there concentrate with Baird. Meantime contradictory orders and the lack of proper discipline among Bragg's division commanders led to such irresolution and lack of concert of action that the attempt to cut Negley and Baird off was abandoned. Cleburne made one attack on Negley, but encountered such a vigorous resistance from two companies of Illinois troops sheltered behind a wall, that he speedily retired, Hindman following him after a short cannonade of the Federal positions. For this failure to make a vigorous attack Bragg severely censured these officers in his report, but he had ordered Hindman, "If you find the enemy in such great force that it is not prudent to attack, then fall back through Catlett's Gap to Lafayette."

Having thus failed to seize upon his opportunity to cut off and demolish Negley, Bragg turned his attention toward Crittenden, who was then marching from Chattanooga down the valley to form a junction with the other divisions of the Union army. Crittenden's corps was split up into three divisions widely separated. "You have a splendid opportunity of crushing Crittenden in detail," telegraphed Bragg to Polk about sunset on the 12th of September, "and I hope you will avail yourself of it at daylight to-morrow. I shall be delighted to hear of your success." Polk was with a whole Confederate corps only three miles from Lee and Gordon's mills, where was General Wood with only two brigades of Union troops. It would have been easy for the Confederate commander to crush this slender force, but he believed that Crittenden was rapidly concentrating his division to attack, and so, instead of marching against Wood, Polk took up a defensive position and telegraphed Bragg, "I have taken up a strong position for defence but need reënforcements." And though Bragg sent strenuous messages to Polk urging an immediate attack, and followed them up by going himself to the front, Polk remained snugly ensconced in his defensive position, while Crittenden marched back and forth before him with what the Confederate General Hill calls, "delightful unconsciousness that he was in the presence of a force of superior strength."

But it was not alone because of his failure to demolish the scattered divisions of his enemy that these movements were unfortunate for Bragg and his cause. The narrow escapes of Crittenden and Negley warned Rosecrans that his antagonist was not making a disorderly retreat but was really concentrating and preparing to give him battle. Roused into frantic activity by the discovery, Rosecrans sent out vigorous orders providing for the immediate concentration of his troops. The whole Union army was almost instantly put in motion. Long and rapid marches were made, and by the 18th the greatest danger was passed and a substantial concentration of the army effected. To all this activity on the part of his foes Bragg was seemingly blind. He

IN THE TRENCHES.

allowed day after day to pass without striking the blow he had ordered Polk to strike on the 13th, and which might have been delivered with equal effect on any one of the two or three days following. So firmly rooted in his mind was the idea that Rosecrans was doing nothing toward rectifying his positions, that, when General Longstreet reported to him some highly important and correct information concerning the whereabouts of the Federals obtained in a reconnoissance by Colonel Baylor, the Confederate commander exclaimed petulantly, "Colonel Baylor lies. There is not a Union infantry soldier south of us." And to this opinion he obstinately adhered until it was too late to prevent the concentration of Rosecrans's army.

The night of the 18th of September saw long lines of blue-clad soldiers, weary with forced marches and dusty and bedraggled with the dirt of mountain roads, swinging into position along the western bank of Chickamauga creek. "The river of death" is the literal meaning of the harsh Indian name by which this stream is known. Through the woods, across broad pastures and cultivated fields that bordered on the rivulet with the sombre name, stretched the Union army; divided no longer but drawn up in line of battle, alert and ready for the conflict.

From the summit of Pigeon Mountain beyond the Chickamauga, Bragg's scouts looked down upon the Federal brigades swinging into line. The Confederate commander himself was there, availing himself of the opportunity afforded to study the exact dispositions of his foe. If Bragg felt any chagrin at seeing thus concentrated before him an army which he might have dismembered he gave no expressions to this thought. Heavy reënforcements had come to him during the day, and now with 70,000 men to 55,000 Federals he felt confident that he could crush his foe.

The plan of battle chosen by General Bragg was substantially the same as that adopted by him at Stone's River. While holding Rosecrans's attention by demonstrations all along the line, he purposed to concentrate his main attack on the Federal left, crushing that by force of men and metal, and swinging the Federals around as on a pivot. Unluckily for the success of his plan he put General (and Bishop) Polk in command of his right wing, while the Federal left was under the command of General Thomas, who proved more than a match for his clerical antagonist.

On the night of the 18th there was little activity among the Confederates. Bragg did nothing more than to push two divisions across the Chickamauga, and issue his orders for the battle of the following day. As it happened, this advance of a small portion of the Confederate force led to the initiative being taken by the Federals in the next day's battle, for a party of Federal cavalrymen burnt the bridge behind the Confederate vanguard and then galloped off to tell Thomas, who had just come up, that a small body of his foes were in his power, cut off from their friends and unable to retreat.

With the dawn of the 19th Thomas is ready for action. He sends forward two brigades toward Reed's bridge to engage the Confederates who have crossed. They meet Forrest's cavalry and easily put it to flight, but two brigades of foot-soldiers in butternut gray come up and check the tide of battle. While the lines are being reformed, Liddell's Confederate division, 2000 strong, and fresh and vigorous after four days of inactivity, comes up and falls furiously upon the Union troops, which give way for the moment in seemingly hopeless disorder. The exultant Confederates rush madly forward with frantic yells. The men of Brannan and Baird's division give way before the assault and rush pell-mell to the rear. Even the three regiments of regulars gave way. Only the artillerists stand sturdily in line. It is too late to escape with their guns, they prefer to die rather than to leave them. Loomis's Michigan battery is one of the two captured. From the beginning of the war it has been at the very front of the line of battle, and the very wood and metal of its guns are dear to its members. Nearly all the gunners die by the side of their cannon, and Lieutenant Van Pelt fights madly against whole regiments with his single sabre until he is cut down amid his guns.

But now the tide of war, which has been setting so strongly against the Federals, turns. Two fresh divisions come up and are thrown into the fight. This enables the Federals to outflank their adversaries and the Confederates are driven in their turn, losing a large number of prisoners and the batteries which they had just captured. Before the advance of the reënforced Federals is checked the Confederates have been driven back to the line of Chickamauga Creek, and though they try time and again to regain their lost ground, nightfall finds them no further advanced than when they went into battle at ten o'clock in the morning. The first day's fighting ends in the triumph of the Federals, for they have held their position and beaten back all efforts to drive them.

That night there was activity along the lines of both armies. The course of the day's battle had clearly revealed Bragg's plan of action to his adversaries, and Rosecrans spent the night in sending heavy detachments of troops over to his left flank, where he felt sure the attack would be fiercest in the morning. Bragg for his part changed the organization of his army, dividing it into two wings and giving Polk command of the right, and Longstreet of the left. Polk was ordered to attack at daylight in the morning. To him was left the weighty responsibility of sustaining the brunt of the conflict. Success in his front meant the cutting off of the Nationals from Chattanooga and the certain destruction of the Federal army. Heavy reënforcements for the Confederates came up during the night, and Bragg felt that at last victory was within his grasp.

Morning dawned. The gray light of early dawn brightened into the rosy flush of the sunrise. The hum of voices and the rumbling of wagons arose from both the hostile camps, but there came no sound of battle from Polk's position, and Bragg paced up and down before his headquarters impatiently listening for the boom of the cannon that should tell him that Polk had gone into action. A staff officer sent to hasten the clerical general brought back the disappointing message: "Please inform the general commanding that I have already ordered General Hill into action; that I am waiting for him to begin; and do please say to General Bragg that my heart is overflowing with anxiety for the attack." Bragg then galloped off in person to find Hill. It was eight o'clock when this officer was found. His troops were leisurely breakfasting around their camp-fires.

"Why have you not begun the attack?" asked Bragg with some indignation.

"I have received no order to that effect," responded Hill with surprise.

"I found Polk after sunrise sitting down reading a newspaper at Alexander's bridge, two miles from the line of battle where he ought to have been fighting," continued Bragg hotly. His orders had miscarried, and as usual he was inclined to charge his officers with flagrant neglect of duty in not having obeyed orders that they had not received.

Soon after Bragg's arrival the battle opened. For a time the Federals were driven back, but Rosecrans hurried forward heavy reënforcements to the aid of Thomas and the lost ground was soon recovered. The Rossville road was the point for which both armies contended, and it was held now by one and then by the other. If the Confederate attack was spirited, the Union defense was stubborn, and the carnage was frightful. But Thomas, whom the Confederate General Hill calls "the savior of the Union army," was equal to his task, and though the fury of the Confederate attack forced his line back, he opposed a stout resistance and successfully blocked Bragg's endeavor to flank the Union line. But his success was won at heavy cost. Though protected by breastworks of logs and fence rails, Thomas still found the Confederate attacks so fierce that he was obliged to send repeatedly to Rosecrans for assistance. In answer to his appeals the divisions of Negley, Van Cleve, McCook and the reserve brigade of Brannan were sent to his assistance, while orders were sent to Sheridan to be ready to follow at an instant's notice. All this weakened the Federal right wing, and when Longstreet, "the hammer," began to send his brigades against that part of the Union line, Rosecrans became apprehensive that his right would be crushed. Seeking to remedy his fancied error he sent orders out for the rearrangement of his lines. One of these was to General Wood, whose division was posted on the right center. "The general commanding," it read, "directs that you close up on Reynolds as fast as possible, and that you support him. This order, written by one of Rosecrans's staff officers, was contradictory in its terms and meaningless. To "close up" in its military sense means to take position beside another body of troops so that the two shall form one continuous line. "To support" means to take a position in the rear. Both could not be done, and General Wood, instead of sending back to Rosecrans for an explanation of the contradictory order, concluded to support Reynolds, and accordingly withdrew his command to a position in the rear of Reynolds. This left a gap in the Union lines directly opposite Longstreet, which was instantly observed by that able commander. Instantly he began to pour his troops into the opening. Bushrod Johnson's three brigades were first into the gap. Hindman and Kershaw followed fast. No raw untried troops these, but veterans who followed Lee and Longstreet and Jackson in all the bloody campaigns against the Army of the Potomac, and who were on their mettle now and anxious to show their Western brethren in arms how the Virginia soldiers could fight. "On they rushed," writes General Hill, "shouting, yelling, running over batteries, capturing trains, taking prisoners, seizing the headquarters of the Federal commander at the Widow Glenn's, until they found themselves facing the new Federal line on Snodgrass Hill. Hindman had advanced a little later than the center and had met great and immediate success. The brigades of Deas and Manigault charged the breastworks at double-quick, rushed over them, drove Laiboldt's Federal brigade of Sheridan's division off the field down the Rossville road; then General Patton Anderson's brigade of Hindman, having come into line, attacked and beat back the forces of Davis, Sheridan and Wilder in their front, killed the hero and poet, General

Lytle,* took 1100 prisoners, 27 pieces of artillery, commissary and ordnance trains, etc."

This, then, was the situation after Wood's fatal blunder: On the left of the Union line Thomas, holding his line gallantly; his men in the breastworks that made a semicircle about the crest of Snodgrass Hill; the enemy to his right, left, and in his front. On the far right of the Union line were Sheridan and Davis with five fresh brigades cut off from all communication with Thomas and practically useless for further employment against the enemy. In the center, where the line had been pierced, was a motley throng of disorganized infantrymen, teamsters, and camp followers all rushing to the rear. The Dry Valley road that led to Rossville, where the Union reserve were posted, was thronged with wagons, empty caissons, ambulance, mounted men and men on foot, all with one thought and one purpose, to escape from the field of battle. In this torrent of fugitives Rosecrans was caught. He had made an attempt to reach Thomas, but found his progress in that direction blocked by the enemy, and was now drifting with the tide toward Rossville. With him was his chief of staff, James A. Garfield, many years afterward President of the United States.

The information volunteered by the stragglers was not encouraging. "The entire army is defeated and is retreating to Chattanooga," said one; "Rosecrans and Thomas have both been killed, and McCook and Crittenden are prisoners," declared another. From the mass of true and false report Rosecrans sifted the one fact that most of the disorderly fugitives were from Negley's division, and that the division had been cut to pieces. As Negley had been sent to reënforce Thomas, Rosecrans reasoned that disaster to Negley meant disaster to Thomas,

---

* General Lytle will long be remembered as the author of the poem, "The death of Mark Antony," beginning :

"I am dying, Egypt, dying,
Ebbs the crimson life-tide fast."

and accordingly concluded that the left wing had been crushed like the right. Believing then that his army had sustained a complete defeat, Rosecrans hastened to Chattanooga, in order to be there to meet and rally the disorganized troops of fugitives that were making for that place.

General Garfield, however, did not feel satisfied with the information gleaned. He wanted to go and find Thomas, and receiving permission from Rosecrans set out. Evading the Confederates by whom Thomas was nearly surrounded, he soon stood at that General's side. He found him stubbornly holding his ground after a bloody contest which had resulted in holding for the Federal arms the spot which was the key to the whole battle field.

When Longstreet pierced the Union center, Thomas was engaged in repelling a spirited attack on his left. Bragg was still anxious to turn his flank, and sent Breckinridge forward to make an attack for that purpose. The officer in command at the point threatened sent in haste to Thomas for reënforcements, and Thomas sent an aide to bring up Sheridan. The messenger soon returned with terrifying tidings. He could not find Sheridan. He could see no signs of the divisions that should have been covering the right of Thomas's line. He had gone but a few rods when he met a long line of men in gray, with skirmishers advanced approaching on the right flank.

Thomas understood at once what had happened. The Union line had been pierced, and he had now to repel assaults on both his flanks as well as in his front. It was a trying situation, but Thomas never faltered. With his men behind his improvised breastworks and his cannon flaming from a commanding hillock in his rear, he set about making a cool, deliberate, stubborn defensive fight, making sure that help would come from some quarter.

Help did come and from an unexpected quarter. Over at Rossville was General Gordon Granger in command of the Union reserves. A soldier of fiery temper, he became restive at being kept in inactivity. When to the sound of the Sabbath church bells of Chattanooga there succeeded the heavy booming of the cannon along the line of battle, Granger grew impatient.

"He walked up and down in front of his flag nervously pulling his beard." It is Granger's chief of staff who tells the story. "Once stopping he said, 'Why the —— does Rosecrans keep me here? There is nothing in front of us now. There is the battle,' pointing in the direction of Thomas. Every moment the sounds of battle grew louder, while the many columns of dust rolling together were mingled with the smoke that hung over the scene.

"At eleven o'clock, with Granger I climbed a high hay-rick near by. We sat there for ten minutes listening and watching. Then Granger jumped up, thrust his glass into its case and exclaimed with an oath, 'I am going to Thomas, orders or no orders.' 'And if you go' I replied, 'it may bring disaster to the army and you to a court martial.' 'There's nothing in our front now but ragtag bobtail cavalry,' he replied. 'Don't you see Bragg is piling his whole army on Thomas? I am going to his assistance.'"

A few minutes later Granger was marching his troops along the dusty road toward Snodgrass Hill, four miles away, where Thomas was holding his own against heavy odds. The column of relief arrived not a minute too soon. Thomas had held his ground bravely and had beaten back Polk's men, who were attacking on his right, with such vigor that Bragg told Longstreet there was no more fight left in them. But Longstreet's troops were better disciplined and were pressing Thomas hotly. Just as Granger came up a force of Confederates were advancing through a gorge, while on a ridge behind a noted Southern battery was unlimbering its guns for an enfilading fire. Thomas had no men to repel this threatening attack, but Granger's arrival gave him new strength. "Can you carry that position?" he asked. "Yes," replied Granger, "My men are fresh and they are just the fellows for that work. They are raw troops and they don't know any better than to charge up there."

The charge was made, Steedman leading it with the regimental colors in his hand. In twenty minutes the gorge was cleared and the ridge carried. The cost in human life was fearful, but the reward was the salvation of the army.

It was soon after this success had been won that Garfield reached Thomas's position. He had expected to find disaster impending, but saw instead a strong position stubbornly held by Union soldiers, who, though greatly outnumbered, still were confident of holding their ground. He quickly started a courier galloping off to Chattanooga to find Rosecrans with a dispatch: "General Thomas holds his own ground of the morning—the hardest fighting of the day is now going on. I hope General Thomas will be able to hold on here till night and will not have to fall back farther than Rossville, perhaps not any. All fighting men should be stopped there. I think we may retrieve the disaster of the morning—I never saw better fighting than our men are now doing. The rebel ammunition must be nearly exhausted, ours fast failing. If we can hold out an hour more it will be all right."

While Garfield was writing his dispatch, Longstreet was massing his troops to try to retake the position whence the Confederates had been driven by Steedman. He sent to Bragg asking that some of Polk's men be sent to aid him. Bragg returned word that Polk's men had been beaten so badly that there was no more fight in them. At that moment Rosecrans and Bragg each thought that his respective army was defeated. Longstreet then tried to carry the position with four brigades from his own command headed by General Preston, but though the assault was gallantly made it was repulsed with fearful slaughter. Nor for the rest of the day, though the Confederates charged again and again, though the National ammunition gave out and the Federals were obliged to rely upon the bayonet, was any gap made in Thomas's lines. The sun went down leaving Thomas still holding his ground. He had saved the Union army and won for himself the name of "the Rock of Chickamauga."

Night was falling over the little town of Chattanooga when a cavalryman came galloping up the street, threading his way among the wagons and ambulances that filled the streets—the advance guard of the rabble of fugitives that was pressing on to seek shelter in the town. He sought out the adjutant-general's office, where he found Rosecrans, dejected and careworn, talking to McCook and Crittenden. The courier produced an envelope—Garfield's dispatch. Rosecrans read it, sprang to his feet and swung his hat above his head with a shout of joy. "Thank God," he cried. "This is good enough, the day isn't lost yet." Then turning to McCook and Crittenden he said, "Gentlemen, this is no place for you. Go at once to your commands at the front." A few minutes later all three were rallying stragglers, directing detached bodies of troops that had lost their way, and sending all organized commands to Rossville where the army was to be concentrated.

That night under cover of the darkness, while the Confederates were jubilating over the victory of the day, Thomas stealthily marched his command away from Horseshoe Ridge, which he had so gallantly held. Before morning the Union army, sorely diminished in numbers, it is true, but reunited, and reinvigorated with a stern determination to let the enemy win no more laurels, was once more drawn up in line of battle confronting Bragg. Twenty-four hours later the second line was abandoned and the whole Union army was concentrated in Chattanooga, where extensive and massive earthworks gave assurance that even with his comparatively small force Rosecrans might hope to hold the town against his enemy.

So ended the battle of Chickamauga. It had been a costly struggle for both armies. "Never have I known Federal troops to fight so well," wrote the Confederate General Hindman in his report, and he adds that he "never saw Confederate troops fight better." To the valor shown by both armies the long lists of the killed and wounded bear testimony. Rosecrans lost in all 16,336 men, of whom 1687 were killed and 9394 wounded. Bragg's loss was, killed 2673, wounded 16,274, missing 2003. Though the battle had been a tactical victory for the Confederates it had been a costly one, as these figures

DRAGGING BATTERY THROUGH A MARSH.

show. Moreover it proved a barren victory, for after all was over Rosecrans and the Union army were in Chattanooga, and Bragg was still outside. And that the victory cost the Confederates so dear, and won for them so little, was due in the main to General George H. Thomas, who, with his 25,000 men on the slope of Horseshoe Ridge, beat back Longstreet and Polk and saved the Union left.

A month passed away. The Union troops, penned up in Chattanooga with the river behind them and Bragg's men in front, began to experience the discomforts of a siege. One rough road, sixty miles long, over rugged mountain ranges, and through a country infested with the enemy's sharpshooters, was the only way by which supplies could be brought to the Union camp. In fair weather the perils of the road were bad enough, but when the rainy season set in the highway became sixty miles of almost fathomless mud. Wagons sank in up to their axles. Mules were mired and died in their tracks, so that the whole road was lined with the dead bodies of these sturdy animals. Meantime Rosecrans's army was eating up its provisions faster than they could be replaced. Soon half rations became the order of the day; then quarter rations, and before long the soldiers became so hungry that they would follow the wagons coming in with provisions, picking up grains of corn and bits of crackers that dropped from them and devouring them voraciously.

Bragg meanwhile strengthened his works on the slopes of Lookout Mountain and Missionary Ridge, and as he looked down upon the white tents of the Union army, thought complacently that he need sacrifice no more of his gallant soldiers to complete the discomfiture of Rosecrans, but would let starvation do the work for him.

But Bragg was not destined to enjoy so easy a triumph. The authorities at Washington knew of the perilous plight in which Rosecrans was placed, and were taking active steps to relieve him. Sherman was detached from Grant's forces near Vicksburg and ordered to Chattanooga. Hooker and Howard with their two corps were de-

tached from the Army of the Potomac and sent to Tennessee
Finally the Secretary of War himself left Washington, went to Louisville, where he met General Grant, who had been summoned thither by
telegraph, and put that officer in command of all the Union armies
between the Alleghanies and the Mississippi. Rosecrans was next
relieved of his command at Chattanooga and Thomas appointed in his
stead.

"You must hold Chattanooga at all hazards," telegraphed Grant to
the new commander.

"We will hold the town till we starve," was the sturdy reply.

Hastening on to Chattanooga, Grant found the situation there
quite as threatening as indicated by Thomas's dispatch. The army had
not ammunition enough for a battle. It had barely enough provisions
to ward off for ten days absolute starvation. Something had to be
done, and that quickly. Rosecrans had already arranged a plan
to open a line for bringing supplies to the army. Bridgeport, far
down the winding river, was the Union base of supplies and there
Hooker's corps was sent. A few miles down the river from Chattanooga was the landing-place called Brown's Ferry, and from the
town to this ferry was a road on the north side of the river, crossing the tongue of land known as Moccasin Point and secure from
the enemy's fire. The task which Grant had to perform was to
sweep the enemy away from the river and the road between Bridgeport and Brown's Ferry, so that both steamers and wagons could be
used to bring supplies to the beleaguered Army of the Cumberland.
This plan, though seemingly difficult, was carried out with but little
opposition from the enemy. Eighteen hundred men under General
Hazen embarked in great flat-bottomed boats built by the soldiers at
Chattanooga and floated silently down the stream at dead of night, past
seven miles of hostile pickets who caught no glimpse of the floating
column. At Brown's Ferry they disembarked on the south side of the
river, driving away quickly the enemy's pickets posted there. A force
of 1200 men meantime had marched across Moccasin Point to the other

side of the ferry, and these were now quickly ferried across. Axes and shovels were called into play, and before the astonished Confederates could attack these intruders, a line of abatis and earthworks was built and the landing-place at the ferry was securely held. Meantime Hooker had done his part valiantly and well. He marched up the road from Bridgeport toward the ferry, sweeping the Confederates aside, and, leaving detachments to guard the exposed points, formed a junction with the troops at the ferry. By nightfall of the 28th of October, supplies for the Union troops in Chattanooga, instead of being carted for sixty miles over an unsafe road exposed to the raids of the enemy, could be brought in over a perfectly well protected road twenty-eight miles long, or could be brought on steamers up the river to Brown's Ferry, and then taken over eight miles of level road to the Union camp. A little steamer which had been made by the soldiers at Bridgeport out of an old saw-mill engine, mounted in a flat-bottomed scow, made the first trip and brought 240,000 rations to the half-starved soldiers at Chattanooga. "It is hard for any one not an eye-witness to realize the relief this brought," writes General Grant. "The men were soon re-clothed and well fed; an abundance of ammunition was brought up, and a cheerfulness prevailed not before enjoyed in many weeks. Neither officers nor men looked upon themselves any longer as doomed. The weak and languid appearance of the troops, so visible before, disappeared at once. I do not know what the effect was on the other side, but assume it must have been correspondingly depressing."

What the "effect was upon the other side," may be judged from the comment of a Richmond newspaper, which said: "The daring surprise in the Lookout Valley on the nights of the 26th and 27th has deprived us of the fruits of Chickamauga."

It must not not be supposed, however, that the Confederates relinquished without striking a return blow their command over the Union line of communication. At midnight of the 28th, Geary, who had been stationed at Wauhatchie, was furiously attacked by Stevenson's Confederate division. The enemy had hoped to surprise Geary, but he was ready for them, and though attacked from three sides at once, held his assailants gallantly at bay until Schurz came to his aid and drove the enemy off. The Confederates sacrificed several hundred men, but the road over which the Union rations were coming was still safe.

There followed a month of inaction. Sherman was coming up from Vicksburg, and Grant's men simply sat in the trenches at Chattanooga and waited. A sort of truce existed between the two armies. At places the picket lines were scarcely a hundred yards apart, but there was no firing on the pickets. Both armies drew water amicably from the same stream. At night the blue-coats about their camp fires could hear the strains of "Dixie" or the "Bonny Blue Flag" floating from the Confederate camps, and would respond with the patriotic notes of "Hail Columbia" and the "Star Spangled Banner." By day the signal flags of the enemy could be seen waving messages from Lookout Mountain to Missionary Ridge, and all the ingenious minds in Grant's army were trying to make out what those messages were.

One day General Grant rode down to the Union picket line. "Turn out the guard for the commanding general," cried the first picket who saw him. "Never mind the guard," said Grant good-humoredly. But the Confederate pickets too had seen who the visitor was. "Turn out the guard for the commanding general, General Grant," they cried, and in a moment a rank of gray-clad men faced Grant and gravely presented arms. He politely returned the salute and passed on.

This tacit armistice between the hostile armies was terminated about the middle of November by Bragg, who sent Longstreet up into the mountains of eastern Tennessee to drive Burnside out of Knoxville. A fatal error this on the part of the Confederate commander, for at the moment when he thus weakened his army by sending away his ablest corps commander, and a heavy body of troops,

Grant was strengthening his army in every way and preparing to drive the Confederates from the lines with which they surrounded him. But Bragg thought his position impregnable, and this over-confidence led to his destruction. Moreover, his sending Longstreet into eastern Tennessee hastened Grant's attack. The mountaineers of that section had always been loyal to the Union, and President Lincoln was very anxious to keep Confederate forces away from their homes. It was thought that the best way to force Longstreet to abandon his expedition against Knoxville would be to attack Bragg vigorously, and this Grant was ordered to do. The result was the battle of Chattanooga, made up of the three distinct actions of Lookout Mountain, Chattanooga, and Missionary Ridge.

It will be remembered that Bragg's lines surrounded Chattanooga on its landward side in the form of a huge semicircle, the ends resting on the Tennessee River on either side of the town. The Confederate right flank was at the point where Missionary Ridge slopes down to the river, the left flank was on the northern end of Lookout Mountain. Grant's plan of action was to wait until Sherman could come up with his full command, then have him cross the river at Missionary Ridge and make the main attack there, while Thomas in the center and Hooker on the slope of Lookout Mountain should attack the enemy with just enough vigor to prevent any reënforcements being sent to the right flank. In the main this plan of action was adhered to, though as we shall see the enthusiasm and the gallantry of the troops under Hooker and Thomas made them really the heroes of the day, and so far from merely acting to divert Bragg's attention from Sherman they themselves won the greatest triumphs of the battle of Chattanooga.

On the 20th of November Grant received a strange message from Bragg. It read, "As there may still be some non-combatants in Chattanooga I deem it proper to notify you that prudence would dictate their early withdrawal."

Grant was somewhat perplexed by this message. He felt sure

that Bragg could not be contemplating an attack. He knew that Bragg was still sending away troops to help Longstreet, and deserters from the Confederate camp gave him information which seemed to indicate that his foe was planning a retreat. He determined to test the enemy's intentions. So, shortly after noon on the 23d, those of the Confederates who were in position to see saw the troops of Granger, Sheridan, and Wood forming in front of the town as if for a review. But those who thought it a mere military pageant were quickly undeceived, for the long blue line swept quickly forward, driving in the Confederate pickets and charging the rifle-pits. Though from all the hills around the Confederate cannon were roaring and flaming, the men in gray could not hold their ground. Before they could hurry forward more troops to the threatened point the line of fortifications hitherto held by them was in possession of the Federals. It took but little time to turn the earthworks to face the other way, and by night the Union line was well entrenched a mile in advance of the position held by it in the morning.

That night Sherman's troops crossed the Tennessee and made a lodgment at the foot of Missionary Ridge. Their orders were to attack at daylight in the morning. Over on the Union right, around the base of Lookout Mountain, were Hooker's troops. They too were to attack at daylight. All were brimful of enthusiasm and confident of success.

Let us watch Hooker's attack first. It is daylight of a wet, chilly morning. A drizzling rain is falling. All the valley and the lower part of the mountain are shrouded in an impenetrable veil of fog that effectually shuts off all that is going on in the valley from the view of the Confederates on the heights. At four o'clock all is life and action in the Union camps. Hooker's men press forward, driving back the enemy's pickets and advance guard until Lookout Creek is reached. Here a serious check is encountered, for the creek is so swollen by the rain as to be impassable in the face of a hostile force. Hooker begins a bridge and at the same time sends Geary with two divisions up the stream to Wauhatchie, telling him to cross there and return down the other bank, taking the enemy in flank. The Confederates having all their attention fixed upon Hooker's bridge fail to notice Geary's movement, and he is soon attacking them in the flank and rear and spreading panic in their ranks. By eleven o'clock Hooker's bridge is finished, his corps has crossed and in conjunction with Geary is scaling the mountain side, beating back the enemy and driving them around the northern end of the mountain. The ground over which the Federals are advancing is rugged—a steep mountain side, covered with bowlders, broken with crags, ravines and rocky crests. To add to its difficulty the enemy had felled trees, over the trunks and through the tangled boughs of which the assailants have to force their way. Yet the courage and indomitable persistency of Hooker's men overcame all obstacles. The troops of the Confederate General Stevenson fly before them. The Union batteries on neighboring hills and one across the river on Moccasin Point throw shells into their disordered ranks. By two o'clock the Confederates have been driven from the northern slope of the mountain and are flying down into Chattanooga valley. Then Hooker halts and fortifies his lines. He has discharged the task assigned him, and he has done more. Ordered to attack the enemy vigorously he has gone on and driven them from a position which, even after his success, looks to all military eyes impregnable.

The fog that hangs over the mountain has hid Hooker's lines from the anxious eyes of the watchers in the town below. Now and then a break in the veil of mist gives a hasty glimpse of the fighting, but for the most part it is a "battle above the clouds." But when the morning of the day after the battle dawns bright and clear, the blue-coats in Chattanooga see floating from the topmost peak of Lookout Mountain the stars and stripes, and a cheer runs along the line of the whole army, for all know now that the backbone of Bragg's position is broken.

Meanwhile, on the Union left, Sherman is doing some hard fighting, and achieving notable results, though no success as marvelous as the taking of Lookout Mountain attends his efforts. He reaches the crest of the hill, advancing all the time in the face of a heavy infantry fire, and finds when he gets there that the enemy has retreated across a gully to another part of the ridge—Tunnel Hill they call it, because pierced to allow the passage of a railroad. Sherman concludes to advance no further to-day, so fortifies the position he has won, and sends tidings of his success to Grant. "Attack to-morrow at daylight," is the order Grant sends in return.

The morning of the 25th comes. No rain or fog now. The sun rises bright so that the officers in Chattanooga can see with their field-glasses all parts of the battle field. Missionary Ridge is to be the scene of the fighting to-day. Yesterday Bragg's line reached from Missionary Ridge to Lookout Mountain. To-day he will make a desperate effort to hold the ridge alone. The advantage of numbers no longer rests with Bragg. He has but 47,000 men left now. Grant has about 80,000, but not all these will be brought into action.

At sunrise the Union attack begins. Sherman moves along the crest of Missionary Ridge and attacks the enemy in his front. Here is the main column of Bragg's army, and though Sherman's attack is spirited he makes little progress. The tide of battle sways backward and forward. It is evident that if Missionary Ridge is to be carried to-day it will not be by Sherman.

Hooker too is on the march early in the day. Grant thought that by sending him down the valley to Rossville, he would threaten Bragg's rear and weaken the resistance to Sherman. But when Hooker reaches the Chattanooga Creek he finds the bridges destroyed and is delayed too long to make any effective diversion in favor of Sherman.

Grant's plans thus seem to be in danger of entire miscarriage. How then is the day to be won? We shall see that when it was won it was won by soldiers, not generals; that to disobedience of orders was due the notable victory won that day for the Union on the side of Missionary Ridge.

On the crest of Orchard Knob stands General Grant. He scans the summit of the ridge where Sherman is fighting and sees that he is making but little progress. His aides bring him word that Hooker is detained by the wrecked bridges. He sees that some other means of assisting Sherman must be devised.

Along the base of Missionary Ridge is a line of earthworks. On the summit are other works well provided with cannon. Between, the ground is steep, rugged, and covered with brush and felled trees. Before the first line of earthworks is a strip of woods crowded with Confederate skirmishers.

Grant determines to take this first line of works. It will at least, he thinks, draw some of the enemy away from Sherman's front. So he orders forward the divisions of Wood, Johnson, Baird and Sheridan—about 20,000 men all told. Let us let an eye-witness * tell the story of the charge that followed:

"At twenty minutes before four the signal guns were fired. Suddenly 20,000 men rushed forward, moving in line of battle by brigades, with a double line of skirmishers in front, and closely followed by the reserves in mass. The big siege guns in the Chattanooga forts roared above the light artillery and musketry in the valley. The enemy's rifle-pits were ablaze, and the whole ridge in our front had broke out like another Ætna. Not many minutes afterward our men were seen working through the felled trees and other obstructions. Though exposed to such a terrific fire they neither fell back nor halted. By a bold and desperate push they broke through the works in several places and opened flank and reverse fires. The enemy was thrown into confusion and took precipitate flight up the ridge. Many prisoners and a large number of small arms were captured. The order of the commanding general had now been fully and most suc-

---

* General J. S. Fullerton, in " Battles and Leaders of the Civil War."

cessfully carried out. But it did not go far enough to satisfy these brave men, who thought that now the time had come to finish the battle of Chickamauga. There was a halt of but a few minutes to take breath and re-form lines; then with a sudden impulse and without orders all started up the ridge. Officers, catching their spirit, first followed, then led. There was no thought of supports, or of protecting flanks, though the enemy's line could be seen stretching on either side.

"As soon as this movement was seen from Orchard Knob, Grant quickly turned to Thomas, who stood by his side, and I heard him say angrily, 'Thomas, who ordered those men up the ridge?' Thomas replied in his usual slow, quiet manner, 'I don't know; I did not.' Then addressing General Gordon Granger he said, 'Did you order them up, Granger?' 'No,' said Granger, 'they started up without orders. When those fellows get started all hell can't stop them.' General Grant said something to the effect that somebody would suffer if it did not turn out well, and then turning stoically watched the ridge. He gave no further orders.

"As soon as Granger had replied to Thomas he turned to me, his chief of staff, and said: 'Ride at once to Wood and then to Sheridan, and ask them if they ordered their men up the ridge, and tell them if they can take it to push ahead.' As fast as my horse could carry me I rode first to General Wood and delivered the message. 'I didn't order them up,' said Wood; 'they started up on their own account, and they are going up too! Tell Granger, if we are supported we will take and hold the ridge!' As soon as I reached Wood, Captain Avery got to General Sheridan and delivered his message. 'I didn't order them up,' said Sheridan; 'but we are going to take the ridge!' He then asked Avery for his flask and waved it at a group of Confederate officers, standing just in front of Bragg's headquarters, with the salutation 'Here's at you!' At once two guns in front of Bragg's headquarters were fired at Sheridan and the group of officers about him. One shell struck so near as to throw dirt on

Sheridan and Avery. 'Ah!' said the general; 'that is ungenerous. I shall take those guns for that.'

"The men, fighting and climbing up the steep hill, sought the roads, ravines, and less rugged parts. The ground was so broken that it was impossible to keep a regular line of battle. At times their movements were in shape like the flight of migratory birds—sometimes in line, sometimes in mass, mostly in V-shaped groups with the points toward the enemy. At these points the regimental colors were flying, sometimes drooping as the bearers were shot, but never reaching the ground, for other brave hands were there to seize them. Sixty flags were advancing up the hill. Bragg was hurrying large bodies of men from his right to the center. They could be seen hastening along the ridge. Cheatham's division was being withdrawn from Sherman's front. Bragg and Hardee were at the center, urging their men to stand firm, and drive back the advancing enemy now so near the summit—indeed so near that the guns, which could not be sufficiently depressed to reach them, became useless. Artillerymen were lighting the fuses of shells, and bowling them by hundreds down the hill. The critical moment arrived when the summit was just within reach. At six different points, and almost simultaneously, Sheridan's and Wood's divisions broke over the crest—Sheridan's first near Bragg's headquarters; and in a few minutes Sheridan was beside the guns that had been fired at him, and claiming them as captures of his division. Baird's division took the works on Wood's left almost immediately afterward; and then Johnson came up on Sheridan's right. The enemy's guns were turned upon those who still remained in the works and soon all were in flight down the eastern slope. Baird got on the ridge just in time to change front and oppose a large body of the enemy moving down from Bragg's right to attack our left. After a sharp engagement that lasted till dark he drove the enemy back beyond a high point on the north which he at once occupied.

"The sun had not yet gone down, Missionary Ridge was ours, and Bragg's army was broken and in flight. Dead and wounded comrades lay thickly strewn on the ground; but thicker yet were the dead and wounded men in gray. Then followed the wildest confusion as the victors gave vent to their joy. Some madly shouted; some wept from the very excess of joy; some grotesquely danced out their delight—even our wounded forgot their pain to join in the general hurrah."

There was reason enough for the exultation of the men in blue. The notable victory on Missionary Ridge marked the triumphant climax of a campaign in which every chance had been against the escape of the Union army. For days before Chickamauga, Bragg fairly held the Army of the Cumberland in his power, and only his failure to act with promptitude saved that army. At Chickamauga Thomas alone stood between it and destruction. In Chattanooga it narrowly escaped starvation. Finally the egregious blunder of Bragg in sending Longstreet away enabled Grant not only to cut his way out of Chattanooga, but to inflict a signal defeat upon his enemy as well. It is no wonder that the Union soldiers went mad with joy. Nor is it strange that the Confederates, who had fought gallantly and were sacrificed by their incompetent leader, were filled with bitter rage against Bragg, and when he rode among them seeking to rally them with shouts of "Here's your commander!" they responded with derisive cries of "Here's your mule," and "Oh, Bragg is bully on the retreat, you bet."

When the difficulties of the situation and the number of men engaged are taken into consideration, it will be seen that the losses in the battles around Chattanooga were not very heavy. In three days of bridging rivers, climbing hills and scaling precipices in the teeth of the enemy's fire the Federals lost only 5616 men, of whom 757 were killed and 4529 wounded. The total Confederate loss was 8684. But the Union could have well afforded to sacrifice twice as many men to accomplish the same result, for the victory at Chattanooga took the war out of Tennessee (Longstreet's expedition against Knoxville being abandoned as soon as the news reached him), drove Bragg out of the

IN THE WAKE OF BATTLE.

State, and opened to the Federal forces the gateway to the south. In another volume we shall see how such a stream of men in blue poured through that gateway as to overflow the whole southland from Atlanta to the sea-coast, stamping out resistance to the Union and wrecking the Confederacy beyond repair.

Moreover the victory at Chattanooga added yet another triumph to the military record of the soldier who, beginning as a simple lieutenant in Missouri, was quietly and without ostentation building for himself a record that ended in his being placed in supreme command of the armies of the Union.

CHAPTER XII.

IN CHARLESTON HARBOR. — CONFEDERATE EFFORTS TO BREAK THE BLOCKADE. — GENERAL GILLMORE IN COMMAND. — UNION TROOPS ON FOLLY ISLAND. — A LODGMENT ON MORRIS ISLAND. — ATTACK ON FORT WAGNER. — BOMBARDMENT OF FORT SUMTER. — THE SWAMP ANGEL. — BOMBARDMENT OF FORT WAGNER. — VICTORY OF THE FEDERALS. — THE END.

THROUGHOUT the war the war authorities of the North had looked with longing eyes upon Charleston and Charleston Harbor. Sentimental reasons had much to do with the desire of the North to take this notable stronghold of the Confederacy. There the doctrine of secession had its cradle. There the palmetto flag was first unfurled and the first cannon shots sent against the stars and stripes. In that harbor was Fort Sumter, over which the Confederate flag had been flying ever since the day when Anderson and his devoted garrison marched out with the honors of war. But reasons other than those of pure sentiment also actuated the Union authorities in their desire to put Charleston under Federal rule. The harbor, with the channels leading to it, was commanded by Confederate guns in Sumter and in the batteries on the shores. This made it a famous port of entry for blockade runners, bringing arms, clothing, and medicines from England and taking out the cotton grown in the Southern States. Though the naval authorities made strenuous efforts to close the port to the blockade runners by keeping a large fleet of cruisers stationed at its entrance, and by sinking hulks in the channels, the swift, stealthy steamers still slipped in and out with great regularity. "Lines of blockade-running steamers entered and left the port of Charleston at regular stated intervals, up to nearly the close of the war," writes General Beauregard, who was in command of the Confederate defenses.

The same reasons which led the Federals to wish to compass the fall of Charleston impelled the Confederates to make strenuous efforts to retain the city and the harbor under their control. General Beauregard, perhaps the ablest engineer officer of the war, was put in command of all the defenses. Fort Sumter was strongly garrisoned and provided with guns of English make, brought in by the blockade runners. Great troops of slaves were taken from the city and down the harbor in boats, and set to work building redoubts and bastions on the sandy shores. Soon there was no bit of land within gunshot of Fort Sumter that was not fortified and held by the Confederates. Torpedoes, the location of which was made known to the captains of blockade runners, filled the harbor, and floating booms and rope obstructions made the possibility of any hostile man-of-war ever entering the port slight indeed.

Nor did the Confederates confine their efforts to preparations for defense alone. In January, 1863, they sent out two ironclad gunboats that gave battle to the blockading fleet and forced two Federal vessels to strike their colors. This occurrence satisfied the Union authorities that the blockade could only be made effective by establishing the Union forces on the sandy islands that bordered the entrance to the harbor and silencing the guns of Fort Sumter.

South of the harbor's mouth were two large islands made up of low swampy land cut off from the main land by the Stono River and several narrow inlets from the sea. The southernmost of these islands is called Folly Island. North of it and forming the southern boundary of the harbor's mouth is Morris Island. A long narrow spit of sand runs northward from Morris Island, and at its very end was Bat-

tery Gregg, the Confederate work which during the bombardment of
Fort Sumter in 1861 had inflicted the most serious damage upon that
work. To defend Battery Gregg from a hostile force which might
land at the southern end of the island and take it in the rear, there
was built Fort Wagner. This was a spacious earthwork spanning
the island, which at this point is very narrow. High bastions of
sand behind a deep ditch kept ever full of water by the tides, spacious
bombproofs able to shelter the entire garrison from bursting shells, a
line of chevaux-de-frise tipped with iron barring the way to the front,
and a long strip of heavy timbers studded with sharp iron spikes—
all these things combined to make Fort Wagner a defensive work of
a very formidable character. In its front the part of the island bordering upon the ocean was fairly covered with earthworks extending as
far south as Lighthouse Inlet, which separated Morris Island from
Folly Island.

In June of 1863, General Quincey A. Gillmore was put in command of the Union forces about Charleston. He found Folly Island
held by the troops under his command, but the Confederates firmly
intrenched in their position on Morris Island. Fort Sumter and Fort
Wagner had recently met and successfully endured a furious attack
by the Union fleet, and the Confederates were calmly confident that
the positions held by them were impregnable.

A skilled military engineer, Gillmore at once brought scientific
engineering to bear upon the problem before him. The experience
of the navy in the recent action had demonstrated that Fort Sumter
could never be reduced by naval guns alone. So long as the Confederates held Morris Island, no Union land batteries could be erected
within effective range of the grim pile of masonry that guarded the
entrance to Charleston Harbor. Gillmore's first task then was to effect
a lodgment on Morris Island. To this end he began the erection of
heavy batteries on Folly Island at points within easy range of the
enemy's works. This was no easy task. The island was covered
with a dense growth of dwarf pine, thickly undergrown with matted

vines and shrubs. "I have never seen such a mass of briars and thorns anywhere else," wrote one of Gillmore's aides. There was not a road of any description, and the only way to pass from one end of the island to the other was along the beach, which was not always practicable at high tides." But though the tangled thickets vastly increased the labor of building the Union works, yet they concealed Gillmore's operations from the eyes of the enemy so that in twenty days from the time the work was begun forty-eight heavy guns were mounted in massive earthworks within range of the Confederate pickets. All had been done without arousing the suspicion of the enemy.

The time was now ripe for Gillmore to throw a force across Lighthouse Inlet. His first step was to divert the enemy's attention from the point actually threatened. For this purpose General Terry started up the Stono River with 3800 men and landed on James Island. This seemed to threaten an advance on Charleston, and Beauregard sent hastily a part of his Morris Island force to meet and oppose this expedition. Meantime General Strong, with a force of about 2000 men in boats, was making his way through the placid winding lagoon, hidden by the tall waving marsh grass, toward Lighthouse Inlet. At daybreak of the 9th of July, Strong had reached the inlet. When the sun rose the Confederates were astonished to witness all of Gillmore's unsuspected batteries on Folly Island burst into full cry. From the dense pine thickets came rapid flashes and jets of smoke and the shells fell thick and fast in the enemy's works. Four monitors, the *Weehawken*, the *Catskill*, the *Montauk*, and the *Nahant*, steamed in close to shore and added the thunder of their guns to the titanic chorus When the cannonade was at its fiercest the boats bearing Strong's storming party pushed out from their shelter and started down the inlet toward the chosen landing-place. They had a mile to go under the Confederate fire, but the Union artillery was well served and the enemy was suffering too sorely to be exact in aim, so but little damage was sustained. At the landing-place the storming party leaped from the boats into the mud and water and rushed up the sandy beach. The enemy fled almost without resistance. At nine o'clock all the Confederate works at the south end of the island, with eleven pieces of artillery, were captured, and Strong's skirmishers had pushed up within musket range of Fort Wagner, where the Confederates were preparing for a desperate defense. But by this time the day had grown sultry. The blazing southern sun was beating fiercely upon the glaring beach of white sand on which the gallant boys in blue had won a foothold. The troops began to show signs of exhaustion, and the Union commander determined to defer for a day or two the assault upon Fort Wagner.

Great was the consternation in Charleston that day when it was known that the Union troops had won a lodgment on Morris Island. Even the most sanguine saw that the city was doomed. The mayor issued a proclamation advising all women and children to leave the city as quickly as possible. The governor of the State called for three thousand negroes to build defensive works. The newspapers were shrill in their defiance of the hated enemy, and the *Courier* said, "Let us resolve on a Saragossa defense of the city, manning and defending every wharf—fighting from street to street and house to house—and if failing to achieve success, yielding nothing but smoking ruins and mangled bodies as the spoil of the ruthless conqueror."

On the morning of the 11th, Strong ordered an assault upon Fort Wagner. Though led with the greatest gallantry the attack was repulsed, and the assailants retired, convinced that they had before them a formidable obstacle not to be lightly swept from their path. The musket and bayonet were now thrown aside for a time, and the troops were set to digging trenches and mounting cannon. Before many days forty-one cannon, rifles and mortars were facing Fort Wagner at short range. Then Gillmore prepared for another assault.

Shortly after noon on the 18th all the cannon in the Union trenches opened fire on Fort Wagner. The Confederates sprang to their guns and answered with a will. From Fort Sumter came the occasional boom of a heavy gun, and all the land batteries on James

THE CHARGE AT FORT WAGNER.

Island sent iron messages of defiance to the men in Gillmore's works. From the Union fleet riding at anchor in the offing the ironclad vessels soon separated themselves and steamed in to take part in the bombardment. Led by the *New Ironsides*, the ponderous floating citadels steamed slowly back and forth before the fort, sending their shells ricochetting along the water to burst beyond the parapet. The flying pieces of iron sought out every nook and corner of the fort. Its defenders were driven from one gun after another, seeking unwillingly the shelter of the bomb-proofs. The front of the fort that had blazed fire soon became silent and seemed deserted. When the sun went down no gun spoke defiance from the embrasures of Fort Wagner, but over its parapet the flag of the Confederacy still floated.

The Union storming party then formed for the assault. It was led by the gallant Strong, who had been the first Federal soldier to set foot on Morris Island. In the van was the Fifty-fourth Massachusetts regiment, free colored men, recently mustered into the service and led by a white colonel, Robert G. Shaw. Three brigades in all followed the Massachusetts men.

When half a mile from Fort Wagner, the order "Double quick, march!" was given and the party rushed forward at a trot. From Fort Sumter and from the enemy's works on James Island a storm of solid shot and bursting shell was turned upon the advancing column. Wagner still was silent, for its garrison was still confined to the bomb-proofs by the accuracy of the Union artillery fire.

But soon the assailants drew so near the fort that the Union gunners afloat and on shore had to cease firing lest their missiles should injure their friends. Then the Confederates sprang from their bomb-proofs and rushed to the ramparts. The whole front of Fort Wagner was instantly ablaze with musketry. Howitzers poured deadly loads of grape and canister into the dark faces of the assaulting troops. Hand grenades and shells were thrown among them as they floundered in the deep ditch or tried to scramble up the steep glacis. General

Strong was struck down with a mortal wound. Colonel Shaw was killed. Union officers fell fast on every side. The command of regiments fell to men who went into the fight simple lieutenants.

There was a flaw in the preparation for the assault. The troops that should have supported the forlorn hope failed to advance. So, though a part of the gallant assailants scaled the parapet they won but a barren triumph. No reënforcements came to widen the breach they had made, and after gallantly defending themselves for a long time against superior numbers they were forced to surrender. Night fell, with the Confederate flag still floating over Fort Wagner, with nearly 400 Federal soldiers prisoners within the enemy's lines, and with 246 dead and 880 wounded men lying where they had fallen before Fort Wagner's towering redoubt. The total Confederate loss was but 174.

The assault had demonstrated, for the first time, that the negro possessed all the soldierly qualities of his white brother, but beyond this nothing was accomplished. Fort Wagner was unscathed and Charleston seemed further off than ever.

Gillmore had now seen enough to convince him that Fort Wagner could never be taken by direct assault, and the tedious labor of a regular siege was begun. With shovels and barrows the troops began to cut the face of the island into trenches, zigzagging back and forth from the water side to the swamp and approaching nearer to Fort Wagner daily. As soon as favorable ground was reached heavy siege guns were mounted and the work of battering down Fort Sumter with guns two miles away was begun. For seven days the heavy breaching cannon pounded away, firing directly over the heads of the garrison of Fort Wagner. "About 450 projectiles struck the fort daily, every one of which inflicted an incurable wound," writes General Gillmore. "Large masses of the brick walls and parapets were rapidly loosened and thrown down. The bulk of our fire was directed against the gorge and southeast face, which presented themselves diagonally to us. They were soon pierced through and through and cut down on top to the casemate arches. The shot

IN A MONITOR'S TURRET.

that went over them took the north and northwest faces in reverse." After seven days of this cannonade, Sumter was a mass of ruins, easily held by a force of infantry, but mounting no guns and useless for offensive purposes. The Confederates had removed from the shattered structure all its guns, and mounted them in other parts of the harbor.

With Fort Sumter now out of the problem before him, Gillmore turned his attention once more to Fort Wagner. While pushing forward his parallels and approaches with all possible speed, he bethought himself of an expedient for forcing the Confederate commander to surrender without further loss of time or effusion of blood. This plan was nothing more or less than to put a battery in position to bombard Charleston, if the Confederate commander refused to evacuate Morris Island. To build such a battery was in itself a most difficult task. Between the Union works on the beach and Charleston was a vast expanse of muddy marsh cut up by deep tidal creeks and lagoons. Somewhere in that broad expanse of mud and water, the battery must be put for its shells to reach the city. An exploring party found the mud at most places too fluid to bear a man's weight, and from fifteen to twenty feet deep. To build a battery of heavy sand-bags, and mount in it a gun weighing several tons, seemed an impossible task, and it is related that the officer to whom the work was assigned made a humorous requisition for "twenty men eighteen feet long to do duty in fifteen feet of mud." But by the exercise of Yankee ingenuity and a good deal of hard work the task was accomplished and a 10-ton gun mounted behind a parapet of sand bags within five miles of Charleston. Then General Gillmore sent to Beauregard an imperative summons to evacuate Morris Island and Fort Sumter, declaring that unless this was done the city would be shelled. To this demand Beauregard gave no attention, and at midnight of August 22, the Union artillerists, who had sighted the gun and fixed the range of the city, pulled the lanyard. There was a roar and then the watchers could see the slender line of fire traced through the air by the fuse of the flying shell. It disappeared, and then in a moment the clanging of bells and the shrieking of steam whistles in the city told the artillerists that the missile had reached its mark. The soldiers dubbed the big gun the "Swamp Angel," and maintained the bombardment until at the thirty-sixth shot the cannon burst and Charleston was safe again. While the bombardment was continuing, the Confederates, finding that they could not silence the Swamp Angel with the guns of Fort Wagner, hit upon the expedient of sending Union prisoners into the quarter of the city reached by the shells, and notifying Gillmore that he was firing upon his friends. One of these officers writes, "When the distant rumbling of the Swamp Angel was heard, and the cry 'Here it comes!' resounded through our prison house, there was a general stir. Sleepers sprang to their feet, the gloomy forgot their sorrows, conversation was hushed, and all started to see where the messenger would fall. At night we traced along the sky a slight stream of fire, similar to the tail of a comet, and followed its course until, 'whiz! whiz!' came the little pieces from our mighty 200-pounder scattering themselves all around."

September came. The work of pushing forward the approaches to Fort Wagner was slow and tedious. The ground was low and sandy. The trenches could hardly be sunk two feet without filling with water. At times the tide washed over the whole of the Union works. From the fort the Confederates kept up a continual harassing fusilade. Gillmore saw that the spirits of his men were drooping, and determined to take steps to hasten the end of the siege.

Accordingly, on the 5th of the month, a furious cannonade was directed upon the Confederate works. From the Union lines seventeen siege and Cochorn mortars threw shells incessantly into the enemy's quarters. Fourteen heavy Parrott guns hurled their missiles against the bomb-proofs. Ten light siege guns sought out every nook and cranny of the fort with their projectiles. During the day the *New Ironsides* steamed close to the fort and added her eight guns to the formidable force of artillery that was pounding away at the

MORTAR BATTERY IN ACTION.

Confederate stronghold. But the shore batteries were silent neither by night or day. When darkness came on calcium lights with powerful reflectors threw their beams toward Fort Wagner, dazzling the eyes of its defenders and making it a prominent and easy target for the Union artillerists. For forty hours this cannonade was continued without cessation.

The Confederates soon abandoned all efforts to respond to this fierce attack and sought shelter in their bomb-proofs. The fort stood grim and silent, an unresisting target. The Union sappers and miners, relieved from all annoyance from the enemy's fire, pushed their work ahead with great rapidity and soon had carried the approaches up to the parapet of the wall. All was then ready for the final assault, and the order was issued for it to be made early in the morning, but during the night the Confederates stealthily abandoned the fort and morning found the Union forces masters of Morris Island.

At this point we may close our account of the military operations of the second period of the civil war. The epoch had opened with the Confederates triumphant and confident; it closed with them despondent and already expecting final defeat. At the close of the year 1863 the Confederates had been driven from both Kentucky and Tennessee; the Mississippi River had been opened from St. Louis to its mouth; the whole Atlantic coast was virtually under the control of the United States forces; Lee had been beaten back from Pennsylvania, and Stonewall Jackson, the greatest of his generals, was dead. All was ready for a speedy restoration of the authority of the United States in all parts of the South, and we shall see in the concluding volume of this series how this was accomplished under the leadership of that great American soldier, Ulysses S. Grant.

.

THE END.

www.ingramcontent.com/pod-product-compliance
Lightning Source LLC
Chambersburg PA
CBHW020240240426
43672CB00006B/591